W9-BWT-411

FIGHT THE POWER

Fight the Power

*African Americans and the Long History
of Police Brutality in New York City*

Clarence Taylor

NEW YORK UNIVERSITY PRESS

New York

NEW YORK UNIVERSITY PRESS
New York
www.nyupress.org

References to Internet websites (URLs) were accurate at the time of writing. Neither the author nor New York University Press is responsible for URLs that may have expired or changed since the manuscript was prepared.

Library of Congress Cataloging-in-Publication Data
Names: Taylor, Clarence, author.
Title: Fight the power : African Americans and the long history
of police brutality in New York City / Clarence Taylor.
Description: New York : New York University, [2019] |
Includes bibliographical references and index.
Identifiers: LCCN 2017060992 | ISBN 9781479862450 (cl : alk. paper)
Subjects: LCSH: Police brutality—New York (State)—New York—History. |
African Americans—Violence against—New York (State)—New York.
Classification: LCC HV8148.N5 T39 2018 | DDC 363.2/3—dc23
LC record available at https://lccn.loc.gov/2017060992

New York University Press books are printed on acid-free paper, and their binding materials are chosen for strength and durability. We strive to use environmentally responsible suppliers and materials to the greatest extent possible in publishing our books.

Manufactured in the United States of America

10 9 8 7 6 5 4 3 2 1

Also available as an ebook

CONTENTS

Introduction

On August 19, 2010, I served as the moderator of a panel examining the 1968 New York City teachers' strike. The event took place at the Museum of the City of New York and was held in conjunction with its exhibition on mayor John Lindsay. Two weeks later, to my surprise, the museum invited me back to take part in a symposium on Mayor Lindsay and policing. I understood why I was asked to host the August 19 event; I had written a book on the teachers' strike and had given several public talks on the fight for community control, a central focus of the strike, but I had never written on policing and John Lindsay. Nevertheless, I agreed to take part.

The symposium's moderator was Sam Roberts from the *New York Times*, and a number of people who had served in the Lindsay administration took part in the discussion. I had thought I would add little to the conversation, but that was not the case. When one symposium participant blamed Lindsay for the bad relationship between his administration and the police, I felt I had to refute him. I spoke about police brutality in black communities, how it had led to civil unrest and mistrust between blacks and the NYPD. I also pointed out that there is a long history of African Americans' efforts to expose the brutality and bring it to an end. The ensuing questions from the audience and symposium participants alike made it clear that they were largely unaware of how the interactions of police and race had been polarizing the city for decades and continued to do so. I decided that evening to write this book.

Police brutality is the use of excessive force by police on citizens when such force is unnecessary. Unjust shootings, severe beatings, intimidation, verbal abuse, and psychological as well as physical coercion are some of its most common forms.[1]

Policing and race have been a major focus of public discourse, with renewed emphasis beginning, perhaps, with the killing of Michael

Brown in Ferguson, Missouri, in 2014. Video recordings of police brutality incidents across the country have resulted in numerous protests and confrontations between the police and citizens—sometimes spreading beyond the cities where the incidents took place. Under president Barack Obama, the Department of Justice investigated a number of police killings of black people. In March 2015 it released a report on the police department in Ferguson which concluded that police there disproportionally targeted African Americans in a number of ways, including unconstitutional traffic stops and arrests and the use of excessive force.[2]

But despite the recent focus on police brutality, there has been little examination by the media of the long history of the abusive imbalance of power between the police and black communities or the early campaigns by black people to expose and eliminate police brutality. Contemporary media coverage that does look at the past does not look very far back. In July 2014 the *Huffington Post* published an article by Matthew Mathias and Carly Schwartz titled "The NYPD Has a Long History of Killing Unarmed Black Men." With the exception of James Powell, who was killed in 1965, all the victims profiled in the article were killed after 1990. In the preface to the ACLU's 1997 publication "Fighting Police Abuse: A Community Action Manual," Ira Glazer, then the organization's executive director, writes of the 1991 police beating of Rodney King in Los Angeles, but with that exception, all the other incidents of police brutality listed in the manual happened no earlier than 1995.[3] In her *Huffington Post* article "Police Violence Has Been Going on Forever: No Wonder People Are Fed Up with It," Natasha Bach writes that the protests in Ferguson, Baltimore, and elsewhere sparked by Michael Brown's fatal shooting were rooted in past brutality cases. Yet the earliest incident she notes was the Rodney King beating.[4] Bryan Burrough, writing in the *Los Angeles Times* on May 2, 2015, compares contemporary public response to police abuse to that of the 1960s and concludes that organized protests have become a lot less violent than in the 1960s and the 1970s, when those opposing police brutality used "terroristic violence."[5]

Missing from all the above examples is any acknowledgment that police brutality against people of color long predates the 1960s, as have the vigorous campaigns mounted to address that abuse. And those few writers who have traced police violence against black citizens back to well before the 1960s have stopped short of informing readers about the various ways people have organized and mobilized to stop the brutal attacks. Jamilah King's April 29, 2015, piece in the digital magazine *Take Part*, for example, examines police abuse cases from the Chicago riot in 1919 up to the 2015 murder of Freddie Gray in Baltimore, but leaves out citizens' organized efforts to respond.[6]

Although police brutality has been a problem since the founding of professional police departments in the mid-nineteenth century, the starting point of this book is the 1940s, when New York experienced a massive wave of black migration from the South and of immigration from the Caribbean. The city's black population increased dramatically from 152,467 in 1920 to 327,706 in 1930. By 1940 it had jumped to 458,888, and by 1950 it reached 747,608. Harlem's black population numbered 341,000 in 1950.[7] By 1960 the city's black population of over one million was larger than the total population of Baltimore (939,024), Houston (938,219), Cleveland (876,060), Washington, DC (763,956), St. Louis (750,026), San Francisco (740,316), and Boston (697,197).[8] As the black population grew, so did related institutions such as religious bodies, political parties, civic groups, civil rights organizations, and the black press. These institutions worked to improve the social and economic conditions of black people in the North and targeted racial oppression, one manifestation of which was police brutality.

As black communities and their institutions grew, the push for equal justice also increased. In the 1920s the Reverend Thomas Harten of Brooklyn's Holy Trinity Baptist Church led protests against police assaults on black citizens. In 1925, for example, he held a rally of two thousand people at his church protesting police brutality. But such events were sporadic, and few black New York ministers in the early twentieth century turned to street demonstrations, rallies, or other forms of social protest to confront police practices.[9] Protracted campaigns protesting police brutality against black people in New York were launched in response to the Harlem riots of 1935 and 1943, which were set off by police assaults on people of color. Both riots helped to spotlight police brutality. The black press, civil rights leaders, and others called loudly for an end to the police officers' practice of brutalizing the citizens of Harlem.

This book examines the activist groups that carried out long campaigns, first sparked by the 1935 and 1943 riots, to end racially targeted police brutality. Those involved represented a wide spectrum of individuals and groups, ranging from the politically secular and religious left in the 1940s, black nationalists and civil rights leaders of the 1950s and 1960s, elected officials starting in the 1960s, and civil liberty groups on behalf of black and brown people who were subjected to the abuses of the policy of stop, question, and frisk beginning in the 1990s.

Activists in the 1940s realized that police brutality was one expression of a form of domination and extreme power police held over citizens, and they rejected the then-popular theory that rogue cops, just a few bad apples, were to blame. They and their successors understood that brutality was not only pervasive but sanctioned by the highest echelons of the NYPD. Until John Lindsay became New York City's mayor in 1966, those in political power did nothing to curtail the police. One major reason, which persists today, was a matter of popular perception: the role of the police was to protect the lives and rights of white citizens, not the lives or rights of "black criminals"; they were control agents and crime fighters placed in the community to stop crime and criminals, not to act as social workers. The positive popular image of law enforcement and the general public's support of police officers is due in large measure to the fact that they put their lives on the line to protect citizens and maintain the peace by confronting the criminals in society. Their public image as a safeguarding force is reinforced by a narrative disseminated by the media, political leaders, popular culture outlets, and law enforcement agencies themselves. Since the 1940s radio programs and films, and later television, have portrayed heroic police saving the public from dangerous criminals. From the mid-1940s to the mid-1960s, Hollywood especially portrayed law enforcement as comprising "men who enforced the law for moral and ethical reasons."[10]

Political leaders also often beat the same drum. President Harry S. Truman outlined to law enforcement officers their role in postwar America: "You should be vigilant to enforce the laws which protect our citizens from violence or intimidation in the exercise of their constitutional and legal rights. The strength of our institutions depends in large measure upon the vigorous efforts to prevent mob violence, and other forms of interference with basic rights—the right to a fair trial, the right to vote, and the right to exercise freedom of speech, assembly, and petition." Reminding his audience of its moral duty, Truman continued, "It is just as much your duty to protect the innocent as it is to prosecute the guilty. The friendless, the weak, the victims of prejudice and public excitement are entitled to the same quality of justice and fair play that the rich, the powerful, the well-connected, and the fellow with pull thinks he can get."[11]

Unfortunately for people of color in New York, not all police took Truman's sentiments to heart. Another reason no action was taken to curb police brutality until Mayor Lindsay took the first small steps was police resistance and the enormous amount of political power the force wielded. Whatever their station in life, those who attempted to take corrective action or were seen as challenging police power were targeted for retribution.

The individuals and groups that challenged police power did so by fighting for greater citizen input regarding how the police operated in their communities and by trying to democratize the process determining who should decide how police should function. They advocated greater racial representation on the force at every level, demanded an independent civilian complaint review board, and proposed innovative measures to try to improve police–community relations—all in the interest of placing in the hands of ordinary people power over the public institution of law enforcement.

The people and groups profiled in this book came from a political spectrum that ranged from the far left to liberal. Their efforts were alternately ignored, received little attention, or were actively resisted, but they made an important contribution to a long and ongoing civil rights struggle in New York and elsewhere. Among the diverse people and groups profiled here, a significant thread of religiously inflected activism should be noted. The black religious community involved in civil rights struggles and freedom from police brutality was diverse, involving men and women across denominations and religions, from high-profile black churches in Harlem to the Nation of Islam. This book showcases religious communities not just as *additions* to the civil rights movement, but as forces that helped, alongside other actors, to *shape* the movement.

Whether religious or lay activists, the experiences of those involved in the struggle against police brutality in New York taught them to distrust the pervasive positive image of the police. They mounted campaigns to end what they saw as unjustifiable assaults on and killings of black people, and to challenge the popular image of blacks as criminals, even claiming that the mainstream press worked hand in hand with the police to denigrate black people and propagate notions of crime waves in black communities. Those profiled here, ranging from civil rights groups and African American secular and religious leaders to the Communist Party and the black press, understood that police brutality was a form of domination, and therefore they were not just attempting to define how police operated in their communities but were also attempting to define a new and active role for citizens to take with respect to the policing of their communities. Yes, they were trying to reduce the extraordinary power of the police, but ultimately they wanted to democratize the operation of a public institution so that it could and would serve all citizens fairly.

The fight against police brutality has been one of the longest civil rights struggles in American history. Black people in New York have had to deal with the crime of police brutality longer than any other racial or ethnic group in the city. This book examines a more than seventy-year period, from the 1940s to the de Blasio era, to trace how black activists have challenged this form of racial terror by the arm of the state. Many of the chapters in this book examine how black people sought ways to reduce the power of the police. Those in the anti–police brutality campaign did not just call for police reform—they wanted to assure that under any circumstances police could not violate them as human beings. On the other hand, this volume also points out the extraordinary resistance by the police and their allies to altering the power dynamics between people of color and law enforcement. *Fight the Power* argues that race was the major reason for police brutality and that false racialized narratives were a major impediment to struggles for change. Police officers, along with many in the general society, equated blackness with criminality and attempted to control black people through brutal force. Police targeting of blacks was more than a problem of rogue cops—it was an institutional problem. The lack of attention paid to addressing it stemmed from the refusal of those who governed the police force to recognize legitimate grievances of black victims. Instead, law enforcement, the white media, and New York City mayors saw it merely as a crime problem. Black communities were depicted by the NYPD, the white press, and city leaders as infested with criminals—so, therefore, police officers were carrying out their duty in aggressively targeting black crime. Indeed, this book argues with strong evidence that the NYPD, the Patrolmen's Benevolent Association, major white publications, criminologists, and a number of city mayors long denied even the existence of police brutality. It was black activists and their allies who challenged the popular portrayal of both blacks as criminals and the police as upholders of the law. This book tells their story.

1

The *People's Voice* and Police Brutality

Since the 1990s, scholars have been investigating the civil rights struggles outside the South and challenging an earlier historiography that depicted the movement as an exclusively southern affair. They have also questioned the 1954 benchmark set as the start of the civil rights movement, citing northern civil rights campaigns inaugurated well before the U.S. Supreme Court found legal segregation unconstitutional in its *Brown v. Board of Education* decision. They argued that civil rights activists outside the South sought more than integration, an end to discrimination in public accommodations, and the protection of voting rights. The campaigns in the North and West, as well as in the South, also sought economic empowerment, fairer distribution of governmental services and resources, and an end to discriminatory practices in both the private and public sectors.

For activists in the North, ending police brutality was a major objective. Historian Martha Biondi argues, for example, that starting in the 1940s, activists in New York City fought for "protection from unreasonable search and seizure, a halt to coerced confessions, the creation of an independent civilian complaint-review board, a law to end police immunity from criminal prosecution, greater accountability and disciplinary procedures within the department, more Black police officers, an end to the media stereotyping of Black men as criminals, a halt to the criminalization of poor, minority neighborhoods, and better, fairer policing of Black neighborhoods."[1]

In New York City, police brutality was a major concern of the civil rights community, and the *People's Voice* newspaper carved out a key political role in one of urban America's most important civil rights battles. The *Voice* framed itself as a champion of black people, particularly in the case of police brutality. It pitted its version of the events in police brutality cases against the official police version and the perspective of the white press, and claimed that it was exposing the latter's deliberate effort to denigrate Harlem and other black communities.

In December 1942, the *Saturday Review* published an essay by Warren H. Brown, former director of Negro relations for the Council of Democracy and once executive secretary of the March on Washington Movement, in which he accused the black press of rushing to judgment when it came to police brutality: "When a Negro runs seriously afoul of the law, the Negro press seldom stops to ask the facts. It goes to town in flaming headlines to turn the matter to race-rousing account." Brown pointed to a case in New York City in which a police officer shot a "demented Negro" who tried to escape arrest. One black weekly, he noted, "did not wait for an official investigation. It chose to ignore that, under the Police Commissioner and the courts of New York, a fair trial can be assured. Instead this paper broke out its blackest type for a 'police brutality' story."[2] The weekly in question was the *People's Voice*.

While one may question Brown's assertion that the black press rushed to judgment in such instances, in the 1940s, when there was dramatic growth of New York City's black population, many African American periodicals did indeed highlight cases of police violence against African Americans and often called for justice for the victims. Social scientist Maxwell R. Brooks contended that even though the white press ignored racial discrimination, "such reports of discriminatory treatment of members of the race are of primary concern to Negro people everywhere." Referring to the black press, he noted that such "news furnishes the raw material for the editorials and personal columns."[3] In his book *The Negro Revolt*, African American reporter and author Louis E. Lomax writes that the "problem is aggravated in areas like Harlem where police brutality is an accepted fact of life. Without such cases to report, Negro newspapers would have considerable blank space."[4]

Although Lomax exaggerated the potential for empty space, he was correct in claiming that black publications spent considerable ink reporting cases of police officers physically abusing and/or killing people of African origins. For example, the *New York Amsterdam News*, the longest-running and largest New York City black weekly, founded in 1909, reported police attacks on black New Yorkers practically every week in the 1940s and 1950s. Al Nall, a writer for the *Amsterdam News*, noted in 1957 that there was not a week in which the paper was not informed of a police brutality case. He claimed that there were so many police brutality lawsuits and financial settlements that police abuse had become quite expensive for the city.[5] In 1953 the NAACP magazine *Crisis* declared that police brutality was an "old story" carried out by police and "conniving supervisors" whose victims were usually blacks and other minorities who had little recourse under federal law.[6] The black press became one of the most important vehicles for informing their readership of police assaults on black citizens.

Of all the black-owned publications in New York City, the *People's Voice* was the most critical of police brutality. Created in 1942 by the Reverend Adam Clayton Powell Jr., who served as editor in chief, and Charles P. Buchanan, the paper's publisher, it joined a long list of the city's black-owned weekly newspapers, monthly magazines, and journals; among the most prominent were the *Amsterdam News, New York Age*, the NAACP's *Crisis*, and the Urban League's *Opportunity Journal*. Despite the crowded field, Powell decided that the city needed another black newspaper in order to address the pressing needs of Harlem. One of the city's preeminent black leaders, in 1936 he was named senior pastor of New York's largest and most prestigious black church, Harlem's Abyssinian Baptist Church. In 1941 he was elected to the New York City Council, becoming the first African American to represent Harlem. Powell's prestige ensured that New York's black press covered his activities. The *Amsterdam News* even invited him to write a column, but he was more interested in a publication that he felt would better promote his image as an effective leader and make the city's black community aware of his activities and accomplishments. While New York's black newspapers of course reported on the political and cultural life of black New Yorkers, Powell accused them of containing too much sensationalism and not enough reporting on vital issues that had an impact on the community. He wanted to create a quality paper that would report on international and national as well as local social and political events.

Powell also wanted his paper to reflect his own political leanings, so he was not afraid to recruit writers on the left. He hired a group of dedicated journalists, including Marvel Cooke, who had written for the NAACP *Crisis* and the *Amsterdam News* and was critical of the latter's sensational headlines. Cooke had joined the Communist Party during a 1935 strike against the *Amsterdam News* by the Writers Guild. Powell also hired the attorney Benjamin Davis, who was a prominent official in the American Communist Party,[7] as well as Doxey Wilkerson, who would officially join the party in 1945 and was well-known for his leftist views. Wilkerson would later become educational director of the Maryland Communist Party, a columnist for the *Daily Worker*, and a member of the party's National Committee.[8] Powell also convinced the managing editor of the *Amsterdam News* and nationally renowned political cartoonist Ollie Harrington to come on board as art director. Harrington may not have joined the Communist Party, but he did support the 1935 Writers Guild strike against the *Amsterdam News*, during which he became friends with Ben Davis and Marvel Cooke and developed ties to the party.[9]

One of the *Voice*'s most important writers on police brutality was journalist and photographer Llewellyn Ransom. Although not a member of any left-leaning organizations, more than any other *Voice* writer he shaped the paper's arguments on the issue of police brutality—in particular with regard to young people. Powell's decision to hire leftist journalists assured that the *Voice* would not dwell on the sensational but would seriously interrogate the problems of Harlem and of people of African origins throughout the nation and the world. Hiring politically dedicated journalists also guaranteed that the *Voice* would present an interpretation of events from the left, one that differed from the more middle-class-oriented *Amsterdam News* and *New York Age*. Furthermore, a left-leaning staff made it certain that the paper would take a position in support of Harlem and the city's other black working-class neighborhoods.

The *People's Voice* wasted little time in revealing its political task. The first edition came out on February 14, 1942, at what it called "modern history's most chaotic hour," with war being waged on "every continent." The *Voice* proclaimed that it was time for those who were elected, selected, or volunteered to assume some portion of leadership: "It matters not how insignificant the role of past leaders may have been, this day and this hour demand the highest, the greatest and the best that all of us can give." Reading like a manifesto, the first edition declared that its mission was to solve "the people's problem," and went on to claim that it was the "people's hour to make democracy real."[10] It also embraced what would later be called the Double V campaign, first called for in a January 31, 1942, letter to the *Pittsburgh Courier* by James G. Thompson, who was a reader of that paper. The twenty-six-year-old Thompson identified himself as an "American of dark complexion" and suggested that "while we keep defense and victory in the forefront that we don't lose sight of our fight for true democracy at home."[11] Thompson's call for victory over racism at home as well as abroad was adopted by the *People's Voice*, which in its inaugural edition envisioned a "world made safe for democracy and also an America made safe." The objective should be a "real democracy, triumphant not only on the scene of battle but triumphant on the scene of civil liberties, racial equality and human justices."[12]

While the *Voice* embraced the tradition of the black press by becoming an advocate of social reforms, it also reflected the left-leaning politics of its staff and distinguished itself from other black weeklies by linking the issues of race and class, asserting that people of African origins faced not only racism but also class exploitation. It declared itself a "working class paper" and African Americans "a working class race."[13] As such, it pledged its full support to the trade union movement and embraced a civil rights agenda that called not only for political democracy but also for economic justice, which included the right to fair wages and an end to discrimination in employment and in the union hall. The *Voice* recognized that the white working class suffered from the plague of racism, and it declared a challenge by announcing that it would see to it that blacks were admitted to all unions. Focusing on issues that crossed lines of race and class, the *Voice* promised to crusade for improved housing, health facilities, better elementary schools, more black faculty members, and support for black businesses.[14] Writer Richard Robbins noted in 1949 that a major difference between the *Amsterdam News* and the *People's Voice* was that the latter was "more militant, more outspoken in castigating white practices, more impatient with the slow rate of amelioration. It is, in the non-invidious meaning of the term, essentially radical."[15]

The *Voice's* weekly circulation ranged from sixteen thousand to fifty thousand copies. This represented a significant percentage of New York black population, but it was small compared to the more politically moderate *Amsterdam News*, whose weekly circulation was over 105,000. But the *Voice's* importance was in its more militant tone,[16] and the issue on which it exceeded all other black publications in militancy was police brutality.

The *Voice* mounted its campaign on police brutality by trying to empower black New Yorkers in the battle against abuse. It published detailed accounts of incidents, using eyewitnesses, in order to counter the police versions that were usually reported in the white press. By providing a counter-narrative, the *Voice* hoped to verify to a larger audience that the police physically assaulted black people without justification. Its mission was to expose police brutality so that an aware public could demand action to end it. To that end, the paper went beyond the details of brutal police assaults on blacks to also provide proposals for altering the power dynamics between police and citizens.

Investigating Brutality Cases on the Behalf of the Victim

The *People's Voice* differentiated itself from the *Amsterdam News* and the *New York Age*, the city's largest black weeklies, by not just reporting police brutality cases but by also serving as an advocate for the victims. It undertook "investigations" to uncover the truth about the incidents and prove to the public the victims' innocence and the culpability of the police. As a victims' advocate, the paper never accepted police versions of what happened, which, it made clear, were at best suspect and at worst a cover-up. In challenging the police versions of events, the *Voice* provided elaborate details on how the police attacked black men, women, and children with impunity. In practically all cases of police assaults on black citizens, the paper took the position that police officers abused their power by targeting black citizens solely because they were black, but it also went further and asserted that police brutality did not just involve the police. In many of its reports and editorials, the *Voice* pointed the finger at the mainstream press for creating a distorted image of blacks as criminals. The *Voice* used a variety of approaches in its challenge to police brutality, including vivid imagery, eyewitness accounts, undermining the police version of events, highlighting attacks on black youth, and challenging what the paper labeled the crime smear. According to the *Voice*, the crime smear was a campaign by the white press to portray Harlem and other black communities as areas plagued by crime and therefore an unsafe place for citizens to reside.

The *Voice*'s reports on police brutality were well researched and always claimed to uncover events concealed by the police. In its efforts to challenge the abuse of power by the powerful, the paper embraced the spirit of investigative journalism by acting as a watchdog and attempting to get the citizenry and government to take remedial action.

In order to win support for its campaign to end police brutality, the *People's Voice* carefully constructed and distributed images of upright, hardworking, law-abiding citizens, innocent of any criminal offense but nonetheless targeted by police. The police were depicted as racist brutes indifferent to human life who inflicted physical pain on black men, women, and children with impunity. The images were intended to shock readers with the viciousness and injustice of police brutality and to create a sense of moral indignation that, the paper hoped, would spur people to take action.

The *Voice*'s reporting on the brutal beating of Palmer Anderson of 118 West 112th Street in February 1942 vividly displayed the paper's advocacy role with its riveting and detailed narrative of victims and villains. According to the *Voice*, Anderson was a forty-nine-year-old war veteran who had gone to the police precinct on 123rd Street in Harlem to report that a woman had robbed him. Although he attempted to file a complaint, he was told to wait, and after some time passed he complained about the long wait, at which point two police officers leapt on him, hitting him with their clubs and fists. Anderson told the *Voice* that other officers joined in the beating, injuring his left shoulder, elbow, and wrist, knocking out several of his teeth, and putting him in the hospital for a month. He was charged with assaulting a police officer.[17]

The article was constructed as a story about a vicious and senseless police assault on a middle-aged man who had put his life on the line for his country in the armed forces. Anderson was portrayed as a responsible citizen who instead of taking the law into his own hands went to the police station to report that he was the victim of a crime—that he did so signaled to the reader that he was a law-abiding citizen. The *Voice* did not speculate about why the police attacked Anderson. Readers are left with the impression that ruthless cops senselessly beat an innocent citizen because he had the nerve to request that a public servant file his complaint.

This type of story of victims and villains was characteristic of the *Voice*. The portrayal of the police as ruthless thugs implied that any black New Yorker was in danger of police assault, as the police simply had no moral conscience when it came to the treatment of black people no matter what the victim's physical or mental condition.[18] *Voice* writer Llewellyn Ransom's report on a mentally disturbed man shot to death by police is a case in point. Harold Reidman, age twenty-five, who was assigned to the Twenty-Fifth Precinct at 120th Street, shot Wallace Armstrong in what the reporter labeled a "cold blooded murder of a mental case about to be committed to Bellevue Hospital for observation." Ransom presented Armstrong as a helpless mentally disturbed individual who was in need of treatment and maintained that the police and "eyewitnesses" agree that Armstrong was "mentally unbalanced." His father had called the police to ask them to take his son to Bellevue Hospital, but when Reidman arrived and attempted to take Armstrong into custody, Armstrong resisted and fought with the police officer. In his article, Ransom admitted that Armstrong displayed a knife, but wrote that he "acted dazed" and made "no attempt to use it." The "crazed" man was actually walking away from the officer, who followed him with his gun drawn and threatened to shoot him if he did not drop the knife, Ransom wrote—characterizing the police officer, rather than Armstrong, as threatening.[19]

Then another police officer, Patrick Smith, came on the scene, knocked the knife out of Armstrong's hand with his club and, along with Reidman, began beating the crazed man. Once the beating started, a third patrolman joined the assault. Then, in a move that is hard to explain, Reidman stepped back and fired two shots into Armstrong's stomach.[20] A mentally disturbed man with a knife would be seen as a threat by most anyone, but Ransom constructed an image of Armstrong as a person whose emotional state made him incapable of inflicting bodily harm and therefore could not possibly pose a threat to police. Ransom's description of the Armstrong shooting represented an effort to speak for a victim of the police. Once the knife was knocked out of Armstrong's hand and he was thrown to the ground and beaten, shooting him became an act of murder, according to Ransom.

Eyewitnesses

A pivotal element for *Voice* reporters writing on police brutality was the eyewitness account. Unlike white-owned newspapers that usually just reported the police version, eyewitnesses provided vital details authen-ticating the *Voice*'s claims that the police perpetrated brutality against innocent black citizens. This is not to say that the white-owned press did not report witnesses who challenged the police version of events, but it did not use those witnesses specifically to discredit the police version. *Voice* articles highlighted the testimony of people who were on the scene and could provide meticulous detail. Eyewitnesses were a key compo-nent in the paper's crusade against police brutality, and at times their testimony to reporters took up many column inches. Eyewitnesses were portrayed as good, law-abiding citizens who were not lashing out at the police but had a sense of justice and wanted to perform their civic duty. The eyewitnesses quoted always gained credence by noting that they were in close proximity to the incident and always had no connection to the victim, thus establishing their impartiality. They were on the scene and therefore could provide elaborate details.

In the police versions of violent incidents involving Harlem citizens, the story was almost always that officers were forced to use deadly force because their lives were in grave danger.[21] However, eyewitnesses helped to authenticate the victims' versions of events far better than a reporter's account could, and the *People's Voice* turned to James W. Douglas in the Armstrong case. Douglas could not be easily dismissed because he declared that he saw the shooting from just a few feet away. He wrote a powerful piece in the May 23 edition of the *Voice* discrediting the police claim that Armstrong came at Reidman with his knife. Douglas main-tained that Reidman simply killed a "helpless man." To establish Douglas as a credible witness, the paper included a portrait photo along with his piece. It showed him looking away from the camera with a serious ex-pression reflecting his somber mood and determination to set the record straight.[22]

To avoid being seen as a person opposed to all police officers, Doug-las wrote that he was sorry to have seen the killing, and his only reason for coming forward was that he was happy to help his fellow Harlem citizens in the campaign to rid the area of "brutal and stupid members of the police force." He insisted that his coming forward was a selfless act to protect the Harlem community from further police killings. In copious detail he noted the time and location of the event and described his proximity to the victim, which put him in a better position to see what transpired than most of the other witnesses. He was so close to Armstrong that he saw him "bleeding profusely from wounds on his head and blood running all over his face and into his eyes." Although the police were ordering Armstrong to drop the knife, Douglas maintained that he was "unable to handle the situation adequately," and despite having been beaten and made helpless, Reidman shot him.[23]

Black Youth and Police Brutality

A recurring narrative in the *People's Voice*'s campaign against police brutality was that of white police officers brutalizing Harlem's African American youth. In a number of reports the paper detailed young people's victimization and attempted to portray as atrocious and immoral the behavior of police toward the community's most precious and vulnerable citizens. Such stories helped to present the image of a community under siege and also served the wider purpose of portraying a different image of young people than appeared in the white press.

Gang violence had become a major concern in the United States by the 1940s, especially in urban centers. Journalists, social scientists, and law enforcement officials argued that thanks to the social ills exacerbated by World War II, juvenile crime had increased.

Juvenile crime was admittedly a problem in Harlem, as it was in other communities. The presiding justice of New York City's Domestic Court, Edward Boyle, commissioned a study titled "The Negro Problem as Reflected in the Functioning of the Domestic Relations Court of the City of New York." It reported in 1934 that crime among black youth had increased 240 percent over a thirteen-year period.[24] The increase in juvenile crime made blacks a target of aggressive policing. In 1936 New York City police commissioner Lewis Valentine advocated that criminals be "mussed up," thus giving police the green light to physically assault suspects.[25]

The *Voice*'s reports on attacks on young people showed that no one in black communities was safe from the NYPD. Llewellyn Ransom's coverage of the James McCullum shooting by detective Thomas Coleman began with the sentence "Another Negro youth was shot in Harlem early Monday morning by what eyewitness called a drunken and irresponsible policeman in plain clothes." McCullum was charged with the attempted robbery of Detective Coleman, which the *Voice* called a "police brutality 'frame up.'"[26] The paper's notion of youth was quite liberal. McCullum, who was wounded in the shooting, was twenty-two, by law an adult. But McCullum was young enough for Ransom and the *People's Voice* to proclaim that a "youth" had been targeted by the police. One likely reason to ignore the legal definition and label men in their twenties as youths was to help to alter the popular image of young black men as criminals and create support for the victim amid a public more inclined to be sympathetic to young people than to adults. Public sympathy would also bolster the paper's campaign against police brutality.

An analysis of the articles in the *People's Voice* would lead one to conclude that the paper's strategy to engender sympathy and support for black youths who were victims of police brutality was to juxtapose the image of the unruly cop who boldly violated proper police procedures with that of a well-behaved young person who was innocent of any crime. Writers and eyewitnesses provided elaborate details regarding police officers involved in assaults on young people, leaving no doubt that the cops were committing criminal acts. An eyewitness to the James McCullum shooting, William Bradsher, told the *Voice* that it was the "same old affair," another case of "ruthless and criminal assault." Bradsher, a parking lot attendant, was reporting to work when he saw a white man physically abusing a youth. Asserting his credibility as a witness, he told the paper that he was close enough to touch McCullum. He described the cop, Thomas Coleman, as "disorderly looking with mucous and spit all over his sleeve. He was obviously drunk and kept yelling" at McCullum. The description was designed to leave no doubt in the mind of the reader that McCullum was being abused by an inebriated, out of control cop. Although the *People's Voice* did not say why the cop attacked McCullum, Brasher's report of verbal abuse using vile language left no doubt that the incident was racially motivated. The cop, Brasher said, ordered McCullum to "get over there you black son of a bitch." McCullum, according to the eyewitness, pleaded, "I didn't do anything."[27]

Though the *Voice* accused the police of keeping McCullum "incommunicado," the December 12, 1942, issue featured an interview with him, giving "the youth's own version of the shooting which may come as a surprise to these police officials." McCullum had gone to New York from Lakewood, New Jersey, to visit his cousin living on 124th Street. He did not see Coleman on the train or on the platform, but when he was almost on the sidewalk Coleman came up behind him. McCullum says, "I did not attempt in any way to rob or molest him." Without explanation, Coleman demanded that he accompany him to the police station and identified himself as a detective when the young man asked who he was. McCullum agreed to go with him, but once they were in the parking lot Coleman began shoving him into a fence, reached for his gun, and threatened to shoot him. McCullum confessed to the paper that he had begged, "Please Mister, don't shoot me. I haven't done anything." But Coleman "turned around towards me again and shot me." McCullum fell to the ground and passed out.[28] His pleading helped flesh out a picture of McCullum as a confused and frightened "youth" who feared for his life.

To prove the victim's decent character the *Voice* noted that he had never been arrested or "in trouble" and was gainfully employed at the Hotel Harmony in Lakewood. "I've held the job open for him and want him to come back to work right away," his employer, Musher Gross, told the *Voice*. McCullum had worked at the hotel for three years and had "constantly been around a large sum of money," thus proving that he was trustworthy. The *Voice* relied on people who were in a position to evaluate McCullum's character much more objectively than a relative or friend. The paper, supported by the employer, painted a picture of an upright young citizen who had "always been trust worthy, well-liked and extremely popular with hotel customers." Mrs. Anna Broudy, identified as another of McCullum's employers, said that he made "excellent tips due to his service." Broudy was identified as "white," which was meant to highlight how McCullum won the support of people across the color line. The paper's mention that McCullum had only twenty-five dollars on him when arrested made the claim that there was a robbery seem even more implausible.[29] With such tactics, the *Voice* worked to dispel the dangerous myth of the young black criminal.

According to the *People's Voice* the police assault on youth was extremely brutal and done with the express purpose of degrading them. The *Voice*'s narrative of police officers' assaults on children presented the cops as torturers. For instance, Llewellyn Ransom wrote about "four polite, intelligent, friendly Negro boys of high school age," who were tortured by the cops, beaten, kicked in the stomach and groin, and forced to urinate on themselves by three police officers in an apartment hallway on 164th Street. They were then taken to the Thirteenth Precinct on 132nd Street and Amsterdam Avenue, where they were beaten some more. The boys told the *People's Voice* that they had been waiting for a friend in the lobby of the apartment building to discuss opening a gym in their neighborhood because the local facility had closed and youths had nowhere to go for recreational activities. Ransom linked the incident to the city's refusal to budget funding for recreational facilities, one solution advocated by Adam Clayton Powell and the *Voice* to the problem of crime in black urban New York.[30]

In its most direct and accusatory article reporting on police assaults on innocent and well-behaved black youths, the *People's Voice* detailed a police roundup of twenty black youth, five of whom were under the age of sixteen. Before the police approached them some of the young people had left the YMCA; others had left the St. Christopher Boys Club of St. Phillips Protestant Episcopal Church. The reader was presented with young people of high moral fiber associated with two of the most prestigious institutions in Harlem. Founded in 1809 in Five Points by free blacks, St. Phillip's is the oldest black congregation in New York City. The church relocated in 1910 to 134th Street and Seventh Avenue, and its parishioners included Harlem's most prominent residents (e.g., W. E. B. Du Bois).[31] Others among the teens were members of the Salem Crescent Club of Salem Methodist Episcopal Church.

Apparently two boys not associated with the arrested teens got into a fight on 134th Street and Seventh Avenue. The altercation ended before the police arrived, but the twenty boys were "swept up" by the police, despite eyewitnesses' insistence that they had had nothing to do with the turmoil and had no weapons. They were taken to the Thirty-Second Precinct and booked for disorderly conduct. For the *Voice*, the impact of the actions of the police had profound consequences. The paper claimed that "these innocent kids would suffer the stigma of a police record as a result of over-ambitious and indiscriminate police activity." The article's title, "Juvenile or Police Delinquency—Which?" indicated the *Voice's* challenge to the public perception of a crime wave in Harlem: juvenile delinquency was not exclusive to Harlem; the problem was the confrontational approach that police took toward black youth.[32]

The *Voice* claimed that the attack on black youths was not to be dismissed as the actions of a group of rogue cops, but reflected police policy. In August 1944 Ransom warned that Harlem was in danger of a "growing menace of mass arrests of its youth" who were "indiscriminately treated as juvenile delinquents." He accused the police of creating a "bogeyman squad" of thirty-four black detectives who lacked a "constructive approach to the problem of juvenile delinquency." Between seventy-four and one hundred young people had been arrested by the bogeyman squad and saddled with a police record that would have an adverse impact on their future. Although most of the young people had been given a suspended sentence, it became apparent to Harlem residents that "anybody's child is subject to [being] picked up." Ransom argued that the police were forging a perspective that blacks were dangerous from childhood to adulthood, and the mass arrests represented a process of criminalizing an entire race. Any black child standing on a street corner was viewed as dangerous, and therefore subject to arrest.[33]

Fighting the Crime Smear Campaign

A prime target of the *People's Voice* in its campaign against police brutality was the mainstream white press, which it accused in numerous pieces of deliberately portraying black communities as crime infested and black people as prone to crime. The press, more than any other institution, had the power to shape public opinion on numerous issues, including race and crime. The white press has a long history of portraying blacks as criminals. For example, a March 11, 1898, article headlined "Woman Attacked by Negro" asserted that Mrs. Lizzie Cousins, twenty-three, of Belleville, New Jersey, "was attacked and nearly killed last night by a Negro."[34] The August 20, 1900, *New York Times* ran a short article, "Negroes Stab a White Man," about a clerk who was walking on 53rd Street and Eighth Avenue when suddenly "two Negroes stepped out." After one of the assailants said, "There is the man," they stabbed him and ran. In the same edition was a piece headlined "Frightened Negro Kills Girl."[35] In these pieces race was the primary description of the alleged suspect—they were always a "Negro."

By the 1930s and 1940s the *Times* was still emphasizing the race of alleged criminals who were black. As an example, a July 1935 article bore the headline "Woman Slain in Park: Stabbed by Negro in Morningside—Her Escort Beaten."[36] Ten years later, a *Times* article headlined "One-Man Offensive Halted by Bullet," typically emphasized race, noting that John Williams, "a Negro, six feet tall and weighing 200 pounds," had battled the police until shot. He was a "giant," with "prodigious strength."[37] Although they lacked evidence of this assertion, some papers announced that "crime waves" had erupted, mainly carried out by youths.[38] The March 27, 1943, edition of the *New York Times* carried a piece headlined "Muggings Are Laid to New Arrivals" in which Kings County judge Peter J. Brancato claimed that the "crime wave involving Negroes could be attributed to recent arrivals from the South and not to those who had been born and brought up in the metropolitan area."[39]

Black publications opposed the mainstream press's portrayal of crime waves in black communities. The NAACP's *Crisis* magazine, for example, ran an editorial in the December 1941 edition titled "Crime Smear." *Crisis* accused the *New York Times* of manufacturing a "crime wave" in Harlem and branding that community's three hundred thousand residents "as criminals." It also claimed that the *Times* and the rest of the white press based its claim on the deaths in a Harlem park of two white youths—one who was stabbed and one who was strangled.[40]

The *People's Voice* joined in the effort to challenge the portrayal of a crime wave in Harlem and other predominantly black communities, in particular stressing that the police and the white media had manufactured the young black criminal primarily in order to criminalize black youth. The *Voice* claimed that the *New York Daily News*, the Hearst papers, and other mainstream papers "consistently blazoned their front pages with sensational stories, usually inaccurate," that maligned "Harlem as a vice area, dangerous to whites, overflowing with criminals, prostitutes, dope fiends, muggers and a whole catalog of law breakers." The *Voice* also blamed the white press for refusing to print any positive stories about Harlem.[41]

When it came to reporting crime, the *Voice* asserted that it would not feature such stories, leaving that to the "unenlightened metropolitan press with its artificial crime waves."[42] The *People's Voice* maintained that it was the obligation of the black press to not only oppose the production of negative images of black communities as crime-infested areas and black people as criminals, but also to provide alternative images showing the majority of black people as model citizens.

Regarding the white press's claim of a crime wave in Harlem, the *Voice* accused the papers of simply fabricating the stories. *People's Voice* reporter Joe Bostic declared that he could not find anyone in a position of authority to support the *Daily News* allegation that the NYPD had placed Harlem off-limits to the Army and Navy for the safety of the armed forces. He wrote that he interviewed "every person I could locate who carried even the slightest shred of authority. The sum total of my many interviews—Harlem is not out of" bounds. Bostic told his readers to "mark it up in your memory as just another smear attempt on Harlem by the local press."[43]

In gathering information to repudiate the *Daily News* story, Bostic interviewed health commissioner Ernest Lyman Stebbins, who told him that not only was there was no reason to bar military personnel from Harlem, but in fact, Time Square, not Harlem, had the highest crime rate in the city. Police commissioner Lewis Valentine also made it clear that he had not received a request to declare any part of the city off-limits to soldiers or sailors. The *Daily News* story, Valentine said, has "erroneously stigmatized the city of New York as an immoral city." According to the police commissioner, there "are no areas or locations within the city that the armed forces are banned from entering."[44]

Adam Clayton Powell Jr. offered a political explanation for the smear campaign by the white press after a Brooklyn grand jury claimed that Bedford-Stuyvesant, Brooklyn's largest black community, was experiencing a crime wave—he maintained that it was racism. The crime wave story, he insisted, was created by a "group of bigoted whites" led by realtor Sumner Sirtl, whom the New York City Teachers Union had labeled a Nazi.[45] Powell wrote that Sirtl's intention was to "impose the Southern pattern [Jim Crow] on Brooklyn." Powell also denounced one of the star witnesses for the Brooklyn grand jury as an "Alabama cracker cop" who supposedly had said the crime wave was due to an "influx of sunburned citizens who came up from the Deep South mistaking liberty for license." Powell insisted that "this cracker cop," David Liebman, should be removed from the NYPD immediately. The fact that an "Alabama cracker cop" was on the force and a star witness for a grand jury was proof to him that New York was a Jim Crow city and black New Yorkers subjugated to the same racial attacks that blacks experienced in the South.[46]

Police assaults on black New Yorkers, Powell wrote, were evidence that the North was a bastion of racial prejudice, and they were part of a larger apparatus to deny black people the right to live in certain corners of the city. In the case of Bedford-Stuyvesant, realtors teamed up with the police to shut blacks out. Just a few years earlier, he contended, blacks were not allowed to reside in Bedford-Stuyvesant, and the "police did everything they could to keep Negroes from even walking the streets." Blacks were not even allowed on the grand jury that pronounced the crime wave.[47]

The *People's Voice* strategy of "exposing" the mainstream press's bias and presenting a more positive image of Harlem and its residents was an essential element in its campaign against police brutality. The paper worked vigorously to combat a sea of negative images from the mainstream press. The *Voice* was fighting what would be later be known as racial profiling of individuals and a community by the police and white press.

Solutions

Although the *People's Voice* was to the left of other New York City black weeklies, the solutions it advocated for ending police brutality were at best mainstream. After the 1943 Harlem Riot, for example, Powell proposed a number of long-term solutions that included building more recreational centers for youngsters, holding a conference of the various youth gangs of the city to allow the "kids to get off what's on their chest," and suggesting that they be allowed to organize their own movement, "however badly they run it themselves." The riot, which began on August 1, was triggered when a rookie patrol officer by the name of James Collins attempted to arrest one Margie Polite outside a Harlem hotel. Army private Robert Bandy intervened in an attempt to assist Polite and got into a fight with Collins, who shot him. Bandy was wounded, but a rumor spread that the police had killed him and Harlem ignited for two days.[48] Naming police brutality as a cause of the riot, Powell wrote that Harlem's citizens stood behind the police when they were right; however, when they were wrong, the citizens were "going to demand investigation and demand the wrong be righted."[49] Powell's recommendations were in line with those of the *New York Times* in its call for action to end violence in Harlem. The *Times* even noted that it embraced some of Powell points, including building playgrounds, recreational facilities, and summer schools in Harlem.[50]

One of the mainstream solutions the *People's Voice* advocated was the hiring of black police officers. Since racism was at the heart of police brutality, it was assumed that black officers would not behave toward the Harlem community like their white colleagues. A more racially inclusive police force would end racial polarization. Moreover, black officers would change the image of the police force from that of a white institution to a racially diverse one that does not discriminate. Perhaps it might also change the view that the police were an abusive force with the mission of keeping blacks in their place. With more black officers, the NYPD could promote a better relationship between black citizens and the police department.

In calling for Commissioner Valentine to hire more black officers, Powell argued that such a move would not just benefit Harlem but the entire city "with a more equally matched force." Hiring one thousand black officers would show the entire city that blacks were capable of serving as police officers, since many of those new hires would be assigned to white communities; it would foster an image of blacks as law enforcers rather than the stereotypical criminals; and it would demonstrate to the entire city that the police department was committed to integrating the force. The Harlem councilman pointed out that the department's record of hiring blacks was pathetic: there was only one black detective, at the 135th Street police station.[51]

The push for more black police officers was not just a campaign for diversity. The *People's Voice* maintained that black detectives could have an important impact on the investigation process. A September 11, 1943, *Voice* article complained that Harlem was "being stripped of Negro detectives," who were then replaced by whites. Of the sixty detectives in Harlem, only five were black, and the lack of black detectives affected police work. Since the basic task of a detective was to investigate, what was needed was the "utmost confidence and forthrightness on the part of both the interviewer and the interviewed." The *Voice* argued that a larger number of black detectives in Harlem could do a better job of policing the area, implying that they were more familiar with the black community and people. It also suggested that blacks would place more trust in black officers than in their white counterparts.[52]

The *People's Voice* called on assistant chief inspector John J. Ryan, who was in charge of assigning detectives to precincts, to explain why there were so few black detectives in Harlem. In the fall of 1943 the paper claimed that its investigation had uncovered that no black detectives had been assigned to Harlem since 1932 The NYPD had only eleven black detectives on the entire force. The *People's Voice* was not promoting segregation—instead, it argued that the entire city could benefit from a well-integrated police force.[53]

The *People's Voice* supported the efforts of civil rights organizations that pushed for more blacks on the force, and it praised the top brass who promised to take action. In its July 10, 1943, issue, the *Voice* reported on a meeting between a committee of New York Urban League and Police Commissioner Valentine, noting that the commissioner agreed with the committee's assertion that one precautionary measure to "prevent racial outbreaks" was to hire black police officers. Valentine said that he realized the significance of black as well as white police officers in stopping racial conflict, but that statement did not demonstrate that he accepted the premise that police brutality was a reality and that the racial attitudes of white officers led to confrontations between the police and black New Yorkers. Valentine didn't even bother to note the racial dynamics of police–community tensions. Instead, he made a color-blind argument by pointing to the contribution both black and white officers made toward stopping racial conflict. Offering no concrete program to integrate the NYPD, Valentine merely claimed that he was willing to work with any organization that was eager to help in attracting candidates to the force.[54]

At times the *People's Voice* placed too much trust in those who ran the NYPD, in the hope that they would work to racially integrate the ranks. Responding to Joe Bostic's inquiry about the declining number of detectives in Harlem, Assistant Chief Inspector Ryan promised that "Harlem will get more Negro detectives and will get them in the very near future." He also promised that he would assure that a "representative percentage" of blacks would be assigned to the new detective squad in Brooklyn's Seventy-Ninth Precinct. He even showed Bostic the files of black police officers he said would be promoted to detectives. The *People's Voice* took credit for Ryan's assurance, labeling it a "promise." Bostic even wrote that Ryan was "sincere."[55]

Bostic's optimism proved naïve, which led to disappointment when no action was taken regarding the "promises." Two weeks after writing that Ryan was sincere, Bostic excoriated the assistant chief inspector for upholding a "Jim Crow policy of refusing to assign a fair proportion of detectives to Harlem." Ryan's "policy," he wrote, confirmed the fears of the Harlem community that "anti-Negro bias" was a major reason why black detectives were not deployed in Harlem. Bostic was infuriated over Ryan's recent decision to appoint three white detectives to area. The appointments "now proved [Ryan's promises] to have been wholly insincere. . . . There was only one conclusion to reach in the light of overwhelming evidence," Bostic wrote—"Harlem is the victim of a flagrant, vicious and un-American Jim Cro[w] policy that has no place in a law enforcement agency."[56] Bostic used moral suasion in an effort to embarrass the NYPD by arguing that its actions were contrary to the American principles of liberty and justice. But his criticism of Ryan reflected despair on the part of the *People's Voice*.

Although Bostic expressed his disappointment that police top officials did not take action to hire black officers, the *Voice* continued to express faith that this would eventually happen. The number of blacks on the force remained low, however, making up less than 1 percent of the NYPD in 1943. Of the total population of sixteen thousand police officers, only 155 were black, just six of whom were sergeants and one a patrol commissioner. Mayor La Guardia and Police Commissioner Valentine, along with the U.S. military, agreed to deploy 1,500 civilian volunteers—most of them black citizens—after the Harlem Riot in 1943, but that group was only temporary. Despite the absence of a proposal by Valentine to attract more blacks to the force, the *Voice* still offered no criticism, and its July 10, 1943, article reporting on the commissioner's speech before the committee of Urban League members, "Valentine Willing to Add More Negroes to Police Force," was optimistic in tone.[57] Without offering any concrete solutions, Valentine told the New York Urban League that he would continue doing what he had been doing for his nine years as commissioner—urging blacks to take the civil service examination for positions in the police department. The police commissioner effectively promised to do nothing. It was the Urban League that promised to take action in announcing that it planned to set up classes at the Harlem YMCA to help blacks pass the exam.[58]

In a 1945 speech before an audience of two thousand at the NYPD's annual St. George Breakfast, Commissioner Valentine declared, "Whether he [a police officer] be Catholic, Protestant or Jew, Republican or Democrat, Negro or white, matters not at all. We are working together in harmony."[59]

The department did make progress by the early 1950s—in 1952 it reported 16,577 white and 564 black officers. This was a significant increase; however, of the 1,139 sergeants, only six were black. By 1953 it had only one black captain.[60]

Why did the *People's Voice* place its faith in the NYPD to open its ranks to blacks and not call for more militant tactics such as civil disobedience, lawsuits, and petition drives? Powell was not unfamiliar with hard-hitting strategies. In the 1930s he had been involved in the "Don't Buy Where You Can't Work" campaign. In 1941 he teamed up with the Harlem Labor Union, the Manhattan Council of the National Negro Congress, and the Transport Workers Union to conduct a two-week boycott against the Fifth Avenue Coach Company and New York Omnibus Corporation, both of which refused to hire blacks as bus drivers and mechanics and mistreated black riders. The protesting groups organized the United Bus Strike Committee, which conducted a bus boycott that kept an estimated sixty thousand Harlem residents off the busses and managed to win major concessions, including the hiring of black bus drivers and mechanics.[61]

One reason Powell did not resort to such militant tactics is that after 1941 he had moved away from protest toward more traditional politics. He had been elected to the city council and already had his eye on climbing the political ladder. In 1944 he ran for and won a seat in Congress but remained editor in chief of the *Voice* until 1946, using the paper to promote himself. Valentine's statement that he wanted to hire blacks was framed as an accomplishment. The *Voice's* enthusiasm to highlight announcements made by the police high brass on their willingness to add more black officers—even if no actual hires were made—indicated Powell's eagerness to show the Harlem community that he was an effective leader who could deliver services from those in power. He also wanted to distinguish his paper from its rivals.

Despite the sharp focus on the issue of hiring black officers, Powell's and the *People's Voice's* solutions to ending police brutality did go

beyond that demand and included suspending and immediately prosecuting officers accused of assaults and ensuring that victims had legal
representation. They even called into question the police and district
attorney's entire investigative process. In his May 30, 1942, "Soapbox"
column, Powell pointed out that when a cop killed or assaulted a citizen,
the district attorney did not conduct an investigation unless there was a
complaint filed. To make matters worse, in cases involving police brutality, when an investigation was conducted, the police usually escorted
the witnesses to the DA's office, implying that such an escort could in-
timidate anyone who might be willing to testify against a police officer.
Another questionable practice was that grand jury hearings were held
behind closed doors, away from the public. Powell noted that blacks
were almost totally excluded from grand juries. Although blacks made
up 20 percent of the city's population, only one or two blacks served on
a grand jury in 1941. The lack of black grand jury members, according
to the Harlem councilman, led to the acquittal of white cops who murdered or brutalized black New Yorkers.[62] Despite his criticism, however,
Powell did not call for an alternative to the grand jury system—instead,
he demanded assurance that blacks would serve on those bodies.

Powell maintained that institutional racism, such as the exclusion of
blacks from grand juries, revealed that racism was more than a regional
problem: "The false democracy of Alabama is dressed up a little bit more
in New York. The basic principles of a full democracy are just about ignored in this 'free' North." Powell's accusation of institutional racism in
New York called into question northern racial liberalism by pointing to
the structural framework of the criminal justice system that led to racial
oppression of blacks. Such a statement was also a means of embarrassing
city officials.[63]

Powell argued that northern racism went beyond the realm of "administration of justice." He acknowledged that some restaurants served
blacks, that there was public school integration and even a few black
teachers in elementary schools, but he pointed out that there were practically no black teachers in the high schools and colleges and that blacks
were excluded from civil service exams in many states. New York City
and State were better, but when "it comes to [a] question of advancement, qualified people are passed over just because they are Negroes."
He wrote, "Ole man Jim Crow is just dressed up in the North."[64]

On occasion, the *Voice* helped to promote rallies and demonstrations. Rallies were an effective way of informing people and showing moral support for the struggle. Large protests were a means of demonstrating to city officials the collective anger of the community. Commissioner Valentine was extremely disturbed by the rally against police brutality organized by Powell in the wake of the Wallace Armstrong killing. Valentine informed Mayor La Guardia of a circular calling for a demonstration on May 17, 1942, sparked by the "unfortunate killing" of Armstrong. Powell was fully aware that the case was going to be presented to the grand jury and that, in Valentine's words, "this type of rabble rousing is dangerous and might result in serious disorders," but he was undeterred. Valentine insisted that Powell "should be advised to cancel this proposed Mass Meeting in the public interest and await the action and decision of the New York County Grand Jury."[65]

Fiorello La Guardia's secretary, Lester Stone, told Powell in a phone call that the mayor wanted to convey to Powell how "dangerous" such an event was and that "if it produced any difficulties you would be held responsible." Powell told Stone that it was impossible to call off the event. He explained that immediately after Armstrong's killing he had sent a wire to both the mayor and the commissioner but received no reply from La Guardia and had only received a wire from Valentine the previous day—forty-eight hours after his own wire had been sent. "That was pretty slow timing," he said. Stone again attempted to frighten Powell by asking if he was aware of the "effect of a meeting of that kind." The Harlem councilman attempted to assure him that if it was handled properly and a committee was appointed to meet with La Guardia, things would proceed peacefully. "The people have a right to petition," Powell told Stone, who replied that the people were already riled up by the flyer announcing the rally, which read "ONE MORE NEGRO BRUTALLY BEATEN and KILLED! Shot down like a Dog by the police." It called for Harlem residents to pack the Golden Gate Ballroom at Lenox Avenue and 142nd Street in Harlem on Sunday, May 17, declaring it "I AM an American Day," and urged people to read about Armstrong in the *People's Voice*. "Don't you think the handbill is inflammatory?" Stone asked. "I think the handling is more inflammatory," Powell retorted. Powell informed Stone that he had affidavits from several eyewitnesses but assured him that none of them would address the rally. Only "elected leaders of the community" would speak: "Republicans, Democrats and American Labor Party, both left and right wing." Powell even went so far as to guarantee to Stone that "there will be no disorders" and that the rally would be "peaceful."[66]

City officials were unable to stop the rally, so the police decided to monitor it. Afterward, deputy police inspector George Mitchell sent a report to Stone providing the names of the twelve speakers, their political affiliation or occupation, and whether they were "white" or "colored." Acting Lieutenant Shilbersky, head of the Criminal Alien Squad, prepared Mitchell's report, which stated that Powell started the event at 5:10 p.m. by saying that on the evening of May 12 Wallace Armstrong, "who comes from an excellent family, was surrounded by twelve members of the police force and unjustifiably killed." Powell claimed that he had affidavits from "twenty witnesses" in his pocket and photostats of the affidavits were placed in two different locations in case the originals were "stolen" from him. Declaring that he had a personal responsibility "to offer leadership," he said he had conferred with District Attorney Hogan and sent wires to Valentine and La Guardia asking for the formation of a citizen's committee to investigate the murder. Powell said that all the community's leaders were united and were going to "elect" such a committee to demand an investigation and would "sit on the steps of City Hall, until the Mayor agrees to meet the representatives of Harlem."[67]

A number of the speakers associated police brutality with the concept of democracy. "Democracy," according to Odel Clark, a leader of the American Labor Party, "means more than riding in the same subway, or in the bus or sitting in the same section with the white man." Clark was asking for the same fair treatment for Armstrong as would be accorded to a fallen police officer. State assemblyman Danny Burrows, an African American, wanted to see "Negroes in every branch of the Government service" and said he had no desire to fight in the armed services "unless it is on equal basis with the white man."[68]

The list of speakers and their statements proved that this was not a gathering of the far left. Nevertheless, the police were disturbed enough to observe the event closely. Despite the fears of the mayor and others regarding the rally, despite the tone of the leaflet and Powell's refusal to call off the event, Powell's reassurance to La Guardia that the event would be peaceful indicated that his militancy would go only so far. He would defy the mayor's request to call off the rally, but he was willing to place a damper on the Harlem community's anger. Limiting the speakers to elected officials further indicated that Powell was more interested in show than in substance.

Conclusion

The *Voice* should be given credit for advocating a number of solutions that would be championed by activists in the 1950s and 1960s, including racially integrating the police department and creating a monitoring agency. Long before video cameras could record police beatings and killings, the *Voice* served as a source of detailed accounts of such brutal attacks. Its pages became the people's record of violent encounters between law enforcement and Harlemites.

The *People's Voice* has to be given credit for making thousands of people aware of important social, political, and economic issues that affected the lives of black people, especially police brutality. The paper's campaign to stop police brutality by offering an alternative narrative to that of the mainstream press and police department, and being able to organize huge demonstrations to protest attacks on civil rights, made it unique among white- and black-owned newspapers. At the heart of its crusade against police brutality was its effort to provide black people with ways of opposing police abuse.

While venues for airing their grievances and seeking justice against police brutality—including city government, law enforcement, and the white-owned media—were closed to black people, the black press took on their cause and refused to allow such oppression to go unreported. In its fight against police brutality, the *People's Voice* portrayed the humanity of black people while expounding on their plight.

2

The Communist Party and Police Brutality

In the early morning of December 7, 1950, twenty-four-year-old Army veteran John Derrick, thirty-five-year-old Zach Milline, and thirty-two-year-old Oscar Farley were returning home from a local tavern where they had been celebrating Derrick's medical discharge from the armed forces. Suddenly patrolmen Louis Palumbo and Basil Minakotis approached the three black men and demanded that they raise their hands in the air. According to Milline, a grocery store owner, and Farley, a private in the U.S. Army, the two white policemen began shooting at them without warning. Derrick, who had been wounded serving his country in Korea, was shot in the heart and died. "Why? Why did they do it? I've never seen anything like it in my life," Milline said.[1]

Police claimed that Derrick had a gun, but affidavits of witnesses said he was unarmed. Nevertheless, the district attorney's office ruled that the two patrolmen were "properly performing their duties." A New York County grand jury reported in February 1951 that "it had found no basis for an indictment."[2]

Many in the Harlem community were outraged by Derrick's slaying and the fact that the two cops were not indicted. Harlem councilman Earl Brown called for Palumbo and Minakotis to be punished and asked that the War Department take a role in the investigation, since Derrick was a veteran. According to Lindsay White, head of the Manhattan branch of the NAACP, the civil rights organization hired a private detective agency to investigate the killing. The *New York Amsterdam News*, one of the nation's largest black weeklies, labeled Palumbo and Minakotis "police killers of Negro veteran John Derrick" and announced a massive rally on January 5, 1951, so that the "people of Harlem will be able to show the police, the district attorney and the grand jury that police brutality in the community will be tolerated no longer."[3] The New York City branch of the NAACP and Harlem leaders planed the rally. U.S. senator Jacob Javits, U.S. representative Adam Clayton Powell Jr., civil rights and labor leader A. Phillip Randolph, baseball great Jackie Robinson, and boxing sensation Sugar Ray Robinson were scheduled to attend the event.[4]

We have seen how the most outspoken black weekly in Harlem, the *People's Voice*, took on police brutality. The reaction to the Derrick killing demonstrated that civil rights activists, prominent leaders, and even celebrated sports figures were also willing to challenge such misconduct. But they weren't alone. The American Communist Party was perhaps the most active political organization in the fight against police brutality. Writing for the *Daily Worker*, the Communist Party's daily newspaper, Abner W. Berry portrayed the Derrick shooting as a cold-blooded racist murder covered up by those in power. "A Negro army veteran only 12 hours out of uniform was lynched by two white policemen in Harlem on Pearl Harbor Day," Berry wrote, charging that the Derrick case was part of a "string of brutal Negro killings by police officers" that had been whitewashed by the district attorney's office.[5]

Communist Party members considered police brutality one of the major challenges facing black Americans. Assessing his tour of Detroit, Cleveland, Chicago, and St. Louis on behalf of the Communist Party– operated League of Struggle for Negro Rights, Harry Haywood, an early black member of the American Communist Party, declared that the "burning civil rights issue in these cities was police terror against the Black Community."[6] American Communist Party member Carl Vedro contended in 1950 that in the "case of the Negro people, the intensification of oppressive measures is all too evident. Whereas the denial of civil rights to the Negro people before the war was expressed in lynching mobs, something new has been added today—the role of the police and the state." According to Vedro, instances of brutality demonstrated that the "police and government directly assumed the role of oppressors."[7]

What did their participation in the campaign suggest about the New York City civil rights struggle? Communists organized campaigns against police brutality, participated in demonstrations, and highlighted police brutality cases in left-leaning publications. They became involved in the campaign. I argue here that the view that Communists had little or no concern about civil rights is incorrect, and I challenge the assumption that Cold War repression marginalized Communists, thus muting their voice in civil rights struggles. The American Communist Party played an important role in the civil rights campaign to end police brutality in New York City from World War II into the 1950s. Indeed, the party gave those involved in the struggle new ways of addressing police brutality by connecting it to a larger national and international movement. For Communists, police brutality called into question the notion that racial terror sanctioned by the state was relegated to the South. In the *Daily Worker* the party characterized police shootings, beatings, and other forms of assaults as "northern lynching" perpetrated by those in power. As a policy aimed at African Americans and sanctioned by the government, police brutality, for the party, was a violation of human rights as well as civil rights.

The American Communist Party analyzed police brutality against African Americans along two dimensions. In terms of class, the police were part of a superstructure used to maintain the capitalist economic structure. Communists contended that police brutality against African Americans happened because the latter were members of the American working class who opposed the systematic effort to exploit their labor. However, American Communists also argued that race was a significant factor in understanding police repression of African Americans because it was used as a means of fragmenting the working class, thus stopping any attempt at creating a unified opposition front to capitalism.

Lynching Northern Style

In the early part of its history, the Communist Party maintained that it was the target of police brutality. African American Communist Party member Harry Haywood said that in the early 1930s "Chicago's police force undoubtedly held the record for terror and lawlessness against workers. They were unsurpassed for sadism and brutality, regularly raiding the halls and offices of the Unemployed Councils, revolutionary organizations and the Party." According to Haywood, "It took courage and on occasion ingenuity to thwart the police terror aimed at forcibly stifling and demoralizing the workers' movement."[8]

Chicago was not unique. According to party members, police also targeted them in New York City. In July 1930, Gonzalo Gonzalez, whom the press described as a "Mexican Communist," was shot and killed by officer Edmund J. O'Brian while walking in a "procession of about 30

Mexican and Spanish Communists." Latino Communists were marching to pay homage to Alfred Luro, an African American Communist who had been killed when hit by a piece of wood thrown from a roof—purportedly by the police. When O'Brian told them to break up their demonstration, he was "struck" by one of the demonstrators. The press quoted witnesses who testified that Gonzales then grabbed the cop's nightstick and began beating him, knocking him down twice. After being knocked down the second time, O'Brian shot Gonzales in the heart.[9]

The deaths of Luro and Gonzalez bolstered the Communist Party's argument that the police were an apparatus of the state, which had "launched a reign of terror" against the working class. A. B. Magil and Joseph North, writers for the Marxist journal the *New Masses*, identified Alfred Luro ("a Negro") and Gonzales as "two workers" who were "killed by New York Finest," demonstrating the "current of struggle" that "swiftened as the bosses feverishly built their dam of fascism."[10]

The Communists' accusations were not unfounded. In a 1931 report, the American Civil Liberties Union found that the "chief interferences by city police with civil rights affect radical meetings and strikers' picket lines." The ACLU stated, "The most conspicuous offender among police departments is New York City, with the longest record of meetings and picket-lines broken up, despite the fact that permits for street meetings are not required in New York. The principal victims were Communists." In particular, "smaller Communist demonstrations, particularly at the City Hall, before foreign consulates, and at other unfamiliar spots, were violently broken up." Despite formal complaints to the police commissioner against such assaults, the ACLU declared that there has only been a "whitewashing" of the incidents.[11]

The Communist Party contended that the police specifically targeted African Americans in order to destroy any effort to create black and white unity among workers.[12] According to the party, black Americans were the most exploited segment of the working class. As early as 1921, the American Communist Party (then called the Workers Party) addressed the oppression of African Americans: "The Negro workers in America are exploited and oppressed more ruthlessly than any other group. The history of the Southern Negro is the history of a reign of terror—of persecution, rape and murder. . . . The Workers Party will support Negroes in their struggle for liberation, and will help them in their fight for economic, political and social equality."[13]

It pledged to "destroy" the obstacles that had been implemented to divide black and white workers.[14] Blacks faced a crueler form of oppression than did other workers, and the party would make a vigorous effort to end racial terror. In 1926 William Z. Foster, who joined the American Communist Party in 1923 and would later became its general secretary, echoed this view when he wrote that the "working class is far from being a homogeneous mass. It is divided against itself in regard to race, nationality, color, creed, age, sex, skill, etc." He wrote that the "problem is still further complicated because the employers have learned skillfully to play upon these differences and to split up the workers disastrously on the basis of them." Foster argued that the inclusion of black workers in trade unions could only be "accomplished by complete suppression of race antagonism in the trade unions and by a loyal defense of the Negro worker's interest." However, realizing the intensity of racism in the United States, Foster acknowledged, "This is easier said than done." Therefore, Communists had to take strong measures to challenge racial divisions.[15]

By the time the Communist Party moved into what it called its Third Period (1928–35), it did take strong action to eliminate racial divisions. According to the party, the Third Period witnessed, in the Great Depression, the radicalization of the American working class as well as a collapse of capitalism. During this time, the party worked militantly to end racial terror in order to assure that the working class would not be fragmented in its struggle for a workers' state.[16] Communists led campaigns to end lynching and played a leading role in the Scottsboro Nine case. In 1931, nine youths ranging from ages thirteen to nineteen were arrested in Scottsboro, Alabama, and accused of raping two white women. All but one were sentenced to death. The Communist Party and the International Labor Defense, a Communist Party affiliate, defended the Scottsboro Nine and led an international campaign to free them.[17] For the Communist Party as well as others, Alabama's decision to execute the teenagers was a symbol of southern whites' racist obsession with interracial sex. Although Ruby Bates, one of the two white women who made the charge that she had been raped, could not identify any of her alleged attackers, and she would later recant her story that she had been raped, an all-white jury found the teens guilty and sentenced them to death.[18]

By 1935, concerned that Nazi Germany was preparing to attack the Soviet Union, Moscow ordered Communist Parties worldwide to drop the argument that socialists, social democrats, and liberals who were opposed to Communism were "social fascists" and to instead build a united front with these forces to confront Hitler. In response, the U.S. Communist Party advocated a "Popular Front" of socialists, social democrats, civil rights groups, and non-Communist labor unions united against fascism and racism. The best example of the Popular Front approach with regard to civil rights was the party's participation in the National Negro Congress, which it joined in 1936. The National Negro Congress was a group of civil rights and religious leaders whose objective was to fight for the civil and economic rights of black Americans. Dropping its more strident revolutionary rhetoric and adopting a more mainstream notion of forming a coalition with reformist organizations, the party focused on the issue of police brutality. At the NNC's founding convention, the eight hundred delegates agreed on a program that included the abolition of both police brutality and lynching. In 1938 the NNC attempted to obtain thousands of signatures for a petition against police brutality in Washington, DC, and submit it to president Franklin Delano Roosevelt.[19]

Despite the American Communist Party's public support for civil rights for blacks, its back and forth positions on the international front sent a confusing message. After the Soviet Union signed a non-aggression pact with Nazi Germany in 1939, A. Philip Randolph resigned from the National Negro Congress, condemning it for adhering to the dictates of the Soviet Union and American Communist Party.[20] The *Baltimore Afro American*, a weekly newspaper, claimed that when the Soviet Union signed the non-aggression pact with Nazi Germany, Communists lost credibility with black Americans.[21] Randolph declared at the April 1940 NNC Convention that for "anyone to take the position that the Negroes should place their fortunes at the feet of the Communist Party, which is subject to such violent and far-reaching shakeups, a party which lacks stability of purpose, and serves an alien master, is passing strange."[22] Some civil rights leaders, including Randolph and Roy Wilkins, who would head the NAACP after 1955, even charged that the Communists were not interested in the civil rights of African Americans at all. Calling for a march on Washington in 1942, Randolph declared, "We cannot sup with the Communists for they rule or ruin any movement. This is their policy."[23]

When William Paterson of the Civil Rights Congress, a Communist Party–affiliated organization fighting for civil rights, reached out to the NAACP to form an alliance, Roy Wilkins responded angrily: "As soon as Russia was attacked by Germany they dropped the Negro Question and concentrated all effort in support of the war in order to help the Soviet Union. During the war years the disciples of the extreme left sounded very much like the worst of the Negro-hating Southerners." Wilkins would later write in his criticism of both the Republican Party and the Communists, "Both have tossed the Brother overboard as soon as they got what they wanted."[24]

Yet, despite its changing positions on war, peace, and revolution, the U.S. party did not abandon its attack on the racial terror aimed at black Americans. After the war, the party press continued to characterize police brutality as a form of lynching. Reporting on the shooting of three brothers in Freeport, New York, by a white police officer, a writer for the *Daily Worker* asserted that "Jim Crow Pulled the Trigger." In February 1946 rookie police officer Joseph Romeika shot the two Ferguson brothers, twenty-five-year-old Alfonso and twenty-seven-year-old Charles, a father of three. Apparently, the bullet that killed Charles ricocheted and also wounded twenty-two-old Joseph Ferguson. The fourth brother, Richard, was arrested and charged with disorderly conduct.[25] Hours after his arrest, he was tried without legal counsel or a jury, found guilty by a judge, and fined $100. Official testimony showed that none of the men was armed. The brothers were celebrating Charles's reenlistment in the U.S. Army Air Force. The *Daily Worker* pointed out that when an owner of the Bus Terminal Tea Room refused to serve them coffee, Charles accused him of displaying a "Jim Crow attitude." Romeika was called on the scene, took the brothers into custody and, according two eyewitnesses, lined them up—at which point the "Negro-hating cop" shot them.[26] Freeport police chief Peter Elar decided not to suspend Romeika, and a Freeport grand jury refused to bring charges, even though the officer admitted lining them up and kicking the brothers in the groin before shooting them.[27]

The Communist Party joined in a campaign to win justice for the Ferguson brothers and covered the story in the *Daily Worker*, calling the killing a "lynching Northern style." The New York Veterans against Discrimination of Civil Rights, an organization that the attorney general listed in 1948 as a "Communist Front," and the United Veterans for Equality organized a conference to help plan a fight for justice.[28]

Although there is no evidence that U.S. representative Vito Marcantonio was a member of the American Communist Party (despite the fact that the House Un-American Activities Committee listed him as one of the "well-known Communists or fellow travelers"),[29] he was of the opinion that Communists had a right to be heard. He and the Communist Party were allied on a number of issues, including civil rights, labor rights, anti-lynching and anti–poll tax legislation, independence for Puerto Rico, and opposition to the Taft-Hartley Act. The latter was passed by Congress in 1947 and restricted the activities of labor unions, such as prohibiting the closed shop and secondary boycotts. Marcantonio also wrote a column for the *Daily Worker* titled "Mark My Words." On one occasion, he wrote that the police killing of John Derrick was the "height of police violence and brutality against Negro citizens," arguing that in "recent years the police have attempted to turn Harlem and East Harlem into a Georgia or Mississippi." Marcantonio sent the message to his readers that the NYPD was no different in its treatment of blacks than law enforcement officials in the Jim Crow South.[30]

Ben Davis and Police Brutality

Two of the Communist Party's black members, Benjamin J. Davis and William L. Patterson, made the fight against police brutality a major focus of their political work, and no party members were more outspoken on the issue. Their passion was due, in part, to Communist ideology. Both articulated the party's position that police brutality was a tool the owners used as a "means of production" to divide the working class. But their arguments came from more than ideology; as African Americans they were responding to police brutality as victims of racial oppression.

Ben Davis was the first declared black member of the Communist Party to be elected to the New York City Council, in 1943. He was a high-ranking party official, serving as chairman of the New York State District. Despite his Communist affiliation, he was elected to three terms and served until he was expelled in 1949, after he was convicted under the Smith Act, a law passed in 1940 making it illegal to advocate the overthrow of the United States government.[31]

Davis was born in 1903 in Dawson, Georgia, a Jim Crow city where blacks were relegated to the lowest social, political, and economic positions. They could not vote or hold office. A black person who talked back to a white person could be playing with his life by doing so. Davis attended a one-room, ramshackle "Negro school," where the term was six weeks shorter than in schools for white children. According to Davis, the black school was a "hazard to life and limb."[32] To provide their children with a better education, Davis's parents relocated to Atlanta.[33] Davis would attend Morehouse College and then Amherst College, where he earned a bachelor's degree, and finally Harvard Law School, from which he graduated in 1933.[34]

Davis was radicalized when he got involved in the Angelo Herndon case in 1933. Herndon, an African American labor organizer and member of the Communist Party, was arrested in Georgia for insurrection when he tried to organize black farmworkers. Serving as one of his defense attorneys, Davis was threatened by white southerners and subjected to racial slurs from the judge.[35]

Davis was so impressed by Herndon's bravery, work, and ideology that soon after the trial he joined the Communist Party.[36] His interest in police brutality stemmed from the Herndon case, during which he witnessed how the state apparatus was used to persecute an African American trying to organize the black working class. Davis considered the police an arm of the state used to crush activism and to discourage unity among black and white workers. He would later write that the "struggles of the Negro people are an inseparable part of the struggles of the working class in America, and of the workers, common people and colonials all over the world." Racial discrimination, he argued, was a weapon of "capitalism to intensify its exploitation of certain sections of the population, to keep down the wages and working conditions of the working class, and to prevent the working people from uniting against the common foe—capitalism."[37]

Davis also articulated the party's position that Jim Crow was practiced beyond the Mason-Dixon Line. Writing in the journal *Phylon*, he maintained that, while Jim Crow had its "sharpest expressions in the South," it had spread "its tentacles all over America, including New York, where I share in common with all other Negroes the denial of my constitutional right to live." The Jim Crow system in the North was evident, according to Davis, "in jobs, civil rights, the slum-infested ghetto, education and other fields—sometimes covertly and subtly, but nevertheless it is there."[38] Capitalism was the "root cause" of racial discrimination, motivated by the need to divide the classes and forestall challenges to capitalist ownership of the "basic means of production and natural resources."[39]

Although he was willing to articulate the Communist Party position, Davis did not hesitate to criticize Communists for their lack of recognition of the black community's leadership on the issues directly affecting it. In his report to the Communist Party's Fifteenth National Convention in December 1950, held in New York City, Davis warned members that they must "overcome a certain sluggishness in grasping the significance of this new quality in the peace and Negro liberation struggles." As an example of independent militancy in the black communities, he pointed to those involved in the black liberation struggle who had created a civilian campaign "for death to the police-lynchers of [John] Derrick."[40]

Davis's twenty-two-page pamphlet *Police Brutality, Lynching in the Northern Style* (actually written by Davis's assistant, Horace Marshall, and published in 1947 by Davis's office) detailed many cases of flagrant police violence in Harlem. Samuel T. Symonette, a forty-two-year-old Harlem businessman, was "savagely" assaulted for thirty minutes by four plainclothes cops on October 18, 1947. Peter Train, a twenty-six-year-old veteran, accused New York City police detective John T. O'Connor of hitting and kicking him without reason. The pamphlet declared that police brutality is the northern "counterpart to lynch-terror against Negroes in the semi-feudal South." One section of the pamphlet defended the Communist Party for its diligence in fighting police brutality: "Often when my [Davis's] Councilmanic office and my party—the Communist Party—have made repeated charges of police brutality, the charges have been labeled as 'empty Communist propaganda,' or, as Police Commissioner Wallander once said, 'a campaign of calumny' against the police department. The cases cited here, show who has been indulging in 'empty propaganda.' They show what experience always proves, namely, that red-baiting is a camouflage to hide the truth." The pamphlet also remarked on the use of police brutality as an attempt to divide black

and white workers: "Numerous cases of police brutality have been oc-
casioned because Negro and white were in company together either
in Harlem or other sections of the city. This represents a direct threat
to the trade unions, which are based upon private and public association of Negro and white, Jew and Gentile, Catholic and Protestant, in
all walks of life." It continued, "As the Negro people, supported by their
trade union and white progressive allies, find it necessary to demonstrate, picket, and fight evictions, the policemen's billet is there to turn
them back."[41]

In an April 2, 1948, press release, Davis argued that the pamphlet
outlined his program of action "to stop this evil and to secure redress
and justice for the victim of police brutality." Echoing a familiar theme
pushed by the Communist Party, Davis noted that the pamphlet warned
of the danger of fascism in the lawless use of violence by police against
citizens. Davis also placed police brutality in a Cold War context: "It is
noteworthy that this vicious treatment of the Negro people takes place at
the moment when the Truman Doctrine and the Marshall Plan to save
the world from Communism are supposed to be spreading freedom and
equality all over the world. There could be no more vivid exposure of
hypocrisy of the Truman Administration and its Republican partisans
than what happens to Negroes in America."[42]

The argument equating police brutality to fascism echoed the party's
position that the police were part of the repressive state apparatus used
against those who challenged the status quo. The attack on the Truman administration and the Republican Party echoed accusations by
the Soviet Union and its allies that the racial terror and discrimination
aimed at black Americans undermined the United States' claim that it
was the paragon of democracy while the Soviet Union was a slave state.
But Davis's arguments were more than Communist propaganda. As we
saw above, Adam Clayton Powell Jr. and the *People's Voice* also compared
northern racism to its southern counterpart.

Davis's comparison of New York City police brutality to southern
lynching drew the attention of police commissioner Arthur William Wallander, who accused the city councilman of equating police with "Georgia lynchers" and carrying out a "campaign of calumny." In response,
Davis declared that the "Communist Party and I and numerous police
victims" would continue to make the claim until the police ended the

brutality, and he warned that if nothing happened, "this city faces a tragedy." He also denied comparing the NYPD to Georgia lynchers—"The
comparison is his [Wallander's] and not mine"—but he then reasserted
his principled point: "While on the subject, the Commissioner should
be reminded that a lynching was narrowly averted in Queens recently."[43]

Even while articulating the Communist Party's positions, Davis also
left room for those who were unsympathetic to the party. He pointed out
that the "growing incidence of police brutality in New York City has become a serious public issue," and in a letter to supporters described three
recent incidents in which police attacked citizens, including World War
II veteran Benjamin Gibbs, who was beaten by patrolman James Fisher
on October 14, 1946, and Samuel T. Symonette: "Unless we act NOW to
check the rising menace to public safety, the Negro people will become
the wholesale victims of Wallander's recent 'muss-em up' order to get
tough with the 'bums and street corner loafers.'"[44] Davis was referring
to Police Commissioner Wallander's order to crack down on criminals
in Harlem in order to curtail the rising crime rate. In a *Brooklyn Daily
Eagle* article headlined "'Muss up' Hoodlums, Wallander Tells Cops."
Wallander was quoted in September 1947 as ordering police to "get all
hoodlums off our streets. I mean get the street corner loafers and get the
easy money men, the ones who never work, day or night, but manage
to keep well dressed and have plenty of spending money. Give them the
proper treatment. You know what I mean by that."[45]

Police brutality would remain a key issue for Davis, even when he and
other top leaders of the American Communist Party became victims of
the Cold War and were charged in 1949 with violating the Smith Act.
When he ran, unsuccessfully, for reelection he continued to stress the
issues of "police brutality ... better housing [and] ... decent jobs."[46]

Cold War Civil Rights?

According to some scholars, by the Cold War period the NAACP had
embraced anti-Communist liberalism and joined an alliance of the federal, state, and local governments, private industry, labor, and others to
remove Communists from the fight for social justice. Historian Penny
Von Eschen writes, "As early as 1946, with the formation of Truman's
Committee on Civil Rights, [NAACP executive secretary Walter] White

and others began to craft the dominant argument of the anti-Communist civil rights liberals. The new argument seized on international criticism of American racism to argue that antidiscrimination measures were necessary for the United States in its struggle against communism. The liberal argument against racism, using anti-Communism to justify the fight against domestic discrimination and or civil rights, conceded the high ground to anti-Communism."[47]

Accusing Walter White, head of the NAACP from 1931 to 1955, of pushing the Communists out of the civil rights struggle, historian Manning Marable argues that he "fought any influence of communists or independent radicals in the organization. He supported the early 'witch-hunts' to exclude communists from all levels of the federal government. . . . Like [A. Philip] Randolph, White attempted to identify the struggle for black equality with the anti-communist impulse."[48]

To be sure, in the 1930s the NAACP had accused the Communist Party of trying to exploit African Americans by pretending to fight on their behalf. But the real aim of the party, according to NAACP officials, was to recruit them to the party and get them to accept Communist ideology. In a 1931 article in *Harper's Magazine*, Walter White accusing the party of exploiting black grievances for its own selfish ends.[49] In response, the party insisted that the oldest civil rights organization in the nation was a tool of capitalists, unwilling to mount a struggle on behalf of the black working class.[50]

Ben Davis, like other party members, did not hold back from criticizing the leadership of the NAACP. In a criticism of president Harry S. Truman, Davis claimed, "All those like Roy Wilkins of the NAACP, who seem to think the Negros are more interested in pulling Truman's Cold War chestnuts out of the fire than they are in stopping the lynch war against black people in this country have simply lost their heads in a mess of partisan politics."[51]

However, Von Eschen and other proponents of what historian Eric Arnesen calls the "new consensus on the domestic cold war civil rights" ignore evidence that at times the NAACP and other liberals actually cooperated with Communists.[52] Historian Patricia Sullivan points out that the "NAACP worked closely with a number of so-called Popular Front groups, since the New Deal era, such as the National Lawyers Guild, the National Committee to Abolish the Poll Tax, the Southern Conference for Human Welfare, and the Progressive Citizens of America. Walter White even warned that communism was less of a threat than professional anti-communists."[53]

In addition, there were Communists in a few branches of the NAACP. At the height of the Cold War, the Brooklyn branch leader worked alongside a Communist member, the Reverend Milton A. Galamison, who became president of the Brooklyn NAACP in 1956; and formed a strong alliance with Annie Stein, a member of both the branch and the Communist Party. Together, Stein and Galamison developed a grass-roots organization called the NAACP Schools Workshop, which helped to cultivate leadership among black and Latino parents to challenge Board of Education policies that many viewed as detrimental to their children's education. The workshop provided opportunities to negotiate with school officials and express parents' grievances to principals.[54] Historian Manfred Berg points out that Communists were members of the San Francisco and Richmond, California; Great Neck, New York; and Philadelphia branches and of a number of student chapters. Despite its misgivings about Communists in leadership positions, Berg found no evidence that the national leaders of the NAACP sought to purge members from these locales.[55]

Despite Ben Davis's party membership, there is evidence that some liberal voices reached out to the councilman for assistance. After he was elected to the City Council in 1943, an editorial in the Republican-leaning *New York Age* titled "Our New Councilman" declared, "When Benjamin J. Davis takes office on January 1, 1944, as City Councilman, he becomes by the very nature of things our councilman, regardless of his or our political affiliation and ties. That is the challenge which Election Day gave to Benjamin J. Davis. We are confident that he will satisfactorily meet that challenge and will acquit himself with credit to the race as our Councilman."[56]

In the winter of 1947, the Reverend Ben Richardson, executive secretary of the Regional Action Committee of *The Protestant*, wrote to the councilman asking for his assistance in the case of Leona Hightower Samuels, who had been physically assaulted by a patrolman the previous September. An eyewitness reported to *The Protestant* that the police officer kicked and punched her to the ground and began choking her.[57] Dorothy M. Hayes, the union representative for Social Services Employees Union Local 19 of the United Office and Professional Workers of America, CIO, also reached out to Davis, complaining about a police officer's "brutal and discriminatory treatment" of an African American woman who was member of the union. Davis assured Hayes that the union had his support and promised to send a letter to both Commissioner Wallander and Mayor O'Dwyer: "This case is apparently another in a whole series of brutal treatment of Negro women by members of the Police Department." Noting that the incident must be protested, Davis contended that the cases of brutality "are directed not only against the Negro people but against the fraternization between Negro and white which is the very foundation of the trade union movement."[58]

Even though there was animosity between the NAACP and the Communist Party, in 1946 Walter White sent Ben Davis a telegram informing him that his organization had requested a meeting with Commissioner Wallander "regarding the tense situation in Harlem growing out of police brutality" and "cordially" inviting Davis to "be one of a small and select group to attend this conference."[59] In 1949, James Powers, head of the Brooklyn branch of the NAACP, informed Davis that the group's executive board had adopted a resolution criticizing the police department "for willful and reckless practices which prevail throughout the police service of invading homes without warrant or lawful cause, of making illegal searches and seizures, and of exercising unnecessary and brutal violence in making arrests." Calling for a wide-scale investigation, Powers invited Davis's "attention to this subject" and said, "We request your interest and support."[60] It is unlikely that Davis attended the meeting; his name is not listed as an under signer in a press release issued by White.[61] Still, the fact that Walter White wanted to include him among a select group of leaders to meet with Wallander challenges the argument that the NAACP had adopted a policy of total exclusion of Communists from civil rights struggles.

Police Brutality as a Form of Genocide

Ben Davis was the leading Communist voice against police brutality during and shortly after World War II, a mantle that passed to William L. Patterson during the Cold War. Rising through the ranks of the Communist Party, Patterson became a member of the Central Committee and the executive secretary of the International Labor Defense (a party-affiliated legal defense organization).

After graduating from high school in 1911 Patterson moved from Oakland to San Francisco and began attending the University of California to study engineering. However, he had a change of heart and decided to study law, so in 1915 he enrolled at the Hastings College of Law of the University of California in San Francisco and graduated in 1919. A few years later he moved to New York City and in 1923 opened a law firm in Harlem along with two friends specializing in civil rights cases, particularly defending those whom he felt had been targeted unfairly by the state.[62]

In New York, Patterson encountered Marxists and socialists, including some early black members of the Communist Party, such as Richard Moore and Cyril Briggs. Patterson noted in his autobiography that he began studying Marxism as a young lawyer, but it was the famous Sacco and Vanzetti case that moved him to embrace Communism. Ferdinando Nicola Sacco and Bartolomeo Vanzetti, two young Italian immigrants who were anarchists, were arrested on April 15, 1920, and accused of a payroll robbery at a shoe factory in Braintree, Massachusetts. They were found guilty of killing two guards and sentenced to death.[63] Many Communists, socialists, and others on the left believed that Sacco and Vanzetti were falsely convicted and launched a campaign to stop their execution. After reading about the case and talking to Richard Moore, Cyril Briggs, Otto Huiswood, Lovett Fortman Whitman, and Grace Campbell, all black members of the Communist Party, Patterson concluded that the trial "revealed to millions the class nature of justice in the United States." He decided to join the campaign to save their lives. He traveled to Boston with others from the International Labor Defense and demonstrated outside the prison where Sacco and Vanzetti were being held. Despite protests throughout the United States and other countries, Sacco and Vanzetti were executed in late August 1927.[64]

The execution had a profound impact on Patterson: "For me, the world had changed. American reaction had won a victory over the bodies of two men, but its effort to stampede the people had ended in utter failure." His faith in the law as a tool for democracy had disappeared: "I could not practice law again, at least not as I had before." Patterson concluded that "Sacco and Vanzetti belonged to white and Black, Italian,

German, English, Jew, Russian, American—they belonged to progressive mankind." If oppression was going to end, then workers must unite. For Patterson, the execution was part of a larger effort by the ruling class to stop blacks and whites from uniting for a common cause. When Cyril Briggs gave him a copy of *The Communist Manifesto*, Patterson said a "door opened for me." He was soon reading works by Communists and speaking to party members.[65] The party was appealing to many African Americans because of its emphasis on fighting racism and white chauvinism and promoting integration. Its willingness to prioritize the fight against racism made it different from the major political parties and even left-leaning organizations such as the American Socialist Party. Eugene Debs, the founder of the Socialist Party, recognized the racial oppression of African Americans. He noted in a 1903 piece titled "The Negro in the Class Struggle" the fact that the "white heel is still upon the black neck is simply proof that the world is not yet civilized," but he insisted that there was "no Negro Question outside of the labor question. . . . We have nothing special to offer the Negro, and we cannot make separate appeals to all the races."[66] While Debs contended that the only important fight was the class struggle, Victor Berger, another member of the Socialist Party, wrote in 1902, "There could be no doubt that that the Negroes and mulattoes constitute a lower race."[67]

Convinced that Communism was the solution to racial inequality in the United States, Patterson joined the party and began taking classes at its Workers School. After a few months there, party officials selected him to visit the Soviet Union. The trip deepened his commitment, as he met students of color from developing nations: "To many thousands of Black, Brown and Yellow students, the effort of the USSR to give them a chance to become acquainted with the real world and with objective truth was a priceless gift. And to the USSR it represented the acceptance of responsibility to mankind, to international working-class solidarity— their philosophy."[68]

In the early 1930s Patterson became a member of International Labor Defense. In 1931, when the ILD defended the Scottsboro Nine, Patterson wrote, "Scottsboro had revealed the role played by the state—the multiple role—conspirator, judge, jury and executioner. If the state failed to carry through its plans, it was because the progressive world was alerted and had rallied to the defense of the hapless victims."[69] Patterson

learned two things from the Scottsboro case: the state, instead of protecting the lives of black people, was guilty of murdering them; and a
well-organized mass movement of interracial workers and progressives
could stop such killings. In 1933 Patterson, who had by then become national secretary of the ILD, declared the Scottsboro case a "legal lynching" but said the efforts of the mass movement, along with expert legal
defense, had forced the state of Alabama not to carry out the executions:
"The ruling class sought through the Scottsboro terror to chill the blood
of the earth crushed Negro masses, but their liberation struggles have
been raised to a higher level." For Patterson, "class war" prisoners had
to rely not only on expert legal defense but also on a vigorous working-
class mass protest.[70]

In 1949 Patterson became head of the National Civil Rights Congress, which was organized 1946 in Detroit when the National Negro
Congress, the International Labor Defense, and the National Federation
for Constitutional Liberties merged. The CRC's major objective was to
challenge racial injustices perpetrated by federal and local governments.
Patterson adopted the same three-pronged approach he used in the ILD
to address racial inequality: "The development of an offensive movement begins with mass democratic action; the broader and deeper and
sharper it is, the greater the defendant's chances. . . . Legal, procedure
and mass action tactics must be coordinated. It is therefore necessary to
prepare the state's intended victim for the activities that are an inseparable part of the campaign."[71]

As early as 1933 Patterson, too, had argued that oppression of blacks
was not a southern phenomenon but a national problem. In a speech
he said, "Tonight speakers have told you that 5,000 Negroes have been
lynched since the Civil War. Yet there have been 5,000 such lynchings,
and the Republican and Democratic Parties have done nothing about
it." He ridiculed the idea that there was no discrimination in Harlem:
"What about that butchers shop, Harlem Hospital? What about the extra
rents you have to pay? What about the restaurants and hotels right in
Harlem that you can't enter?"[72] But it would not be until the 1940s that
the term genocide was used to describe the United States policy regarding African Americans.

The *Chicago Defender* and the *New York Amsterdam News*, two of
the country's largest black weeklies, suggested soon after the creation of

the United Nation's Genocide Convention that the term genocide might apply to the treatment of African Americans, especially when it came to southern lynchings.[73] But Patterson and the Civil Rights Congress went further. World War II and the horrors of Nazism convinced Patterson to compare the United States' treatment of blacks to Germany's policy of genocide: "I could not fail to recognize that just as the United States, under cover of law, carried out genocidal racist policies in police murders of Black men, framed death sentences, death that came from withholding proper medical care to Black people, just so had Hitler built and operated his mass death machine made under cover of Nazi law. It goes without saying that this analogy was not clearly seen by the masses in Western countries and by the masses of Americans."[74]

The CRC's petition, *We Charge Genocide*, was presented to the UN General Assembly in 1951, but the CRC was not first to solicit in that forum. In 1946 the National Negro Congress drafted a petition calling on the UN to address the oppression of black people throughout the United States. In 1947, the NAACP submitted a petition calling on the UN Commission on Human Rights to probe U.S. racial discrimination.[75] However, the CRC's petition went further in that it accused the United States of implementing a policy of genocide against black Americans. Patterson and members of the CRC prepared the petition, including Communist Party members Elizabeth Lawson and writer Howard Fast, and the folklorist, writer, and antiracist crusader Stetson Kennedy, who had joined the Young Communist League.[76]

The CRC adopted the definition of genocide employed by the Genocide Convention of the UN's General Assembly: "Any intent to destroy, in whole or in part, a national, racial or religious group." The creators of the *We Charge Genocide* petition insisted that "we maintain, therefore, that the oppressed Negro citizens of the United States, segregated, discriminated against and long the target of violence, suffer from genocide as the result of the consistent, conscious, unified policies of every branch of government."[77]

Ninety-three people signed the petition. Most were from New York City, and some were in the Communist Party. Among the Communists were Isadore Begun, who in the late 1920s and early 1930s was a leader of the Communist-led Rank and File Caucus of the New York City Teachers Union; Harry Haywood, one of the party's early black American leaders; James W. Ford, vice presidential candidate on the Communist Party ticket in 1940; Claudia Jones, who became a member of the National Committee of the Communist Party in 1947; Maude White Katz, a party activist; William Alphaeus Hunton, a professor of English at Howard University who became head of the African Affairs Council and joined the party sometime in the 1930s; Ferdinand Smith, second in command of the national Maritime Union; Benjamin Davis; and author Howard Fast.[78] W. E. B. Du Bois, who would join the party in 1959, and Paul Robeson, who never joined but remained close to its leadership, also signed the petition.[79]

The authors of the petition relied on newspaper accounts of police and gang killings and of "masked men" motivated by hatred. The petition specifically pointed to the killings of blacks by members of the law enforcement establishment: "Our evidence concerns the thousands of Negroes who over the years have been beaten to death on chain gangs and in the back rooms of sheriff's offices, in cells of county jails, in precinct police stations and on city streets."[80]

The CRC argued that the killing of innocent blacks was not limited to any specific region of the country but happened in New York, Cleveland, Detroit, Washington, DC, Chicago, Memphis, Atlanta, Birmingham, New Orleans, and Los Angeles. Both lynching and the "policeman's bullet" were responsible for the murders.[81] "We submit that the evidence suggests that the killing of Negroes has become police policy in the United States," they wrote, "and that police policy is the most practical expression of government policy."[82] Of the hundreds of cases of police brutality from 1945 to 1950 described in the petition, fifty-seven involved police shootings and beatings of blacks in New York City. Race, according to CRC, was the major reason blacks were targeted. The victims in New York ranged from some of the most well-known, such as John Derrick and the Ferguson brothers, to a case involving an "unidentified" black man into whom police "emptied their guns." The police involved were never prosecuted.[83]

Although few in the academic community and legal profession supported the *We Charge Genocide* petition, a number of black journalists, ministers and civil rights activists added their names. Among the signers were Charlotta Bass, former owner of the *California Eagle*, who served as director of the Youth Movement of the NAACP and was selected by the Republican Party to serve as the western regional director of Wendell Willkie's presidential campaign; Roscoe Dunjee, owner and editor of the *Oklahoma Black Dispatch*, one of the most prominent black newspapers in the country; William Edward Harrison; editor of the famed *Boston Guardian*; Mary Church Terrell, a leader of the Black Women's Club Movement; and the Reverend Charles A. Hill of Hartford Memorial Baptist Church in Detroit.[84]

Conclusion

The growing scholarship on anti-Communist liberalism describes how groups such as the NAACP and anti-Communist black intellectuals and leaders protected the civil rights movement from being taken over by the party.[85] Anti-Communist liberals did indeed join the Cold War effort to eliminate the Communist Party, but it is inaccurate to argue that the party lacked all liberal support or that it was a nonfactor in the civil rights struggle. The fact that Ben Davis and the CRC received support should make us rethink the notion that the party was completely marginalized by and/or alienated from non-Communist activists. Even the staunchly anti-Communist NAACP reached out to Davis. In addition, scholars who have promoted the notion of Cold War repression have provided a clearer picture of how such actions devastated the Communist Party, its members, and the black freedom struggle.[86]

To be sure, the Communist Party's loyalty to Moscow, its efforts to control the National Negro Congress, and its shameful decision to support the "non-aggression" pact between the Soviet Union and Nazi Germany all helped to bolster the argument that the organization was less concerned with social justice than with supporting the Soviet Union. But these decisions on the part of the American Communist Party should not obscure its work in the field of civil rights, including the effort the party and its members made in the fight against New York City police brutality.

Ben Davis's formulation of police brutality as "lynching" and William Patterson and the Civil Rights Congress' classifying police assaults on black people as human rights violations that government had a responsibility to address, helped many to conceptualize police assault on black people. The refusal of the city government and police department to take serious action against such violence made those with power to act culpable of violating the constitutional and human rights of the victims. By classifying police brutality as state-sanctioned violence, Davis and Paterson provided those engaged in the anti–police brutality movement with a means of pressuring the federal and local governments to respond.[87]

Depicting police brutality as a form of lynching and as genocide has influenced later campaigns for social justice. In Chicago, a coalition of grassroots organizations called We Charge Genocide, after the name of the 1951 petition, has targeted police brutality by sending a report to the UN Committee against Torture on November 13, 2014, asserting that the Chicago Police Department is torturing young black people. Robert Taylor of the Millions for Reparations, a Brooklyn-based organization calling for reparations for black people, has said that We Charge Genocide was the antecedent to his campaign.[88]

On January 29, 2016, the United Nations Working Group of Experts on People of African Descent released a statement to the media comparing police brutality to lynching: "Contemporary police killings and the trauma it creates are reminiscent of the racial terror of lynching of the past. Impunity for state violence has resulted in the current human rights crisis and must be addressed as a matter of urgency."[89] In a July 2016 speech at a church in St. Paul, Minnesota, Cornell Williams Brooks, president of the NAACP, compared the recent killings of young black men by police to lynching during the civil rights movement: "We will stand up and stand against police misconduct, police brutality, and we will bring the 21st Century lynching to an end."[90]

Davis and Patterson's work also refutes the argument that the civil rights movement was a regional phenomenon. Instead, it reminds us today, as it did in the 1940s and 1950s, that the movement was national in scope. A variety of organizations were involved, including civil rights groups, religious communities, and political forces that extended from those who embraced racial liberalism to more radical elements, including the American Communist Party. The party played a role in the northern civil rights struggle by leading campaigns and framing a broader interpretation of civil rights concerns. In fact, it was the Communist Party, more than any other political organization, that connected the issues of race and class when it came to police brutality.

3

The Nation of Islam and Police Brutality

According to New York City Police Department records, on April 14, 1972, eleven police officers from the Twenty-Eighth Precinct rushed into the largest and most famous Nation of Islam Mosque in the United States, Temple No. 7 on 116th Street in Harlem,[1] after receiving an anonymous phone call reporting that a police officer, a Detective Thomas, needed assistance. It eventually was revealed to have been a fictitious claim. Officers Phillip Cardillo and Vito Navarra were the first to enter the mosque. Hearing a disturbance on the second floor, Navarra ran up the stairs and was met by ten to twelve members of the Nation of Islam (NOI), who forced him back down the stairway. Six other NOI members confronted Cardillo, who had remained on the first floor. A fight erupted inside the mosque between the officers and NOI members. One officer was knocked to the floor, and Cardillo was shot. He would die from his wound a few days later. The police detained sixteen NOI members, but tensions remained high outside the mosque, where many onlookers had gathered. Eventually Louis Farrakhan, the minister of Temple No. 7, and U.S. representative Charles Rangel arrived, and Farrakhan used a police loudspeaker to ask the crowd to disperse. He would later complain to the NYPD that the police had raided a place of worship, and on May 13 police commissioner Benjamin Ward issued an official apology to the NOI for having invaded the mosque, noting that errors were made on the part of the police.[2]

"What was so extraordinary about the 1972 incident," writes historian Rasul Miller, "was the Muslims' ability to leverage their influence to address the situation." To help pressure the NYPD to stop its brutal policing of black Muslims, the NOI organized a "unity rally" to protest the police behavior: "Sunni Muslims were in attendance, including the world-renowned Egyptian scholar and Qur'an reciter Sheikh Mahmoud Khalil al-Hussary. Muslims of differing theological opinions came together to oppose repressive policing of Muslims and people of color." It was not the physical confrontation between the police and NOI members that struck Miller but the ability of the group to use its "power" to generate an apology from the commissioner.[3]

Many have written about the Nation of Islam, its many confrontations with police, and its efforts to stop police brutality, but scant attention has been paid to those of its strategies that did not involve physical confrontation. The historical record shows that the NOI did confront the police with force and that its leading figures advocated self-defense, and many have focused on Malcolm X's call for black people to arm themselves and fight back against physical assaults by white racists and the police. But NOI leader Elijah Muhammad insisted, for both practical and religious reasons, that his followers not engage in physical clashes with the police, though almost nothing has been written about his many nonviolent strategies, including attempts to negotiate with police officials, seek legal redress, and employ public pressure through the media.

These were all means of empowering and mobilizing black people to take action against state dominance. The NOI was a pivotal force in the 1950s and 1960s that helped shape the responses of those involved in the struggle to end police violence.

The Origins of the Nation of Islam

Beginning in 1920, a huge wave of southern black migrants, and to a lesser extent black people from the Caribbean, began moving to northern urban centers, resulting in a dramatic economic and social transition as cities became divided by race and class. Between 1920 and 1930 the black population of New York City grew from 152,467 to 327,706. Most of the newcomers came from the upper seaboard states of Virginia, North Carolina, and South Carolina, with a large number also from Georgia and Florida.[4] Coinciding with the rapid influx of blacks into Harlem in that ten-year period, nearly 119,000 white residents left Harlem for other boroughs. The black population, however, continued to grow dramatically over the next two decades. Whites composed the majority in central Harlem in 1920—67.4 percent of the 216,026 residents. By 1930 they constituted only 29.3 percent of a population of 209,663. The black population jumped from 32.4 percent in 1920 to 70.2 percent in 1930 and to 89.3 percent of 221,974 residents in 1940. By 1950 blacks made up over 98 percent of the 237,467 central Harlem residents.[5]

The migrants flooding into Harlem and other northern urban centers got an economic boost, as they were able to secure industrial jobs
that paid far more than those in the South. And by moving from agri-
cultural work to become "proletariats," migrants' children could receive
the education denied to them back home. Nonetheless, conditions in
the northern cities were harsh, and economics and racism meant living in overcrowded, dilapidated housing with few city services. During the Depression Harlem became a ghetto. Historian Gilbert Osofsky
notes, "Harlem was transformed from a potentially ideal community to
a neighborhood with manifold social and economic problems called 'deplorable,' 'unspeakable,' 'incredible.'" While employment opportunities
were better than in the South, the new black residents nevertheless experienced high levels of unemployment and underemployment. Although
the national unemployment rate was close to 25 percent at the height of
the Depression in 1933, in Harlem it was 50 percent. Another 43 percent
of the population were on relief, and family income dropped by nearly
50 percent from 1929 to 1933.[6] To make matters worse, Harlem had the
highest infant mortality, TB, and general mortality rates in the city.[7]

The wave of migration into Harlem created overcrowded schools.
Even though a new school had not been built in Harlem since 1909,
the neighborhood received no school funds from the city or the federal government. By contrast, despite a 1934 request by the city asking
the federal government to provide funding for 168 new schools, no new
school was planned for Harlem. The city only planned to build a school
annex for the Harlem community.[8]

One way the urban black poor responded to their socioeconomic pre-
dicament was to form their own spiritual and religious organizations.
They challenged racial repression by creating community among their
members, providing black men and women with an avenue to leadership, and offering opportunities to take on important roles in the new
religions in urban centers. In *Black Gods of the Metropolis*, his 1944 study
of the new urban working-class religious bodies, anthropologist Arthur
Huff Fauset wrote that race consciousness was a drawing card for the
new black nationalist religious groups. He also wrote that the new religions offered black southern migrants a way of practicing their religious beliefs not allowed in the larger churches of the black elite.[9] The
new religious movements in urban America, wrote sociologist Erdmann

Doane Beynon in 1938, arose "out of the growing disillusionment and race consciousness of recent Negro migrants to northern industrial cities."[10] Some of the new religious groups provided their followers with explanations for their social circumstances that framed black people as the people of God and challenged white supremacy by blaming whites for black misery.

The group that would become the most well-known black-nationalist organization was the Nation of Islam, formed by Wallace D. Fard in 1930 in Detroit. Beynon interviewed several followers of Fard, who told him that in the 1930s Fard first went to the houses of black Detroit residents selling raincoats and silks. Once he had developed a relationship with his customers, he began expounding his nationalistic Islamic teachings that black people were the Lost Tribe of Shabazz and white people had stolen their language and culture. He preached that black people's original religion was Islam, that the Quran was their holy text, and that they must regain their religion, including adopting a number dietary practices such as not eating pork or shellfish and abstaining from alcohol. Fard referred to whites as devils who kidnapped black people, the "original" people from Mecca.[11]

After Fard's mysterious disappearance in the summer of 1934, Elijah Robert Poole, who would change his name to Elijah Muhammad, became the NOI leader. Born in Sandersville, Georgia, in 1897, he left Georgia as part of the Great Migration, settled in Detroit, and was one of the handful of black people there attracted to Fard's teaching. He joined the Nation of Islam in 1931 and became a close ally of Fard. After the founder's disappearance, he declared himself the new NOI leader, claiming that Fard was Allah, had told him all the secrets of life, and had named him as the last prophet. A number of members of the black Muslim movement rejected these claims and the organization split into factions. Fearing for his life, Elijah Muhammad fled to Chicago, where he led his faction of the NOI.

The Nation of Islam was not the only black nationalist religious sect operating in black urban centers in the early twentieth century. Others included the Moorish Science Temple, an Islamic group founded in 1913 by Noble Drew Ali; and black nationalist groups that embraced Judaism, including the Commandment Keepers of the Living God, known also as the Black Jews of Harlem, and the House of Israel, which taught that black Americans were the original Jews.[12] However, the NOI was the most successful of the sects, and while other groups largely faded from the scene, by the 1960s it was estimated that the NOI had between one hundred thousand and three hundred thousand members, a far cry from its few hundred in the early 1950s. The Federal Bureau of Investigation estimated that the NOI operated thirty-eight named temples and over thirty unnamed temples throughout the country.[13] It owned dozens of businesses, including restaurants, bakeries, and farms, and published one of the largest black weeklies in the nation, *Muhammad Speaks*, boasting a circulation of over one hundred thousand by the mid-1960s.[14]

A major reason for the NOI's popularity was its black-nationalist message, which appealed to many working-class African Americans. It adopted a psychological approach toward eliminating black low self-esteem, arguing that blacks were of a noble race and were not the cause of their own socioeconomic failure. Teaching that Allah was God and black people were his chosen people was a counter to the denigration of people of African origins and their resulting feelings of worthlessness. Similar to the Garvey movement, the outward appearance of the NOI's neatly dressed men and women promoted racial pride. As scholar and member of the Malcolm X Project at Columbia University Wayne Taylor has contended, the "Nation of Islam propagated a Black theology of liberation that spoke to the contemporary plight of African Americans in urban centers."[15]

Another reason for the NOI's success was its eschatological view that the six-thousand-year reign of white people over Earth was coming to an end. This position highlighted believers' special relationship with a supreme being that was willing to destroy the white "devils" and elevate the "righteous" to their proper positions as rulers of the planet. It also accentuated the urgency of the moment; if one wanted to be saved, one needed to join the righteous in a timely matter or else face doom.[16]

Yet another reason for the organization's growth was the charismatic Malcolm X. Malcolm, as many knew him, joined the NOI while in prison in the 1950s. Elijah Muhammad named him head minister of Temple No. 7 in 1955, as a reward for him becoming the organization's most articulate spokesperson. Malcolm publicly challenged those in power on issues of race, colonialism, national liberation struggles in Africa, Asia, and Latin America, and contemporary global and national politics.

His ability to destroy his opponents in debates became legendary, and his willingness to attack white people for their inhumane treatment of black people led many to accuse him of spreading hate and advocating violence. However, his fiery language attracted countless admirers, and during his time in the NOI membership grew by tens of thousands.

A Sleeping Tiger

One extremely influential group promoting the view that the Nation of Islam comprised fanatical, dangerous religious zealots bent on physical confrontation with police was the Federal Bureau of Investigation. In 1955 the FBI prepared a lengthy internal report on the history and beliefs of the NOI which maintained that "Muhammad and ministers of the NOI take pride in citing the fearless nature of its members. They speak with pride of various incidents where the NOI members have engaged the police." The report claimed that when a large number of NOI members gather in a place where there are whites, "there seems to be a sort of eagerness to demonstrate their fearlessness." According to the FBI report, it was the police and not the NOI who demonstrated restraint when provoked by the black Muslims.[17]

The FBI report maintained that in the 1930s the Detroit Board of Education tried to prosecute NOI parents for violating state education laws because they refused to send their children to the city's public schools. When some parents were jailed, members of the NOI "banned together and stoned the prison. To avoid a race riot, the judge issued orders for the prisoners' release."[18] The report also described a 1950 confrontation between the San Diego Police Department and NOI members: when officers arrived at the home of a man whom they were attempting to serve with a warrant, two men in the house reported that the suspect was not at home. When the police tried to enter to search the house, "they were ruthlessly attacked. This perpetrated a near riot. And necessitated the calling out of additional cars and approximately twenty officers." Officers reported that before the subject was taken into custody, someone fired three shots into a police car. The police later learned that the subject and the two men who first confronted the officers were members of the San Diego NOI temple.[19]

By 1959, the FBI became so concerned about the confrontations between members of the NOI and the police that it issued a second volume of its report. In this one, it compared NOI members to a sleeping tiger: "When you awake a sleeping tiger, you must put a harness on him also, otherwise he may do a great deal of damage."[20]

The media also promulgated the view that the Nation of Islam was a violent organization. In 1959 WNTA-TV in New York aired the documentary *The Hate That Hate Produced*, produced by journalists Mike Wallace and Louis Lomax. Wallace introduced the documentary by claiming that the organization called for "black supremacy" and predicting that sometime between 1959 and 1970 its leader, Elijah Muhammad, would "give the call for the destruction of the white man."[21] The press labeled the NOI "black supremacists" and "purveyors" of "cold black hatred." *Time* magazine asserted that Muhammad preached a "virulent anti-Americanism and anti-Semitism" and that his "doctrine of total hate found a ready medium in some newspapers which began to exploit Negro hopes and fears of the Emmitt Till case."[22] In another issue, *Time* quoted James Curran, Maryland's superintendent of prisons, who warned that the black Muslims were growing steadily stronger and more troublesome: "They are vicious fighters, quick to take offense, and in their self-sacrificial way, they don't care what happens to them."[23]

Civil rights leaders also denounced the NOI as irresponsible. Thurgood Marshall, legal counsel for the NAACP, labeled the NOI "vicious and a real threat to the FBI, the NAACP and state law enforcement agencies." The organization, according to Marshall, was "run by a bunch of thugs organized from jails."[24]

Various scholars have also insisted that the NOI posed a real threat. Lee P. Brown—who was elected the first black mayor of Houston in 1997 and served three terms—wrote an article in 1965 in which he called the NOI a "radical movement" that "poses a problem to the police" and claimed it "can be compared with the Ku Klux Klan; but its philosophy is a reversal of the doctrines postulated by the Klan. The KKK advocates as their premise, white supremacy; whereas the reversal of this doctrine is employed by the Muslims in that they employ the doctrine of black supremacy." According to Brown, law enforcement was in danger from the NOI "because it has been reported that the cult conceives of the police as a representative of the white man's authority," and a major concern for the police "is that it has been reported by many sources that the Muslims are prone toward hatred and violence. It has been reported that they have arsenals throughout the country, and are trained in the use of firearms. They supposedly have as their target the law enforcement agents of the country."[25]

C. Eric Lincoln, author of *Black Muslims in America*, the first scholarly book on the Nation of Islam, also promoted the view that the NOI adopted a violent approach. Lincoln claims that the Black Muslims were "neither pacifists nor aggressors." However, "they do believe in keeping the scores even, and they have warned all America that 'an eye for an eye and a tooth for a tooth' is the only effective way to settle racial differences."[26]

Obey the Law

Without a doubt, the NOI did see the police as an adversarial force bent on killing black people, a position rooted in its racial religious doctrine. In explaining why there were a number of confrontations between his members and white police, Elijah Muhammad, who led the NOI from 1933 until his death in 1975, argued that white officers attacked blacks because "by nature" black people were peaceful and "by nature white people are for war, bloodshed, are destroyers of high morals." From the NOI's perspective, structural factors played no part in brutal attacks on black people; rather, these acts were purely an expression of white people's evil nature. According to Muhammad, "They [white people] have no respect for people who want to be at peace with them. They have no respect for the laws or justice," and they "have made trouble all over the world with people who were at peace among themselves."[27] When writing on the 1963 confrontation between NOI members and police in Flint, Michigan, Muhammad declared that the "enemies" of black people "have ruled and killed us for the past 4,000 years and especially during the last 400 years." The NOI's analysis of the cause of police brutality ruled out the left's contention that the police were part of a repressive state apparatus used to crush any challenge to the power of the ruling elite. For the NOI, human nature, not structural inequality or policy, was the root cause of black suffering.[28]

If assaults on blacks were an artifact of white cops' "evil," what caused black police officers to attack black people? While some anti–police brutality activists argued that one way to end such practices was to hire more black police officers, the NOI rejected this. Unlike advocates of hiring more black police officers, who argued that black people would not be brutal to their own, the NOI maintained that black police were not loyal to their race. The simplistic psychology of the NOI's answer declared that it happened because "Uncle Toms" were willing to betray their race to gain favor with whites. "In the past and maybe the present," Elijah Muhammad wrote in *Muhammad Speaks* in December 1968, "the white officer chooses among the Uncle-Tom-like men to serve as law enforcement officers over us." Black police provided no useful service to the black community, and the black cop "makes more trouble in the community than the trouble that is made by the community, because he wants to be loved and honored by the white officer at the expense of mistreating his Black people."[29] Muhammad went as far as to accuse the white police of monitoring the behavior of black officers by riding with them in the black community in order to assure "that the Black officer mistreats his people as he would do himself." Consequently, the black police officer did not get the cooperation of his "Black brothers," because they were "divided by the third [white] man."[30] Although Muhammad criticized black police officers, he did not hold them responsible for the bad relationship they had with the black community. That was the doing of the white officer who refused to select a "Black Man who loves his Black People."[31]

On occasion, Elijah Muhammad warned that if Muslims were attacked, they would retaliate. Speaking of the April 27, 1962, murder of NOI member Ronald Stokes by the Los Angeles police, he said he hoped that the "police will not send their trained dogs against my followers. The white man is absolutely heartless; they are murderers of each other; what can we expect from them?"[32] In a May 18, 1963, piece in *Muhammad Speaks*, the leader of the NOI cautioned, "We will fight like hell (the brave ones) with those who fight against us. This is the very law of nature—self-defense—and it is recognized by God and man."[33]

Such rhetoric could easily be interpreted as confrontational, thus providing his opponents with ammunition. The FBI, the white media, and others ignored Muhammad's consistent message to his members to *avoid* conflict with the police and to obey the law and those in authority. He emphasized that his followers were nonviolent and would not engage in retaliation against police brutality. Responding to police brutality against

NOI members in Detroit, Muhammad told an audience in January 1958 to "obey those who are in authority."[34] He wrote in his book *Message to the Blackman in America*, "We are not going to take part in any violence whatsoever. We're not going to do anything other than what we are doing. . . . We have stripped ourselves of arms to let you know that we are not people of violence. We don't intend to attack you. We have no idea or knowledge of anything like that coming in the future."[35]

Such words were not just a plea for restraint—they reflected policy. Point 3 of the Nation of Islam's "Laws and Instructions" commands members to "obey the laws of the land or government you must live under for if you cannot keep these laws how can you obey the laws of Allah (God)?"[36]

Muhammad was not contradicting himself in the 1963 *Muhammad Speaks* statement quoted above saying both that "we will fight like hell" and that Muslims would not retaliate if attacked and would not attack the police out of revenge. He was referring to spontaneous response to an attack, not asserting an official position of the organization. His qualifying remark, noting that the "brave ones" would fight back, indicates that some members would, out of sheer bravery, risk death. However, he was not encouraging his followers to strike back, given NOI's official no-retaliation policy.

Muhammad also offered an additional, quite practical reason for not responding with violence when attacked by the police: "Because if we attacked you, we would have to have superior weapons to attack you with, and we don't have factories nor earth to dig metals to manufacture tools or weapons such as you have."[37] In an April 1963 interview with a *New York Herald Tribune* reporter, Muhammad emphasized that not only would the NOI not participate in any violence, it would continue stripping its members of arms "to let people know that they are not violent people." The Nation of Islam was not stockpiling weapons with the intent of organizing an attack, for such an effort would lead to the NOI's demise. His members were not allowed to carry weapons, and he urged them to "clean themselves up," by which he meant giving up any activity that was considered immoral or antisocial and attempting to live a religiously devout life free of violence.[38] "If you come to the door shooting," Muhammed explained to whites, "we have no guns here to shoot back with, so therefore the right is with God, as it is written in the Book."[39]

Muhammad's declaration that the "right is with God" was also a theological argument that it was God's job to defend Muslims against police violence, and that it was simply against God's will for Muslims to take part in any violent action against such attacks. In *Message to the Blackman*, he insisted that "God forbids us even to accept weapons and even to carry anything like weapons to fight with."[40] As to why God would deny his people weapons to defend themselves, Muhammad argued that taking action against the devil was in the hands of God, not Muslims: "Allah wants to make Himself known in the Western Hemisphere that He is God and has come to save us from the hands of our enemies and place us again in our own country and among our own people. He has said that He would do this job of delivering us and destroying those who have destroyed us. This is prophesized almost throughout the Bible."[41]

This reference to biblical scripture that he claimed was in line with his teachings was an attempt to convince an audience outside the Nation of Islam of the legitimacy of his leadership among black people. Black Christians, after all, far outnumbered those who practiced Islam. Here, he was tapping into a tradition of divine retribution espoused by numerous religions, including Christianity, Judaism, Hinduism, Buddhism, and Islam. In a 1964 article on police brutality, Muhammad claimed that God "would make clear to everyone his plans to destroy the white devil race."[42]

Muhammad's message of restraint in the face of police violence remained consistent throughout his leadership of the NOI. Even during the Black Power era, when black nationalist and revolutionary groups called for armed struggle against police, he remained steadfast in arguing that Muslims must rely on Allah for protection. At a 1972 press conference, he reemphasized that he did not "believe in carrying weapons. When a man puts weapons in his pockets or a gun, I will make clear it takes his mind off God's protection and puts it on the gun to protect him. This I have taught my followers ever since God [Fard] left me."[43]

Muhammad even pushed the notion of predestination as an explanation for his insistence that his followers avoid confrontation with law enforcement, arguing that persecution by the criminal justice system was part of black people's fate: "But actually our people in Los Angeles, New York or any other place, here in Chicago, they have been mistreated right along. They go to prison and the federal penitentiary. But that is all given to us. The trial of the Black Muslims in America must come to pass. We must be tried." This otherworldly message accentuated the notion that it was God's plan that Muslims endure persecution, and thus, any attempt to fight back violated God's wishes.[44]

Muhammad was well aware of the consequences of NOI members responding violently to the police, but his insistence that they remain peaceful went beyond cautioning self-preservation. He recognized that physical disengagement as a collective response could be a useful solution to police violence. While the police, media, and FBI were busy painting the NOI as an organization of thugs, the Nation of Islam was busy challenging that image through speeches, writings, and the principles of the organization, presenting the police, not NOI members, as the perpetrators of violence. Disengaging could demonstrate to the world the humanity of victims who were being depicted as culprits. At the same time, it reinforced the NOI's argument regarding the cruelty of white people.

This was not a strategy of nonviolent civil disobedience as represented by the boycotts, sit-ins, strikes, marches, and demonstrations designed to pressure those inflicting violence on the black population of the South to end their repressive measures. The objective in the South, as characterized by the Southern Christian Leadership Conference, was not to "humiliate the opponent, only to win him."[45] The NOI, however, was far more concerned about its own survival then about transforming those who were doing it harm. The NOI's form of nonviolence was to demonstrate to nonwhites the brutality of white people. Wallace Muhammad, the son of Elijah Muhammad who became head of the NOI after his father's death in 1975, claimed in an interview for the 1994 PBS documentary *Malcolm X: Make It Plain* that the 1960s civil rights struggle benefited the NOI because "the sixties showed us the white man in the image that the Nation [of Islam] cast him in." The 1963 police campaign in Birmingham, Alabama, that turned water cannons and dogs on nonviolent demonstrators, for example, "helped the Nation of Islam's charge against the white race"[46]—it made the case that the NOI held the moral high ground.

Malcolm's Views

In contrast to Elijah Muhammad, NOI minister Malcolm X called for direct and confrontational action, and his speeches and interviews advocated that black people strike back when they were physically assaulted. He constantly ridiculed civil rights leaders, calling them Uncle Toms who foolishly subjected their followers to brutal attacks by racists.

Unlike Elijah Muhammad, who claimed that God would arrange for retribution, Malcolm placed that responsibility in the hands of black people. In a 1952 letter Malcolm wrote, "All over the world the Dark people know that the devils' time was up and those Dark people want to swoop down like a huge tidal wave and wash the devils from this planet." Allah, he said, was holding back until all black people had heard his message and had had the opportunity to accept or reject it, after which time Allah will allow his "'sea of Black Soldiers' to swoop out of the East and make the entire hemisphere a 'sea of blood.'"[47]

When NOI women were the victims of police brutality, Malcolm was even more emphatic about using self-defense. An FBI agent reported in a March 1954 memorandum that Malcolm had told a Detroit audience that black men "went to Korea to fight for the devil but they would not go help their women when their sisters and mothers are being raped by the devil in the street." The minister was reported to have gone on to claim that 1954 was the last year for the white man to rule, because black men were "united all over the world to fight the 'devils.'"[48] In a June 1959 talk in New York, Malcolm told the story of "Sister Roberta," who was mishandled and arrested by New York City police when she attempted to intervene as police officers were arresting her husband. According to Malcolm, Sister Roberta's husband was in a store when a woman came in charging that he had raped her daughter. The police were called and arrested the accused man. Sister Roberta learned about the arrest, went to the store, and spoke to the woman who had made the charge. The woman recanted her story, but when Sister Roberta then begged the police to release her husband the arresting officer hit her in the face and placed her under arrest. At the police station the same officer again struck Sister Roberta in the face. Malcolm told his audience the couple's cases were coming up in a week and urged Muslims to make it their business to attend the trial, because when a single member of NOI was in trouble, all members were in trouble. Although this was a call for moral support, Malcolm then declared that as a rule, anybody who strikes one Muslim woman should not be given the opportunity to strike another.[49]

The differences between Elijah Muhammad and Malcolm X's responses to police brutality were evident in the NOI's most noted case, the April 27, 1962, raid on the NOI temple in Los Angeles. During the raid, police beat members inside the temple and shot seven NOI members, including Ronald Stokes, the temple's secretary, who was attempting to raise his hands in surrender when he was killed. Manning Marable argues that Malcolm was distraught over the raid and in response organized a group of Fruit of Islam members from Temple No. 7 to kill the police officers involved in the murder. The Fruit of Islam were NOI men trained in martial arts whose job was to protect the NOI leadership and its temples. However, Elijah Muhammad ordered him to drop that idea.[50] At an August 10, 1963, "Harlem Unity Rally," Malcolm accused the Los Angeles police of shooting Stokes in the heart, then beating him in the head as he lay dying. Malcolm said angrily that Stokes, an unarmed Korean veteran who fought for the United States, came back and "was shot down like a dog. . . . Not in Mississippi but in Los Angeles, California; not in the South but the North, in the West."[51]

Malcolm warned the Los Angeles Police Department, "You don't shoot one of us and then grin in our faces. . . . Someone has to pay." But payment, he said, would not come from legal action. "A black man can't get justice in the court system in America. The only way you get justice is the streets, the only way you get justice is in the sidewalk. The only way you get justice is when you make justice for yourself. You'll never get justice in the white man's court. No not me. I never want them to take me to court. . . . I've seen what they have done right here in New York City." He reminded NOI members to obey the law, but said that if a white man puts his hands on you, "take him off the planet."[52]

Malcolm's public accusation that black civil rights leaders and his critics were "Uncle Toms" whose milquetoast-like, nonviolent approach was selling out black people helped to foster his own image as a no-nonsense revolutionary advocating armed self-defense. This led some civil rights leaders to portray him as out of control and irresponsible. Although he did not refer directly to the Nation of Islam or Malcolm X, NAACP leader Roy Wilkins spoke out in a letter to famed baseball player and civil rights activist Jackie Robinson saying he didn't envision "the Negro employing hate as a tactic" to "mobilize support or win a set of objectives." Wilkins argued that "the basic battle will not be won by noise makers and name-callers and race baiters but by men and women mature emotionally as well as physically. We are lost if we adopt Klan methods in the name of exalting black people."[53] In an August 1959 speech to the National Bar Association, Martin Luther King Jr. referred to the NOI as "one of the hate groups arising in our midst which would preach a doctrine of black supremacy. . . . Black supremacy is as bad as white supremacy. God is not interested merely in the freedom of black men and brown and yellow men, God is interested in the freedom of the whole human race."[54]

Malcolm X's more militant message of self-defense, as compared to Elijah Muhammad's promise of divine retribution, helped to portray the former as uncompromising toward police brutality. However, his pronouncements regarding the use of force in response to police brutality obscured the fact that he and members of the NOI also adopted far less militant approaches toward police assaults—including meetings, negotiations, and the courts—which have received far less attention than his calls for armed self-defense.

Malcolm X and the Johnson X Hinton Case

The Johnson X. Hinton case provides an example of Malcolm's willingness to use nonviolent approaches in the fight against police brutality. Hinton was a member of the Nation of Islam and belonged to Temple No. 7 in Harlem, headed by the then thirty-one-year-old Malcolm X.

On the evening of April 26, 1957, Hinton, also thirty-one, had left the temple and met a friend, twenty-three-year-old Frankie Lee Potts, at the corner of 125th Street and Lenox Avenue. At 10:15 p.m. Hinton and Potts were walking when they came upon patrolmen Ralph Plaisance and Mike Dolan beating Reese V. Poe, who had been in a confrontation with an acquaintance by the name of Martha Andrews. The police action attracted a crowd of fifty people, including Hinton and Potts. Hinton, clearly disturbed by the beating, asked the officers, "Why don't you carry the man to jail?"[55]

Hinton said in an affidavit that he did not interfere with the arrest but moved back into the crowd. Additional police officials came on the scene and began asking people to move away. Officer Dolan decided that Hinton was not moving fast enough and began beating him over the head with his nightstick, knocking him to the ground. Hinton screamed and shouted, "Allah au Akbar" (Allah is great), at which point other cops rushed over and also began striking him. "Blood gushed from my head and all over my clothes," he reported, "but they still kept beating me." He also accused a police officer of kicking him in the "stomach." Eventually he was handcuffed and put into a police car, where, he claimed, "blood was running all down my head" as he kept repeating "Allah au Akbar." Hinton said one cop threatened to break his neck if he did not "shut up with that damn praying."[56]

Hinton said that given his condition he thought the police would take him to the hospital. Instead he was taken to the Twenty-Eighth Precinct, placed in a back room, and handcuffed to a chair. Hinton noted in his affidavit that when he started to pray once again, one cop punched him in the mouth, kicked him the stomach, and then stomped on him while another cop began hitting him across the knees.[57]

The police version of events claimed that Hinton was arrested after refusing to leave the scene when the police ordered the crowd of on-lookers to disperse. The police claimed that the spectators grew restless, causing the officers to call for assistance. NYPD officials accused Hinton of helping to create a disturbance by taunting the police. When the police attempted to place Hinton under arrest, he resisted and therefore was struck. Eyewitnesses, however, insisted that the police assault on Hinton was unprovoked.[58] One police justification of the beating that would later be used in Hinton's lawsuit against the city was that once he resisted arrest, the police used a nightstick to subdue him. Any injury Hinton suffered while being subdued cannot be blamed on the police because "once a nightstick is brought into use, neither the force nor the effect of a single blow can be regulated. The only reasonable use is for the wielder of the weapon to hit with whatever force he is capable of bringing to bear in the particular situation. Nothing else is practicable nor, in the vast majority of instances, even possible." Moreover, the police denied ever beating Hinton in the police station.[59]

A woman who witnessed the attack ran to a restaurant owned by the NOI and alerted those inside. After a number of telephone calls were made, Malcolm and a group of NOI members went to the precinct and demanded to see Hinton, but they were told that no one by that name was in custody. Malcolm was accompanied by fifty members of the Fruit of Islam. According to *The Autobiography of Malcolm X*, the police could not believe what they were seeing: FOI members standing in "rank formation" outside the police station with residents of Harlem arrayed behind them. "I said that until he [Hinton] was seen and we were sure he received proper medical attention, the Muslims would remain where they were," Malcolm noted, adding that the police were "nervous and scared of the gathering crowd outside."[60]

James L. Hicks of the *Amsterdam News*, who witnessed the exchange between Malcolm X and the police, wrote about it in his paper. Hicks was also chairman of the Twenty-Eighth Precinct Community Council, created in the 1940s to facilitate better communications between the police and community, and someone from that precinct asked him to meet with an Inspector McGowen, deputy commissioner Walter Arm, and deputy inspector Robert J. Mangum, an African American, in hopes of quelling a confrontation between the police and the Nation of Islam. The meeting took place later that day at Hicks's office, and he was asked if he knew Malcolm X. He let them know he did, after which he set up a meeting between Malcolm and the trio of law enforcement officials, during which Arm insulted Malcolm by claiming that the police could "handle any situation that arises in Harlem, and we're not here to ask anybody's help."[61]

Malcolm walked out; Mangum asked Hicks to persuade him to return, which Malcolm did, although he told Arm he had no respect for him or the police department. On the condition that Malcolm would dismiss the crowd outside the precinct, the three police officials consented to Malcolm's terms: he wanted to see Hinton and be assured that if he needed medical attention, he would be taken to the hospital. According to Malcom, "The police were saying, 'We can't handle it without you.' Nobody got down on his knees. But they [the police] bowed."[62]

Hinton described to Malcolm the brutal treatment he'd suffered outside and inside the precinct, and Malcolm insisted that Hinton be taken to the hospital. The growing crowd of Harlem residents, which was raising police fears of a riot, followed Hinton to Harlem Hospital. Hinton wrote in his affidavit that he was still in a daze when a doctor saw him and put him on an operating table, where "they sewed up my head." His mouth and knee were also treated. Despite his injuries, and though he still felt sick, the hospital authorities released Hinton to the police, who took him back to the precinct and put him in a cell. According to Hinton, "Up to this time the police had never asked me my name or where I lived." The crowd had followed Hinton from the hospital back to the precinct, which further alarmed the top brass, and they sent for all available reinforcements.[63]

Hicks wrote in the *Amsterdam News* that many NOI members stood in an organized line a half-block long: "Their discipline amazed police, and more than one high ranking officer expressed growing concern." Over two thousand people were still on the street at 2:30 a.m. when Malcolm X reappeared and was asked to dismiss the crowd: "Malcolm stood up and waved his hand, and all those people just disappeared. . . . One of the police people said to me, 'Did you see what I just saw?' I said 'Yeah.' He said 'This is too much power for one man to have.' He meant one black man. I'll never forget that." Malcolm, along with attorney Charles J. Bearers, arranged bail for Potts and another member of the NOI named L'Pysli Tal, who had also been arrested. When Bearers saw Hinton, he asked that he be taken back to the hospital, but the police refused, contending that Hinton had to be arraigned in the morning. The police even refused Bearers's request for Hinton to be given a pillow because he was unable to stand.[64]

Many subsequent retellings of this case romanticized the gallant warrior image of Malcolm and the FOI, thus juxtaposing their militancy with the nonviolent, peaceful protests and negotiations of the civil rights movement just getting underway in the South. Hicks's article in the *New York Amsterdam News* (quoted above) was headlined "Riot Threat as Cops Beat Moslem: God's Angry Men Tangle with Police," invoking an image of fearless black men battling abusive police officers. Filmmaker Spike Lee's version appeared in his movie *Malcolm X*, which shows an uncompromising Malcolm not only demanding to see the wounded man but insisting that Hinton be taken to the hospital before he would tell the FOI and the angry crowd to disperse. Once his demands were met, Malcolm signals with a hand gesture and the FOI march away in military formation, at which point, the Harlem crowd also walked away peacefully. Lee's version emphasizes the defiant Malcolm X while ignoring the one who was willing to compromise with the police.[65] Historian Fredrick Knight wrote that the Johnson X. Hinton case helped to spread the message among black New Yorkers that the "Nation of Islam was nothing to play with."[66] A 2012 piece titled "The Day That Malcolm Won Harlem Over" claimed that Malcolm "stood up to the NYPD and won."[67] As late as May 2015, the Hinton case was cited by Justin Charity as proof of Malcolm's and the Nation of Islam's defiance of and victory over the police.[68] Although the romanticized warrior construct counters the image of out of control fanatics bent on attacking law enforcement, it also plays into the larger narrative of Malcolm X and the NOI as violent and confrontational individuals who only addressed police brutality by force or threat of force.

However, a closer look at the Hinton incident reveals that Malcolm X was more pragmatic and willing to make concessions than the popular version of Malcolm would suggest. Despite the inflammatory title of Hicks's report, the text noted that there was a give and take between the police and Malcolm. Malcolm was accompanied to the Twenty-Eighth Precinct not only by members of the Fruit of Islam but also by attorney Charles J. Beavers, who attempted to get Hinton released. In what he called "excellent public relations work on the part of police," Hicks wrote that the department "persuaded the Moslem leader that every effort was being made to correct any wrong on the part of police, and the meeting ended with an implied, though not expressed, promise that the Moslems would not cause any trouble Monday night." In an effort not to inflame police–NOI tensions, Malcolm ordered members of his temple not to appear at Hinton's' arraignment in felony court.[69]

The FBI files contain numerous detailed reports on Malcolm's activities, including a version of the Hinton case as reported by an unidentified man at a Boston NOI temple. The individual is said to have told the temple that New York police officers had beaten Hinton with sticks and that Malcolm had taken along "hundreds" of NOI members when he went to see him. The speaker claimed that while talking to Hinton, Malcolm had been surrounded by police and that Muslims from several cities had come to Harlem, "and Brother Malcolm had a hard time keeping the peace because the Muslims were ready to fight." The Boston contact then asserted that the "devil is not playing with you or me so be ready, but don't run out and antagonize the devils now or be stupid on the job. Each Muslim must keep the other Muslims in line but they must unite for strength."[70] The mention of Malcolm's difficulty in maintaining peace strongly suggests that his intention was to maintain order and to not provoke physical confrontation with the police. The unidentified speaker's warning that the "devil is not playing" and to not be "stupid on the job" also seems to have been urging temple members to remain peaceful and not to precipitate physical violence.

In November 1959 the grand jury refused to indict Hinton for disorderly conduct and refusing arrest; Potts was cleared of the disorderly conduct charge, and Tal's sentence for disorderly conduct was suspended. Relying on a November 9 article from the *Amsterdam News* about the decision, the FBI reported that afterward Malcolm sent a telegram to Commissioner Kennedy saying that the two officers involved in the beating should be dismissed from the force. Malcolm argued that their continued presence in Harlem was a "potential powder keg." He did not threaten retaliation by the NOI but tried to convince the commissioner that the Harlem community might react violently if the two continued working in the area. Just as important, Malcolm reminded Commissioner Kennedy that during the April 29 negotiation between himself and Deputy Commissioners Arm and Magnum they had promised a fair and impartial investigation of Hinton's beating.[71]

In response to Malcolm's telegram to Kennedy, Arm, according to the FBI, confirmed that he did indeed promise an immediate investigation but had suspended it during the grand jury proceedings. Arm promised that since those proceedings were completed, he would continue the NYPD's investigation.[72] What was important about Malcolm's telegram to Kennedy was the former's ability to get Arm to agree to an investigation of the Hinton assault.

Other details of the Hinton affair also reveal that the police were able to negotiate with Malcolm to defuse trouble before Hinton was eventually released from police custody and the Muslims took him to Sydenham Hospital. Unlike Harlem Hospital, where Hinton was first taken to by the police and a number of people waited outside, Malcolm asked NOI members not to stand outside of the hospital and not to "start trouble," indicating an effort to distance the NOI from some teens who had appeared on the scene and were rumored to have zip guns. Although the FBI had claimed that a riot almost occurred because the Muslims had "marched" on the Twenty-Eighth Precinct to get "their Moslem Brother," an FBI report on Malcolm noted that when reporters questioned him on the still-recent Hinton incident, his response was that Islam is the religion of peace. Black people, he said, must "wake up" and realize that assaults by the police on members of the NOI were not aimed at any particular group but followed a "general pattern" against all black people.[73] Such details, often buried in reports about the Hinton case, counter the popular image of the NOI's uncompromising militancy and readiness to resort to physical altercations when opposing police brutality.

Not by Any Means Necessary

Hinton's beating was just one of a number of incidents in which Malcolm advocated an approach other than self-defense. In April 1958, for example, he and John Ali, secretary of Temple No. 7, met with deputy police commissioner Walter Arm to request that the NYPD investigate detectives Joseph Kiernan and Michael Bonura regarding their arrest earlier that year of four NOI members: Betty X; John Mollette and his wife, Yvonne Mollette; and Minnie X. Simmons. The FBI, reporting the police version, wrote that several police officers along with a postal inspector had arrived at 25-46 Ninety-Fourth Street in Queens on March 19, 1958, to serve a federal warrant on one Margaret Dorsey, who along with four NOI members was charged with assaulting two of the officers.

Malcolm told the *Amsterdam News* that the two detectives who should be investigated illegally entered John and Yvonne Mollette's house while looking for Margaret Dorsey. Witnesses claimed that they saw the police beating John Mollette, who was arrested along with the other three defendants. After a three-week trial, two of the people arrested were cleared of charges of assault on police officers. However, the jury failed to reach a decision on the Mollettes and a mistrial was declared.[74] The Mollettes then charged the police with false arrest, malicious prosecution, violation of their civil rights, breaking and entering, assaulting women, and property damage.[75]

Malcolm did not threaten violent retaliation in trying to convince the police to discipline the officers but instead filed an official complaint, contending that the detectives illegally entered John and Yvonne Mollette's house. While the FBI report portrayed Malcolm as provocative, it ignored his negotiation with the police.[76] The FBI version of events also did not report that Deputy Commissioner Arm told Malcolm and Ali that the police would investigate the arrest, and if the NOI's allegations were valid there would be a departmental trial of the officers. The *Amsterdam News* referred to the meeting as a "conference" at police headquarters and noted that Nicholas Gaffney, supervisor of the Civilian Complaint Review Board, also attended.[77] The black weekly later reported that many top police officials took part in the subsequent investigation.[78] Again, the Malcolm who emerges in this episode is someone who used dialogue to resolve a police brutality issue and was willing to seek redress through compromise.

In late June 1959 Malcolm complained in the *Amsterdam News* that he had had to waste his time and miss his train to Philadelphia being forced to wait to see commissioner Stephen Kennedy to discuss police brutality incidents against black women. Deputy Commissioner Arm, Malcolm explained, had told him he had arranged the appointment with Kennedy days earlier, but Arm had never informed the commissioner. After waiting for an hour, Malcolm said he was told that the commissioner did not have time to see him. He accused Arm of having stalled him and his companion, John X, for that hour before informing them that the "deal was off."[79]

Though Malcolm did not explain what it meant that the "deal was off," he responded to Arm by saying that if "we can't get justice from the law, then we'll have to seek justice elsewhere. We do not intend to let any man, regardless of race, police or otherwise, molest our women." He said that the Muslims waited for the police to provide justice, but added, "I'm not responsible for anything that happens."[80]

Although he threatened to seek "justice elsewhere," Malcolm had first tried to discuss his community's grievances with the commissioner, and his reference to a deal indicates that he believed he and the NYPD had reached some agreement. Clearly, Malcolm and members of the NOI were willing to address police brutality issues by holding discussions with the police. Why not simply turn to violence if meetings and conferences had actually been dismissed as a waste of time? Because Malcolm and the NOI were more interested in conflict management than in having a violent dispute that would result in the injury or death of NOI members. Meetings provided NOI leaders with a venue to express their discontent with those who held power.

When police were accused of attacking NOI members, Malcolm occasionally felt it necessary to remind the followers of Elijah Muhammad not to take the law in their own hands, as happened in the summer 1961 case of NOI member Raymond Quarles of South Jamaica, Queens. Quarles, who sold custom jewelry, had two cases of merchandise with him when the police approached and questioned him as he was about to enter his uncle's house. Quarles told the *Amsterdam News*, "I pleaded with the officers to take me in the home to verify" that he was a custom jeweler, 'but they refused. I was virtually thrown into the patrol car where the policeman with the badge number 130822 assaulted me with his billy." The officer then went into Quarles's uncle's house and began searching it without a warrant. The uncle phoned Joseph Gravitt (Yusuf Shah), captain of the Fruit of Islam in New York, who soon arrived at the house and questioned the police. He was informed that Quarles would be booked on a charge of vagrancy and disorderly conduct.[81]

Gravitt spoke to lieutenant Francis McFee and arranged a meeting with captain G. H. Seery of the Jamaica precinct. Commenting on the incident, Malcolm X told the *Amsterdam News*, "We Muslims, followers of Elijah Muhammad, obey the law. Our brothers are instructed to obey the police, not to resist in any shape or form and to move quickly and peacefully when ordered." The leader of Temple No. 7 said the assault on Quarles, who had been beaten until he was limp just because he was black, was unjustified, but the situation could have been worse had this man not been a Muslim. "The Muslims," Malcolm said, "respect and obey the law and we as a group demand respect."[82]

Malcolm was reiterating what had become a common theme by the time of the Quarles case: Muslims obey the law and respect authority. On April 26, 1959, he told a New York City NOI meeting that he "again must tell the brothers that they should not resist any law enforcement officer at any time. The NOI is not against the laws. . . . If the law enforcement officer is wrong, he must still be obeyed because Allah will take care of him." According to an FBI report on a May 29, 1959, FOI meeting to plan for a visit of Elijah Muhammad in Washington, DC, Malcolm told the gathering that if local police ordered them to "move on" while they were handing out flyers announcing the event, they should do "as instructed by the police, as the NOI wanted no trouble while Muhammad was in Washington."[83]

Malcolm's willingness to negotiate with police did not stop him from expressing his disdain for and distrust of law enforcement, an institution he considered so viciously racist that he associated white police officers with the Ku Klux Klan. Malcolm substantiated this connection at a September 9, 1959, FOI meeting in New York City. According to the *Amsterdam News*, Malcolm said that he had gotten hold of an August 6, 1959, letter sent from J. B. Stoner, imperial wizard of the Christian Knights of the Ku Klux Klan, to Police Commissioner Kennedy. In it, after noting, "We are working to unite all of the forces of White Christendom in the struggle to preserve the great White Race," Stoner claimed a New York City police officer who was "one of our Klansmen" had told him that the "nigger Muslims are in rebellion against White law and order" and that blacks had "no respect" for the "honest White Christian policemen." Stoner offered the NYPD the support of his organization: "You and I must join forces to stop the black Muslims now or they will soon drive every White person out of New York City. The largest city in the world will then be an all nigger city of black supremacy where White people will not be allowed to live." Stoner offered his "dear friend," Commissioner Kennedy, "5,000 Klansmen" who along with the police could "clean up Harlem" if Kennedy gave the Klansmen badges and police uniforms: "They will leave their Klan robes at home so the New York niggers won't know that your police reinforcements are White Christian Klansmen."[84]

Malcolm used Stoner's letter to accuse members of the NYPD of membership in the KKK, and he linked several cases of police brutality to Stoner's willingness to take care of the "nigger Muslims." Malcolm did not consider Stoner's informant within the force to have been a quack, and he insisted, according to an FBI report, that "if Police Commissioner Stephen Kennedy can't provide the people of Harlem with protection against the lawlessness of white police officers who show definite evidence of Klan-like thinking in their methods of dealing with the people of Harlem, then the people of Harlem demand that Mayor Wagner take already overdue investigation action immediately."[85]

Although he had no evidence linking police officers to the Ku Klux Klan and the letter allegedly written by Stoner was not proof of NYPD affiliation with the white supremacist organization, Malcolm used it to pressure the police department to take action against officers who brutalize blacks. He submitted the letter to the *Amsterdam News*, which published it in its entirety on the front page. The article also quoted extensively from a statement by Malcolm accusing members of the police force of Klan membership and pointing to a number of incidents that led him and others to suspect it—including the Hinton episode and the Mollette case in Queens. "We feel that there is physical evidence to indicate the KKK is very active on the New York police force, as this letter suggests," the statement continued, and it went on to claim that despite a number of cases of police brutality, the department had "never found any evidence of brutality against Negroes." Tellingly, instead of saying that the NOI would retaliate, Malcolm again insisted that the "Moslem record in Harlem has been one of courtesy and law abiding. We have never given a hint or sign of any kind of violence; yet, for the past few weeks, we have been the target of some of the most vicious anti-Moslem propaganda, which leads us to believe that we are being penalized for being law-abiding citizens."[86]

Stoner's claim that NYPD officers were Klan members lacked proof, but Malcolm was basing his reaction, in part, on observed behavior rather than hard evidence. He argued that when police officers could murder and beat black people with impunity, it was equivalent to the Klan's onslaught of racial terror. He was attempting to make black New Yorkers aware of the NYPD's unwillingness to address those problems in any serious way.

Despite his verbal attacks on the department's methods and tactics, historian Manning Marable writes that Malcolm took a "deferential approach to the police." Marable gives the example of an ad hoc working committee meeting of Unity for Action, organized by A. Philip Randolph in 1961, at which Malcolm said "that he would encourage 'his people' to obey the law, denied that NOI members had participated in any recent 'uprising in Harlem,' and denounced the call for a 'march on the 28th Precinct Police Station,' which had been outlined in a leaflet distributed through the crowd. 'We do not think this will accomplish anything,' he declared."[87]

Most likely Malcolm was not making an argument that punishment should be left to Allah; it's more probable that he was referring to the evil nature of white people, thus implying that protesting their behavior would result in little if any substantive change. Demonstrating or boycotting were just not an effective way of confronting police brutality, and

Malcolm was simply rejecting that particular approach. Legal action, on the other hand, seemed more effective.

The Legal Approach

Malcolm and the NOI teamed up with a number of lawyers to take on the issue of police brutality. These included NAACP attorney Edward Jacko, who attended Howard Law School from 1939 to 1941 and was strongly influenced by that school's dean, Charles Hamilton Houston, who emphasized that the law should be used to defeat segregation and racial discrimination. In 1946 Jacko joined the NAACP legal redress team and helped to shape its approach to police brutality. He adopted the methods of the New York NAACP State Conference under its head, Jawn A. Sandifer, and filed civil law suits against New York City with the intent of making police brutality cases so costly that the NYPD would be forced to address the issue substantively.[88]

This strategy was used in the Johnson X. Hinton case. After the grand jury refused in November 1959 to indict Hinton, the decision paved the way for a lawsuit, and Malcolm retained the services of Sandifer and Jacko for Hinton and the NOI, on whose behalf they filed a $1.125 million suit against the city.[89]

In May 1960, an all-white jury, after deliberating for four hours, voted unanimously to award Hinton $75,000, the largest settlement granted to a victim of police brutality in New York City up to that date. Attorneys Jacko and Sandifer provided what the *Amsterdam News* described as a "vigorous cross-examination of police revealing inconsistency in the official records. Dr. Thomas Matthews, a prominent neurosurgeon, told the press that Hinton suffered permanent emotional and behavior disturbances, loss of his ability to handle speech and memory of words and loss of sexual desire. He was unable to rebuild his brain capacity to learn and as a result of the beating a metal plate was placed in his head. Hinton's wife, Christine Hinton, testified that her husband was unable to help support their four children and the family had to go on welfare."[90]

While those who focus on the Hinton case stress the NOI's propensity to physically confront the NYPD, the group's willingness to use a legal path to stop police brutality is the more significant aspect of this story. Fighting in the courts may seem less courageous than physically confronting vicious attacks by the police on unarmed black civilians. However, the NOI's legal pursuit demonstrated that it was willing to use a means that could gain greater public support, financially hurt the city, and help bring substantive relief to victims.

Conclusion

The Nation of Islam was an important force in the challenge to police assaults on black people in postwar America. It was not, as the common narrative suggests, a group of black racists bent on confrontation with law enforcement or a disciplined paramilitary force ready to use self-defense when confronting police brutality. Rather, it adopted nonphysical but forceful de-escalation strategies such as meetings, negotiation, and lawsuits to address law enforcement's intimidation and physical assaults against black people.

De-escalation was one of the greatest yet most often ignored legacies of the NOI's fight against police brutality. It prevented what would most likely have been catastrophic outcomes of confrontations with the police. Some writers have overlooked the evidence of Malcolm's de-escalation tactics while highlighting his call for manly self-defense and physical confrontation. There is no doubt that had the NOI turned to retaliation instead of de-escalation in the cases outlined here (and a number of other incidents throughout the 1950s and 1960s) there would have more beatings, arrests, and even deaths among NOI members.

The NOI adopted de-escalation as an approach before police departments themselves embraced de-escalation training in the twenty-first century as a strategy to curtail the number of violent incidents between officers and citizens. The NOI's de-escalation approach represented an attempt to change the mind-set of black America with respect to police brutality, especially given that many men in the their twenties and thirties were members of the NOI, and that age group was statistically the most likely to have physical confrontations with police. Beginning with Elijah Mohammad, de-escalation as used by the NOI did not indicate compliance or submission to police assaults but reflected an attempt to get NOI members to understand the power dynamics at the moment of confrontation. Police power is immense. Besides possessing an ample supply of deadly weapons, officers have the legal right to use force, including lethal force. In New York City in the 1950s and 1960s, they also had the backing of the courts and the support of the mainstream media and a vast majority of the public. Black citizens, including those profiled here, were at a great disadvantage when confronting police brutality. Muhammad's declaration that those who carried guns would turn to the gun for protection instead of turning to God, was an effort to foster a conscious and alert perspective among FOI members, many of them young men and most from poor working-class communities who had already had encounters with police. The Boston member of the NOI who said that the "devil isn't playing with you and me" was not encouraging NOI followers to back down but to realize the power dynamics at the moment. De-escalation did not represent submission because the NOI turned to other means of fighting the police, including the use of protests and the courts.

Elijah Muhammad's public announcements of NOI policy and the group's emphasis on its religious beliefs were also an attempt to challenge the popular image of the Nation of Islam as a hate group. By promoting an image of the NOI as law-abiding and making it known that their religious doctrine forbade them from carrying weapons and defending themselves against the police, Muhammad showed he understood that the battle with law enforcement meant taking on NOI's negative public image in a propaganda war in which NOI's moral righteous had to be asserted and proven.

Both Malcolm X and to a lesser degree Elijah Muhammad contributed to formulating useful nonviolent strategies in that battle against police violence. Like the black press and the Communist Party, they challenged the racist images of blacks used by law enforcement to justify using excessive force when dealing with black people. Negotiation, lawsuits, and Muhammad's attempt to change the mind-set of young black men so they would not physically confront police officers laid the groundwork for later activists. Using the courts and negotiating with city and state officials would lead to major achievements in the anti–police brutality movement.

4

Civil Rights, Community Activists, and Police Brutality

As World War II wound down, police brutality remained a critical issue for civil rights activists. In 1945 the Brooklyn branch of the NAACP reported that between May and July of that year nine black people had been brutally assaulted by the police. The chapter's major focus by the 1940s was police brutality. It publicly denounced alleged cases of violent police assaults on black people, sponsored rallies against such violations, and in 1949 urged governor Thomas Dewey to appoint a special prosecutor to investigate police brutality. In addition, the Brooklyn branch provided attorneys to victims of police assaults.[1] In May 1948, disruptions erupted on 116th Street in Harlem after rumors spread that a white police officer had killed a black woman. In its efforts to improve relations the NYPD promised to hold hearings on police brutality. The New York NAACP demanded that such hearings be public.[2]

As we have seen, many New York City political activists were depicting police brutality as a civil rights issue long before the rise of the civil rights movement in the South. New York City civil liberties organizations, political leaders, and activists all maintained that the killing and maiming of unarmed black citizens by police was as much a violation of their civil rights as being denied the vote or adequate public accommodations.[3]

By the postwar period there was a growing outcry among civil rights organizations and others demanding that the city take action to end police abuse of citizens. Among the solutions that activists and black leaders continued to push for were increasing the number of African Americans on the force as a way of determining who should police the black communities of the city and creating a civilian complaint review board as a means of determining how they will behave in communities. As police brutality became a major focus as a civil rights issue in New York City, civil rights organizations turned to advocating for an independent review board as the primary means of addressing the problem.

Based on the complaints received, the agency would conduct investigations and decide on the punishment of any officer found guilty. Those who called for creating a review board argued that to ensure that police did not abuse the tremendous power they had over citizens, it should offer a place where citizens could file complaints away from police department premises and should have the power to conduct investigations, subpoena police officers and witnesses, hold hearings, and decide appropriate action, including bringing police to justice when they break the law. Such a review board was seen as a way to ensure that citizens' constitutional rights would be protected. Just as important, it would democratize policing in the city by giving citizens a means of monitoring police actions and would empower citizens of color to compel police to treat them just as they did white New Yorkers.

Just as the campaigns against police brutality continued into the 1950s, so, too, did police resistance. The activists made no headway, as the NYPD and city officials consistently ignored all requests to address police brutality in any serious manner. By ignoring police brutality, the practice was de facto sanctioned by the state, and as long as it was not addressed seriously, tensions increased between the police and minority communities. The activists, however, maintained their resolve on the issue.

Along with the black press, the American Communist Party, and the Nation of Islam, civil rights and community activists in Harlem worked to pressure the NYPD to adopt serious solutions to police brutality. Their focus on a civilian complaint review board as a primary means to make the police accountable to the communities they served raised an important new question: What should be the citizens' role in policing? The activist citizens thought that playing a prominent role would defuse tensions and decrease brutality. The police and other opponents of a review board argued that an independent monitoring agency would undermine law enforcement, and therefore monitoring should remain within the department and citizens should play no role. Countering this resistance was the challenge activists took on.

The Early Call for a Civilian Complaint Review Board

The struggle for a civilian complaint review board began decades before the 1950s. After the 1935 Harlem Riot, mayor Fiorello La Guardia, who served from 1934 to 1945, formed a commission to study the causes of that event and to make recommendations. The commission criticized the city for having stationed extra police in Harlem, which it claimed was a "show of force." One of the commission's recommendations was the formation of a Citizens' Public Safety Committee, which would be delegated to receive complaints of alleged police brutality. The recommendation read as follows: "That the commissioner of police arrange for the appointment of a committee of from five to seven Harlem citizens of both races [black and white] to whom colored people may make complaint if mistreated by the police." The commission assumed that the police commissioner was likely to respond to this suggestion by claiming that there would be little he could do if complaints were not made directly to the NYPD. In response, the commission wrote, "But to this the reply is that the citizens are fearful of making complaints lest there be unpleasant consequences to them and they thereby gain the ill of the police." The commission also pointed out that complaints were routinely sent back to the precinct where the brutality originally took place and were simply "pigeon-holed": "We feel that the situation would be greatly improved if there were a body of citizens to sift all complaints and to take up with the commissioner, personally, if necessary, such cases as merit attention."[4]

The Harlem Commission did not wish to challenge the power of the police commissioner, but it did want the reviewing body to be independent of the NYPD. To that end, it recommended that such a committee be advisory in nature so that the commissioner could be made aware of how citizens regarded the police and of what steps could be taken to improve the police–citizen relationship. To further assure the body's independence from "political or police domination," the Harlem Commission suggested that it include "one of more men who are dissenters from established institutions and also men who are likely to have contact with victims of injustice." It also reasoned that any officer who violated the law should be investigated and punished by the department; therefore it recommended "that in every case of a shooting by the police a most careful investigation should be personally made by one of the highest officials in the department."[5] Mayor La Guardia ignored the recommendation that a citizens' committee be formed because he feared a harsh reaction from the police.

Eight years later, Mayor La Guardia again refused to set up a monitoring agency after another riot took place in Harlem on August 1, 1943. As discussed in chapter 1, on that day Robert Bandy, a private in the United States Army, came to the aid of a black women who was involved in an altercation with a white clerk in the lobby of a hotel. When Bandy intervened, a white police officer attempted to arrest him, and when he allegedly resisted arrest, the officer shot and wounded him. When word spread that a white cop had shot and killed a black soldier, a riot erupted.

In response to the 1943 Harlem Riot, La Guardia did not set up a special commission, and civil rights leaders and groups did not advocate for a citizen's review board. The lack of advocacy for a board was due, in large part, to the wartime focus on maintaining national unity in order to help defeat the Axis powers. Achieving unity meant that racial strife was downplayed even by those who had called for a civilian review board after the 1935 riot. Many people realized that there would be backlash from the NYPD if there were calls for a board, which would be seen as challenging police power and authority. Instead of antagonizing the police, there was praise for their actions at the hotel. On August 7, 1943, Adam Clayton Powell's People's Voice, for example, ran the headline "No Detroit in New York" over an article blaming Private Bandy, who "precipitated in Sunday night's disturbances." In a separate Voice article, Llewelyn Ransom claimed that the "police bent backward to prevent the riot, brutalities and the vandalism experienced in Detroit, and for this Harlem was grateful."[6] Ransom declared that Mayor La Guardia should receive "commendation for the highly efficient manner in which he handled the situation, particularly for his restraint of the police," and noted that the mayor "stayed in Harlem until morning" along with Walter White and other prominent black leaders. Voice reporter Marvel Cooke also credited the police "who followed to the letter Mayor LaGuardia's order not to shoot."[7]

Although there was no call for the creation of an oversight panel after the 1943 riot, activists did push the mayor to address the deplorable social conditions in Harlem. Among the remedies suggested by the People's Committee, which met at Abyssinian Baptist Church where Powell was the senior pastor, were a call for rent control, "the breaking down of Jim Crow" in the armed forces, "the expansion of the OPA program in Harlem, and unity of the Negro people."[8] The U.S. Office of Price

Administration (or OPA), created in 1941 through an executive order of president Franklin Delano Roosevelt, had the power to place ceilings on the price of commodities and on rents.

Public Relations, Not Police Brutality

After the end of World War II civil rights activists wasted little time before taking on the NYPD by renewing their demand for a police monitoring board and promoting other ways to stamp out police brutality. Under pressure from civil rights groups to act, in 1948 police commissioner Arthur W. Wallander created a new "advisory committee to investigate complaints of police brutality in Harlem." It would focus on seven aspects of community life, including improving the welfare of Harlem residents and conditions affecting the enforcement of the law and addressing situations that might erupt into racial conflict. The committee was made up of members of the black elite: Dr. Dan Dodson, director of the Mayor's Committee on Unity; the Reverend John H. Johnson, a Harlem clergyman and police chaplain; attorney Madison Jones of the NAACP's national staff; Edward S. Lewis, executive secretary of the Urban League; and businessman Chilian B. Powell.[9]

Placing no trust in the NYPD to seriously address the brutality problem, the New York branch of the NAACP announced the formation of its own Committee of Action against Police Brutality, which would investigate and take action on police brutality complaints. The committee was organized at a February "mass meeting" of the New York branch, at which a number of people described their encounters with police and requested help from the NAACP. Located at 2272 Seventh Avenue, the Committee of Action's office was open Monday, Wednesday, and Friday to hear complaints, and the NAACP also promised to have an attorney on hand if legal action was needed. The committee's head, Herbert Hill, claimed it would take a new approach to an old problem by combining the provision of legal counsel for victims with organizing direct mass action.[10]

The issue of creating an agency to monitor police was again raised in 1949, when mayor William O'Dwyer appointed a special commission to investigate police brutality headed by Franklin Delano Roosevelt Jr. In response to the deaths of three citizens at the hands of police, this commission reiterated earlier recommendations for the creation of a monitoring agency, but O'Dwyer ignored it.[11] Although city officials remained uninterested in dealing with police brutality in any serious manner, civil rights groups continued their efforts to eliminate police assaults on black people.

William P. O'Brian, who became police commissioner in 1949, responded to demands that he address police brutality against black and Latino citizens by attempting to direct the focus away from police abuse of citizens. It was reported in the *Journal of Criminal Law and Criminality* in 1950 that O'Brian declared that the primary problem between the police and the community was poor public relations. To improve matters, the journal noted, the NYPD's Bureau of Public Relations would inform citizens about the department's good deeds. For O'Brian, the solution to improving police–community relations lay in cultivating trust. According to the journal, "The mutual advantage of a friendly relationship between the people of a community and their police force should be widely understood and more fully appreciated. The success of a police force in the performance of its duties is largely measured by the degree of support and cooperation it receives from the people whom it serves. It is of paramount importance, therefore, to secure for this Department the confidence, respect and approbation of the public."[12]

The journal noted that O'Brian listed four factors for determining good police–community relations, including the police attitude "toward the people of the community, . . . the attitude of the people toward their police force and law enforcement in general," and racial and "religious attitudes." He emphasized that the police officer should "strive to train himself to habits of acceptable conduct that will merit approval." Thus it was left up to the individual officer to develop behavior that a community would find acceptable.[13]

The fact that the commissioner lumped racial attitudes and religious attitudes as one category points to a lack of understanding or a strategic downplaying of the racial tension between New York's police and black communities.[14] That was the extent of O'Brian's efforts to deal with racial tension. Each officer was issued the revised edition of the procedures manual that highlighted the push for better public relations and offered "practical" ways of improving interactions between the police and the "general public, the press, and the organized groups which espouse civic, fraternal and other causes." According to O'Brian, the "more people who are acquainted with our aims, the greater will be the possibility of our achieving them."[15]

Scandal and the Creation of a "Civilian" Complaint Review Board

By the late 1940s it was apparent to many that the police had won the struggle between civil rights and police brutality. Despite two riots in Harlem; the recommendations from appointed commissions; and meetings with civil rights, political, and community leaders urging that steps be taken to end police violence against black and Latino residents, the NYPD and the city still refused to act. This intransigence highlighted how difficult it was to challenge institutional racism and made it clear to those leading the anti-brutality campaign that the department and city were not going to act unless forced to do so.

One such coercion strategy was to take the path of litigation. A number of lawyers, some affiliated with the NAACP, argued that if the city were legally compelled to pay out large sums awarded in jury trials or settlements, it would be much more eager to take action against brutal cops. In the spring of 1948 Jawn Sandifer, head of the New York State NAACP Legal Redress Committee, announced that the organization was launching an intensive campaign to halt police brutality and would pursue civil suits against police involved in violence against citizens: "In criminal cases police enjoy almost complete judicial immunity in the courts. By filing both civil and criminal suits at the same time, we have a much better chance of checking brutality." Two weeks later, Sandifer expressed optimism when he told the *People's Voice* that police officials were "ready to cooperate with the NAACP" in investigating police brutality complaints. "These complaints of police brutality are our biggest headache now," Sandifer asserted, pointing out that the great majority of such cases were never reported, and even if taken to trial, the "NAACP has found that the courts will very seldom find a policeman guilty in cases of this sort."[16]

In 1946, before becoming the Nation of Islam's lawyer, Edward Jacko joined the NAACP legal redress team and helped to shape its approach to police brutality.[17] Jacko won a number of such cases, including that of Ben Fields, a thirty-one-year-old construction worker shot on June 22, 1959, by police officer Harold "Davy Crocket" Stewart. Fields was in a candy store on 126th Street trying to get change for a twenty-dollar bill when Stewart saw him displaying a large sum of money. Stewart approached and questioned the young black man and then took the money from him. When Fields demanded its return, Stewart punched Fields in the face, slammed him against the wall, and shot him in the stomach at close range. Hospital authorities reported that Fields also suffered a head injury that would leave him partially paralyzed for life. New York State Supreme Court justice Mitchell D. Schweitzer awarded Fields $50,000, and a few months later, a six-person jury found Stewart guilty of second-degree assault.[18]

One of Jacko's most notable cases brought to the public's attention a secret agreement between the New York City police commissioner and the U.S. Department of Justice that shielded the NYPD from a federal investigation on police brutality. This revelation would eventually force the NYPD to create a civilian complaint review board later in the 1950s. The case in question began with an assault on Jacob Jackson, a black truck driver who was beaten by officers from the Fifty-Fourth Precinct. On August 9, 1952, after chasing some men caught gambling in the streets, officer William J. Brennan arrested Jackson at his home on 52nd Street. In court, Jackson claimed that once at the precinct, Brennan beat him so badly that he had to be rushed to the hospital, where he underwent two brain operations. While in the hospital Jackson was charged with felonious assault of a police officer, though the charge was later changed to disorderly conduct. He was convicted but given a suspended sentence.[19] According to the NAACP, Jackson arrived at the precinct a "sound, healthy man" but "left in an ambulance."[20] Jacko, who represented Jackson, and the NAACP were aware that the U.S. Justice Department was at the time conducting an investigation of police departments to see if civil rights laws had been violated in acts of police brutality. The NAACP sent the U.S. attorney general a telegram requesting that the Justice Department investigate the Jackson case.[21]

When investigating Jackson's brutality claim, the FBI asked to interview the officers involved in the case. Police commissioner George P. Monaghan refused to cooperate, citing a previous agreement between the NYPD and former U.S. attorney general James P. McGranery. However, once McGranery, who served under President Truman, left office, his successor, Herbert Brownell, serving under President Eisenhower, learned of the agreement and refused to renew it, despite a plea from Monaghan.[22]

Civil rights leaders and city officials alike expressed outrage over the agreement. The executive board of the NAACP released a press statement arguing that "civil rights is a national issue. The responsibility of the Federal Government to secure these rights to all citizens is as imperative in New York as it is in Alabama." The NAACP demanded the removal of local and federal officials who were responsible for the agreement. Ella Baker, president of the New York branch of the NAACP, and Jacko called the agreement a "conspiracy." The NAACP and others demanded that mayor Vincent R. Impellitteri fire the police commissioner.[23] The NAACP claimed in a March 1953 edition of the *Crisis* that it "had already taken effective action to prevent any future secret agreements between the police and Justice Department to suspend federal intervention in cases involving abuse of civil rights by police officers." The organization noted that it had sponsored a February 19 gathering of "seventeen civic, labor, church and minority group organizations to consider plans for protest and action against the non-repudiated agreement between the New York City Police Department and the U.S. Department of Justice."[24]

U.S. representative Adam Clayton Powell Jr. and U.S. senator Jacob Javits both insisted on a congressional investigation. Rudolph Halley, president of the New York City Council, asked for a public inquiry to find out if Monaghan had made a secret deal with the Justice Department. If such an agreement existed, Halley said, it was "vicious." In a statement to the press, Halley claimed that "every citizen of New York should know whether the FBI made an exception here in police cases involving alleged violations of civil rights." City Council member Earl Brown, representing Harlem, said he would present a resolution calling for the formation of a five-person committee to investigate the policies and practices of the NYPD in addressing citizen complaints of police brutality.[25]

Mayor Impellitteri declared that there was no need for a city inquiry, noting that the House of Representatives' Judiciary Subcommittee, headed by New York Republican Kenneth B. Keating, was investigating the agreement. Manhattan borough president Robert F. Wagner Jr. called for a "full report" by the Board of Estimate on the incident, saying that unless it was demonstrated that civil rights laws were equally enforced in the United States, "Radio Moscow will blare forth that we have legalized lynching right here in New York City." The Board of Estimate oversaw many domains, including the city budget, land use, and city contracts, and it is not clear why Wagner asked for a report by that particular agency. The Reverend Donald Harrington, pastor of the Community Church and chair of the Coordinating Committee on Police Practices, told the press that he was "shocked by the immoral practices revealed concerning the denial of fundamental rights to American citizens" that had been "allegedly committed by police officials and allegedly condoned by our highest police officials."[26]

James McInerney, special assistant to Attorney General Brownell, verified that there was indeed such a deal.[27] Knowledge of the secret agreement made civil rights advocates more determined than ever to address police brutality. The NAACP invited twenty-five civil rights and civic organizations to its national office to discuss the police brutality problem.[28] Civil rights groups, city officials, and the House Judiciary Subcommittee called for an investigation by the city and for Monaghan to step down.

The public exposure of the secret deal and the widespread criticism forced the NYPD to take action. It decided to create what it officially called a Civilian Complaint Review Board (CCRB). True to the implications of its title, it was a board where civilians could file complaints against police officers whom they claimed had committed improprieties. However, no civilians were themselves involved in the operation of the board, which was made up of three deputy police commissioners—one who was in charge of legal matters, one in charge of community relations, and one who acted as board chair.[29]

Complaints filed with the board had to be promptly investigated by the commanding officers of the echelon above that in which the accused was a member. The Civilian Complaint Review Board chair had to attend the hearing and could participate by questioning witnesses. Even though the accused officer and the complainant might be present at the hearing, only the officer conducting the investigation and the civilian complaint supervisor were allowed to question witnesses. After the hearing, the officer in charge of the investigation had to submit a transcript of its proceedings and a report with recommendations to the civilian complaint supervisor, who then had to review the report and refer it with his own recommendations to the chairman of the CCRB. The board was required to order the investigating officer to prefer charges if it concluded that the accused officer was guilty of impropriety. The accused would then be arraigned, and a trial would take place following procedures similar to those in the criminal court of the state of New York. The police commissioner could request that the corporation counsel present the department's case. The accused officer could be represented by an attorney, and witnesses had to be sworn. After the trial, the board was to submit its report with recommendations to the police commissioner: "The police commissioner within his discretion makes the final determination and disposition. By provision of the New York City Charter he has complete jurisdiction over the disposition and discipline of the members of the force."[30]

The Continuing Saga of Police Abuse

The creation of a police-operated unit to monitor complaints of police brutality did nothing to lessen the demands that the NYPD address the issue of police brutality. Critics rightfully pointed out that the review board and the entire review process were in the hands of the police, and therefore the new CCRB could not be trusted. The complaints of unfair treatment of blacks and Latinos by the police would continue throughout the 1950s, and the black press kept the issue alive with ongoing reporting. There seemed to be no shortage of incidents to report on, and in practically all cases, including the most sensational, the police officers in question were not brought to justice. The *Amsterdam News*, for instance, reported in May 1955 that Elbert Dukes, a nine-year-old child, was beaten across the face by a police officer from the Twenty-Eighth Precinct who, Dukes claimed, took him into custody while he was waiting for a train and attacked him at the precinct. Two weeks later, the *Amsterdam News* reported that a grand jury had exonerated detective John McEnry in the death of forty-seven-year-old Edward Johnson, who, the detective claimed, had been standing at 106th Street and Central Park West and was "looking suspicious." When the detective attempted to search him, Johnson began kicking him. McEnry claimed that during the confrontation Johnson fell and suffered a skull fracture and hemorrhage. The attorney for Johnson's family, Henry Williams of the NAACP Legal Redress Committee, argued that it was impossible that Johnson could have kicked the detective in the groin because Johnson had suffered from severe arthritis in both legs since 1943.[31] In April 1955 patrolman Herbert Fisher and city marshal Morris Heyman were accused of "clubbing, shoving, flooring, kicking and beating" Cleo McCaskill, a pregnant mother of five. McCaskill, who was being evicted from her apartment, had objected to the marshal placing her furniture in the street. She was arrested "at gun point" and charged with assault.[32]

Fame and wealth did not protect black people from police assaults. The internationally famous jazz artist Miles Davis was made a victim of police brutality in the summer of 1959 while performing at the club Birdland. According to one witness, detectives Don Rolker and Gerald Kildof attacked Davis because they saw him escort a woman with blonde hair to a taxi. Davis told the *Amsterdam News* that Rolker starting "beating on my head like a tom-tom—his breath reeking with liquor." Arrested and charged with assaulting a police officer, Davis was released after posting $1,000 bail. He claimed that the incident began when Kildof approached him and ordered him to move on. Davis told the officer he was working at Birdland and had just come outside for some fresh air. The cop called him a wise guy and once again ordered him to move on. When Davis asked why he had to do so, Kildof grabbed and pushed him. It is not clear what took place next. According to Davis's version of events, when he saw the officer go for his club, he decided to "protect himself." But it is not clear what he meant by that. Rolker then came over and began beating Davis. Both officers cursed at Davis and dragged him to the police car in front of dozens of witnesses. He was then taken to the Fifty-Fourth Precinct and charged with disorderly conduct and assault and later was taken to the hospital, where he received stitches for a head wound. What was not in dispute was that the officers had used excessive force. Witnesses told the *Amsterdam News* that the cops had been simply brutal.[33]

The *New York Times* reported the police version, which alleged that when Kildof told Davis to move on, the jazz artist argued with the cops and then "grabbed the patrolman's night stick." Rolker was just passing by the jazz club when he noticed the commotion, came to Kildof's assistance, and only began striking Davis in the head after the jazz artist pushed him.[34] The *Times* did not carry any eyewitness accounts of the events. The *Amsterdam News*, on the other hand, said it received numerous calls from witnesses who described the incident, and it even quoted two of them. Charles Chambers, a bass player for the Miles Davis Quintet, said, "I've never seen anything like it. The cop, who is a regular at Birdland, brought down the blackjack on Davis' head like he was beating a drum." Another witness said that Rolker ran toward Davis and just started beating him "on his head."[35]

In April 1964 Theodore Weiss, a reform Democrat city councilman from Manhattan, hoped to end the practice of the police investigating the police and recommended the creation of an all-civilian nine-person board to be appointed by the mayor. Weiss's version of a CCRB would have the authority to investigate and conduct hearings, and its findings would be sent to the mayor and police commissioner. However, it would have no enforcement power and could only offer recommendations.[36]

While civil rights groups were supportive of Weiss, the New York City police establishment was outraged by his proposal. The police commissioner at that time, Michael J. Murphy, said that the NYPD was under a "planned pattern" of attack with the intent to make it ineffective. Although Murphy did not identify any individual or organization carrying out the attack, it was clear he was speaking about civil rights groups. In a speech before the Engineers Club in Manhattan, he said that amid the civil rights confrontations, the police "bear the brunt of the resentment of civil rights activists" and were subjected to "unfair abuse and underserved criticism from some quarters in what I can only regard as a planned pattern to destroy their effectiveness and leave the city open to confusion."[37]

Conclusion

Black and Latino communities repeatedly asked the NYPD to address issues of police brutality; discrimination in the hiring, promoting, and assigning of officers of color; and preferential treatment of white lawbreakers. The police department systematically ignored or rebuffed these requests, and in doing so lost many valuable opportunities to develop a cooperative relationship with these communities.

Despite recalcitrance on the part of civil officials and the police department to offer any meaningful solutions, civil rights groups did not let the matter drop. They continued to push for a number of reforms, including a civilian-led complaint review board. The tide would turn in 1964 with civil rights demonstrations in New York; the creation of civilian complaint review boards in Philadelphia, Rochester, and other cities; and no letup in the cases of police abuse, including the killing of a fifteen-year-old junior high school student in upper Manhattan. The eruption of riots in the city's two largest black communities in the summer of 1964 would only intensify the pressure for a CCRB staffed by civilians.

5

Police Brutality, the Harlem and Bedford-Stuyvesant Riots, and the National Civil Rights Movement

Ella Baker, president of the New York City branch of the NAACP, asserted at the organization's Eastern Regional Training Conference in March 1953 that police brutality was not a new issue and stressed that over the past ten years the organization had received complaints of "incident after incident." Al Nall of the *New York Amsterdam News* noted in September 1957 that not a week went by when that black weekly wasn't informed of "some instance of alleged police brutality."[1] In the May 18, 1957, edition of the *Amsterdam News*, Milton Nallory's "Sidewalk Interview" column questioned Harlem residents about the issue, asking "Should policemen found guilty of brutality in the cases where suits are won be automatically fired from the force?" All the respondents were in agreement: yes. Owen Ridges of Manhattan said that they should not only be fired "but should be arrested and prosecuted the same as any other criminal." Bruce Buffins insisted that police who commit brutality "should be classified as inhuman or insane." Respondent Maceo Owens placed police brutality in a broad setting: "Harlem is constantly the victim of police brutality. Race riots usually start from the cruel acts of thoughtless police. The dark world today is a powder keg. Harlem could be the fuse and police brutality is the spark to set it off."[2] Owens was prescient.

It was a pivotal moment for the national as well as the New York City civil rights movements when NYPD lieutenant Thomas Gilligan killed fifteen-year-old James Powell on July 16, 1964, triggering violence that would force a broad spectrum of civil rights leaders to pay attention to the problems blacks in urban centers faced—including police brutality. The Harlem and Bedford-Stuyvesant riots—pitched battles between police and those neighborhoods' black residents—lasted from the day of the shooting until July 22 and occurred during what has been remembered as the high point of the civil rights movement. It had been eleven months since the historic March on Washington for Jobs and Freedom—which president John F. Kennedy told the organizers was a great success. It had been just one month since the start of the Mississippi Freedom Summer Project, which brought over a thousand out-of-state, college-educated, and mostly white young people to work alongside thousands of black Mississippians to end the legal apartheid system popularly known as Jim Crow, and just two weeks after president Lyndon Baines Johnson signed the 1964 Civil Rights Act, which, with the 1965 Voting Rights Act, helped to formally eradicate that regime. President Johnson also launched his War on Poverty in 1964, creating a number of programs and providing billions of dollars to end poverty in the United States. In December of that year, Martin Luther King Jr. would be awarded the Nobel Peace Prize, giving international recognition to what he proclaimed was a movement committed to the "unrelenting struggle" for freedom. However, several days of rioting in two of New York's largest black communities, Harlem and Bedford-Stuyvesant, as well as riots in other northern cities that summer, raised concerns among civil rights leaders that a white backlash would occur to jeopardize the newly won civil rights gains. In 1964 police brutality became one of the most important civil rights issues.

The presidential election scheduled for November that year was one reason concern about white backlash had been triggered. President Johnson, a liberal who was supportive of civil rights, was running against senator Barry Goldwater of Arizona, a Republican conservative who was antagonistic to the movement and its objectives. Martin Luther King Jr. and Bayard Rustin of the Southern Christian Leadership Conference, James Farmer of the Congress of Racial Equality, Roy Wilkins of the National Association for the Advancement of Colored People, Whitney Young of the National Urban League, and other national civil rights leaders all became involved in events in Harlem and Bedford-Stuyvesant and expressed their concern about the impact riots and demonstrations would have on the electoral outcome.

However, not all civil rights leaders were on the same page when addressing the rioting and police brutality in New York, and their opinions on the causes and the action that should be taken brought to the surface a deep division within the civil rights community. King, Wilkins, Rustin, and others stressed that the federal government's commitment to ending racial and economic inequality was at stake and argued that continued demonstrations could lead to Goldwater's election. Therefore, they called for a moratorium on all protests. Others, including James Farmer, struck a more militant tone, maintaining that protests and demonstrations were needed to assure that those in power would continue to act to bolster civil rights. Thus a major question facing movement leaders was how black New Yorkers should respond to police brutality in the face of the ever-deteriorating relationship between the NYPD and the black community. The crisis in Harlem and Bedford-Stuyvesant reinforced the understanding that civil rights were not just a southern concern.[3] City officials and the NYPD had for decades refused to earnestly address black and Latino grievances regarding police violence and had ignored demands and action proposals from civil rights and political leaders. The problems were allowed to fester, and Harlem and Bedford-Stuyvesant became ground zero for confronting the issue of police brutality.

The Riots in New York

On the morning of July 16, 1964, a number of students attending summer school at Robert F. Wagner Junior High School on East Seventy-Sixth Street were hanging out in front of the school building and others were across the street in front of two apartment buildings. Many black students were assigned to the junior high school in that predominantly white area on the Upper East Side of Manhattan to retake courses they had failed during the regular school year. The superintendent of the two apartment buildings, Patrick Lynch, was watering the flowers and plants when he either purposely or accidentally sprayed water on the students standing in front of the building. Some student witnesses claimed that he called them "dirty niggers," a charge he vehemently denied.[3]

Many of those black students may have been reminded of events the previous year in Birmingham, Alabama, when civil rights protesters demonstrating to end segregation in that city conducted sit-ins and marches and launched a boycott of downtown merchants. In response, director of public safety Eugene "Bull" Connor set police dogs on the nonviolent demonstrators, turned firehoses on them, and sent hundreds of demonstrators to jail, including high school and junior high school students. Regardless of whether the New York City students made this connection, the superintendent's actions angered them, and they responded by hurling garbage can lids and bottles at Lynch, forcing him to retreat into the apartment building.

Ninth-grader James Powell, along with two of his classmates, ran after the superintendent. A number of students who later appeared before the grand jury investigating the case testified that Powell did not have a weapon. However, other witnesses said that when Powell ran after Lynch they saw him with a knife. One teenager said that just before Powell pursued Lynch, he asked him, Harris, to give him the knife he had been holding for him.[4]

Off-duty police lieutenant Thomas Gilligan, a sixteen-year veteran with several citations, was in a television repair shop near the incident when he saw what was taking place and ran to the scene. According to Gilligan, Powell did have a knife. When he approached the fifteen-year-old, he fired a warning shot and Powell lunged at him, nicking him in the right arm; he then fired two additional shots. Witnesses, mostly other students at the scene, said that Powell did not have a weapon. One fourteen-year-old witness said the "cop just hit Jimmy and spun him around" and then shot him twice. One bullet went through Powell's right forearm, entered his chest above the right nipple, and lodged in his left lung; the other hit him just above the navel, piercing his abdomen and a major vein. Either shot would have been fatal. Powell, who was five feet six inches tall and weighed 122 pounds, fell to the ground. The fourteen-year-old witness claimed that Gilligan "kicked him over" and called him a "dirty nigger." Beulah Barnes, a nurse, said she saw Gilligan come out of the repair shop holding a revolver and that he shot Powell "twice and then the boy fell to the sidewalk." When Powell's body was first searched, no weapon was found. However, a knife was later found eight feet from where he was shot and fell.

Not all the witnesses agreed. A bus driver who saw the incident testified to the grand jury that he did see Powell with a knife. Another witness asserted that he heard Gilligan identify himself as a police officer and order Powell to stop. The NYPD did not help to clarify matters. According to the *New York Post*, the police refused to allow newspapers to photograph the knife. Soon after the killing, about three hundred students poured out of Wagner Junior High into the streets near the scene and began throwing bricks and bottles. Close to a hundred police were rushed to the area to restore order,[5] and their presence stopped the students' violent reaction. Although a confrontation was avoided the day of the shooting, the situation would be different in Harlem two days later.

On July 18, the Downtown, South Jamaica, and East River branches of the Congress of Racial Equality (CORE) held a rally at 125th Street and Seventh Avenue calling for the suspension of Lieutenant Gilligan. The original purpose of the rally had been to protest the murder by the Ku Klux Klan and law enforcement in Mississippi of Andrew Goodman, Michael Schwerner, and James Chaney, participants in the Mississippi Freedom Summer Project, but the organizers decided instead to focus on the killing of James Powell. After the rally, participants in the larger demonstration, led by Charles Saunders of East River CORE and Chris Sprowal of the Downtown chapter, encouraged people to march to the 123rd Precinct to take part in a nonviolent protest. About 150 did so, though by the time they reached the police station, they numbered 250.[6] Officers set up barriers a block away from the precinct; when the protesters tried to get past them, the police responded with their nightsticks. Harlem erupted in rebellion. According to the *New York Times*, thousands of people took to the streets, breaking windows and looting stores, pulling fire alarms, throwing bottles and other debris, and firing weapons. Over five hundred police officers were assigned to halt the rioting and fired thousands of shots into the air—and, according to some, at people as well—as a means of crowd control. Many protesters were clubbed or beaten by police, and thirty were arrested that evening.[7]

The riots lasted four days and drew worldwide attention. Calling it the worst outbreak in twenty-one years, the *Asahi Evening News* in Japan reported on the fighting between blacks and "steel-helmeted" police in Harlem, writing that hundreds of blacks "hurled bottles, bricks and Molotov cocktails at police who fired hundreds of rounds of warning shots . . . through the heart of the nation's largest Negro community."[8] The *Windsor-Star* in Canada estimated that a crowd of one thousand had broken through police barricades and wrote that the crowd tossed bottles while the police used their nightsticks. It claimed that on the second night "virtual guerrilla warfare had erupted in strife-torn Harlem."[9]

Three days after the violence erupted in Harlem, rioting started in Bedford-Stuyvesant, Brooklyn's largest black community, when police fired in the air in an attempt to stop demonstrators from setting off firecrackers and breaking windows—largely triggered by what many saw as a police assault on black people in Harlem. As of July 21, one person had been killed and seventy had been injured as a result of the clashes between police and civilians in Bedford-Stuyvesant. The police reported that fifty-three officers suffered injuries.[10] The number of protestors was estimated at a thousand. By July 23, eighty-two civilians had been injured and over two hundred people had been arrested. In addition, 117 businesses were damaged. In Bedford-Stuyvesant ten civilians and twelve police officers were injured.

The mainstream press, city officials, and the police all pointed at black militants as the cause of the riots. *Time* magazine blamed "hate-preaching demagogues" who "took to the street corners" and "raunchy radicals" who "issued inflammatory broadsides." Pointing to what it called a "pro–Red China outfit called the Progressive Labor Movement," the magazine blamed that group for labeling the police as "Fascist and racist." But it was the "most restless elements of Harlem," *Time* asserted, who were "bristling for a fight." The magazine went on to describe how the police tried to hold back the "screaming mob" that marched on the police station and "swarmed through the streets" but were unable to do so, and told its readers, "Roving bands of rioters—most of them kids—surged through the districts, aimlessly, desperately pursuing their urge for violence. . . . Some hoodlums lobbed Molotov cocktails into the battalions of pursuing police." Black nationalist militants, *Time* said, used irresponsible rhetoric, as did CORE leader James Farmer, whom it criticized for saying that white cops were "united against the black man."[11] On the third day of the riot, the *New York Times* reported that "groups of Negroes roamed the streets, attacking newsmen and others" and were also on rooftops hurling bottles and bricks at police on the street, who responded by firing warning shots "over the attackers' heads."[12]

The official city response to the rioting was at first in the hands of the acting mayor, Democrat Paul Screvane, head of the City Council and formerly the Sanitation Department commissioner. When the riot in Harlem erupted, Mayor Wagner was in Geneva attending a conference on automation and unemployment, at which he was to give a speech on poverty and unemployment as "related to discrimination and civil rights."[13]

The acting mayor gave his approval to take "all necessary steps" to maintain "law and order." He assured New Yorkers that the shooting of

Powell by Gilligan was being investigated by the Civilian Complaint Review Board (CCRB) and Manhattan district attorney Frank Hogan and said, "Our civic survival depends upon on the rule of law as enforced by the police and courts."[14] Screvane missed the point that Harlem residents did not have any faith in the police-controlled CCRB. At the heart of the problem for many blacks and Latinos was their unfair treatment by the very same forces that Screvane declared were there to preserve law and order.

While in Switzerland Wagner was in contact with Screvane, and the reports he received led him to decide to return to New York a little over one hundred hours after leaving. Speaking for the city government at a news conference on July 21, Screvane blamed the riots on "fringe groups, including the Communist Party." According to the *New York Times,* he praised President Johnson for assigning FBI agents to investigate whether federal statues had been violated and recommended that the FBI look at some of the demonstrators' financial sources, citing some "very inflammatory . . . anti-American . . . and seditious statements." When asked by a reporter if he could verify that Communists were responsible for the riot, he replied, "Well, I don't think there's any question about it. Some of the people have been involved in some of the meetings and rallies that have been called by people who are known Communists, and I don't have any doubt about that." Referring to one rally that had turned violent, the acting mayor claimed that anyone attending it could see firsthand that outside agitators controlled the entire operation. Deputy police commissioner Walter Arm also spoke at the press conference, and the *Times* quoted him as saying that the police had been "investigating very closely indications of leftwing incitement and were in no position to discuss it at this moment." The "extremist groups" under investigation by the police were accused of trying to capitalize on black aspirations; they included, in addition to the Communist Party, the Harlem Progressive Labor Party and its leader, William Epton, and members of the Socialist Workers Party.[15] The Progressive Labor Party, a Maoist group advocating the "Chinese brand" of Communism over the "Soviet brand," had distributed leaflets calling on black people to defend Harlem from the police. Some of its members had even traveled to China and met with China's leadership, including premier Chou En-Lai, to be educated in Maoist dogma.[16]

Blaming Communists for racial disorder was nothing new. Southern segregationists blamed them for civil rights protests in the South and consistently labeled the NAACP and other civil rights groups as Communist organizations. Some southern state legislatures even "investigated" the NAACP in an attempt to prove that it was a Communist outfit. Individual civil rights leaders were also called Communists, Martin Luther King Jr. being the most prominent. FBI head J. Edgar Hoover insisted that King was a Communist and persuaded U.S. attorney general Robert Kennedy to wiretap his phone. The focus on Communism proved an effective diversion from the real causes of protest in the South and the demonstrations and disturbances in New York and other northern cities. While Roy Wilkins contended that the violence gave Harlem a black eye, he also claimed that "raising the Communist cry won't solve very much at this time."[17]

While the mainstream press and city officials blamed black nationalists, Communists, and the Harlem community for the riot, Harlem residents and civil rights leaders blamed the police. Over one hundred people were treated at Harlem and Sydenham hospitals as a result of the July 18 riot. Patients at both hospitals accused the police of brutality. Doris Berry told the *New York Times* that she was out on the street, looking for her mother, who had been lost in the mob near her home, when a white policeman aimed his gun at her and shot her in the right knee: "I thought they were just shooting blanks until I got hit in the leg." The cops, she claimed, "just left me, and I had to take a taxi to the hospital." Thessolonia Cutler, who was treated at Harlem Hospital, told the *Times* she was shot in the back as she headed home after leaving work. The police, she said, "were beating up everyone and there was nothing but smoke and gunshots for blocks around."[18] By the third day of the riot, the police had fired so many rounds that they had exhausted their ammunition supply.[19]

Simone Montgomery, who lived in Harlem, sent a letter to Mayor Wagner and Police Commissioner Murphy detailing her experience on July 19 between 4:00 and 4:30 a.m. She had heard shots and as she looked out her window saw fifteen or more cops "running up and down the block firing shots in the air and chasing people." Two of them looked at her and shouted, "Get the fuck out of the window." Then, she wrote, they "fired directly at me." One bullet just missed her head, traveled through her drapes, grazed a wall, and ricocheted off the ceiling to the floor of her apartment. The second bullet smashed through a windowpane and into the ceiling. She gave both bullets to the detectives who responded to her complaint: "There is no doubt that the officers fired directly at me, as can be evidenced by where the bullet struck in relation to where I was standing." She also claimed that the words she heard one officer say to the other was further proof that she was a target: "We might have got the black bastard." Montgomery wrote that although a riot was taking place, the only disturbance on her block was created by the police.[20]

James Farmer and CORE

By 1963, well before the Harlem and Bedford-Stuyvesant riots, the most outspoken national civil rights figure on the issue of police brutality and the need for a CCRB was James Farmer, who had served as chairman of CORE from 1942 to 1944 and was reelected to that post in 1961. CORE was a small organization competing with more prominent national civil rights groups such as the NAACP and Martin Luther King's Southern Christian Leadership Conference (SCLC). CORE did not have their respected reputations nor their funding sources—the NAACP, for example, relied on dues from a much larger national membership as well as on a host of philanthropic organizations such as the New World Foundation and the Field Foundation, both of which provided money for litigation.[21] Neither could CORE rely on a network structure that, like the SCLC, received donations from black churches and ministerial organizations.

Farmer realized that for CORE to be on a par with the larger civil rights organizations, it would have to take the lead in civil rights campaigns that would grab public attention and have a national impact. In 1961 he decided the way to do this was to challenge segregation on public means of interstate travel. Although in 1946 the Supreme Court had handed down a decision in *Irene Morgan v. the Commonwealth of Virginia* that banned racial discrimination in interstate travel, the decision was not enforced in the South. CORE decided to pressure the federal government to enforce the Supreme Court decision by amassing a team of thirteen interracial volunteers to travel on buses throughout the South as a challenge to de facto segregation. However, when the Freedom Riders on two different busses were beaten in Alabama in May 1961, CORE bowed out of the campaign. Members of the Student Nonviolent Coordinating Committee (SNCC) continued it, however, eventually forcing the Kennedy administration to take stronger measures to enforce the Supreme Court ruling.[22]

Backing out of the Freedom Ride movement was a failure for CORE and certainly wasn't the type of publicity Farmer was seeking. As one SNCC member would comment decades later, "Your parents tell you don't start something that you can't finish. Finish it!" The Harlem and Bedford-Stuyvesant riots offered Farmer an opportunity to jump out in front of a civil rights issue that had gained national attention. Becoming the lead spokesperson on police brutality, an arena where other nationally prominent civil rights organizations had not had much to say, pushed Farmer and CORE into the national spotlight and helped elevate Farmer as a legitimate voice with the clout to negotiate with city officials and be interviewed on national news programs. As for how to halt police brutality, both Farmer and CORE took up a well-known refrain from the black community: empower citizens through a CCRB.

Just speaking publicly on an issue was not enough to establish himself and CORE as key players in the civil rights movement. Farmer realized that he would have to produce results, and in order to do so he would have to confront city officials directly. First Farmer called for meetings with the city in an attempt to win their support for a civilian review board. If they were not willing to support an independent board, CORE would pressure them by carrying out street demonstrations. In late April 1964 Farmer requested and was granted a meeting with Commissioner Murphy. It did not go well, and to Farmer's dismay, Murphy defended the already existing internal board. However, Murphy did say he would consider Farmer's request,[23] but that was certainly not enough for CORE to claim success.

Farmer told the *New York Times*, "There will be demonstrations involving schools, housing, and jobs" during negotiations with the NYPD and said it was going to be "a long hot summer." For his part, Murphy characterized the issue of widespread police brutality as bogus. He admitted to the *Times* that there might have been some "isolated" cases, but claimed there was no pattern to them and they were not necessarily directed at blacks and Latinos.[24]

Soon after the killing of Powell, the NAACP and CORE said that they would conduct their own investigation of the incident, and NAACP lawyer Jawn Sandifer declared that Wagner and Murphy must realize that there were officers who had to be weeded out of the force.[25] Farmer told the press that he had attempted to contact governor Nelson Rockefeller to urge him to call out the National Guard to protect the people of Harlem from the police. However, the governor was vacationing in Wyoming and was not available. Famer accused the police of firing indiscriminately into crowds. He denounced the brutality of the police and blamed them for being "hysterical, and I must say that the Police Commissioner in the posture which he had adopted in the last few months of self-congratulations for the Police Department must assume part of the responsibility." He told the two hundred people attending a rally at a Harlem church on July 19 that the Harlem riot was "New York's night of Birmingham horror."[26]

Farmer claimed that on the day rioting erupted, he had watched the police carry out a "blood orgy" by firing into the windows of tenements and the Therese Hotel. According to Farmer one woman who had approached the police for help was shot in the groin and then taken to Harlem Hospital. The *Times* confirmed that Barbara Barksdale, age twenty-three, was treated there for a superficial gunshot wound in her left thigh.[27]

What Should Be Done

In an attempt to stop the violence, on July 20 acting mayor Paul R. Screvane, deputy mayor Edward F. Cavanagh Jr., Manhattan borough president Edward R. Dudley, police commissioner Michael J. Murphy, and other city officials met with Farmer, Percy Sutton (an attorney for CORE), the Reverend Eugene Callender of the NAACP, and a delegation of other civil rights leaders. The latter group insisted that Officer Gilligan be suspended from the force and arrested, and Farmer once again called for a civilian review board. He also complained that almost all the police in Harlem were white and demanded greater racial integration of the NYPD.[28]

Screvane met later that day with Richard A. Hildebrand, president of the Manhattan branch of the NAACP, and three other civil rights leaders. In response to their demands, Screvane announced at a press conference that Gilligan's case would go to a grand jury and also promised to assign more black police officers to Harlem. Deputy Mayor Cavanagh, he said, would review how the NYPD addressed police brutality charges.[29]

The acting mayor may have promised to place additional black police officers in Harlem, but Police Commissioner Murphy made it clear that they would not be there on a permanent basis. Murphy confessed to the *Times* that he did not know what percentage of the police force was black and explained that although he had withdrawn some of the white police officers who were sent to Harlem to quell the violence, that did not signal a policy change. The department would remain "colorblind in its hiring."[30]

In the same *Times* piece, Farmer criticized Deputy Mayor Cavanagh's promised review process as "insufficient to insure fair play for the minority community" and stressed the desirability of a truly independent civilian review board and "intensive recruiting of Negro police." For his part, the NAACP's Hildebrand called for the creation of a committee formed outside of city governmental officials to investigate the Powell shooting.[31] Two days later, Adam Clayton Powell Jr., noting to the *Times* that he was speaking as the only elected official of Harlem, said the violence would continue unless six demands were met: the creation of a civilian review board, assigning three black captains to Harlem, suspending Gilligan, expanding the jurisdiction of the grand juries investigating gambling and corruption to include police misuse of their authority, ending the assignment of rookie police to "sensitive areas in Harlem," and ceasing the use of live ammunition to stop violence in Harlem. Powell, not one to mince words, said of the police, "What has happened in Harlem is without precedent in the history of any police department in any city, including the Deep South. New York City ought to hang its head in shame."[32]

Dr. Arthur C. Logan, chairman of the board of Harlem Youth Opportunities Unlimited, issued a press release blaming the conflict in Harlem on a "long-standing feeling of powerlessness and its resultant frustrations, coupled with the inadequate training and unreasonable behavior of the Police Department, evidenced by the numerous, documented accounts of unprovoked assaults upon peaceful citizens, including personnel employed by this agency." Logan's agency, created in 1962 by Kenneth Clark, a professor of psychology at City College, recommended Gilligan's "immediate suspension" and the "creation of an independent civilian complaint review board which shall meet as a body and personally hear cases. This board shall be appointed by the Mayor and report only to him." Logan also called for the "immediate promotion of a Negro Police Captain to the rank of Inspector, to be assigned as Commanding Officer of the Division covering Central Harlem," stationing additional black officers in the community, discontinuing the placement of rookie police officers in Harlem, and creating an "effective community relations division in the Police Department."[33]

Civil rights activists fighting for a civilian review board found an ally in the New York Civil Liberties Union, which circulated a statement in late July predicting that further riots would erupt unless the issue of police brutality was addressed. The organization argued that a civilian complaint review board would improve relations between the police and community and thereby reduce the risk of future riots. It attacked the existing review board and the NYPD for not making public the nature and number of complaints received.[34] Two years after the Harlem riots, the NYCLU's parent organization, the American Civil Liberties Union, published *Police Power and Citizens' Rights: The Case for an Independent Police Review Board*. In by-then urgent tones it warned that "time is running out. Impartial review is required now to help lance the festering infection in police–citizen relations, and to assist in halting violations of civil liberties at the hands of a defensive and beleaguered law enforcement system."[35]

Soon after his return from Geneva, Mayor Wagner spoke to city and Harlem leaders and, along with Police Commissioner Murphy, toured the areas hit by the riot. In a July 21 statement, he said he saw the "boarded up windows. I saw the crowds, the itinerant gangs, the residents clustered on the stoops, and looking fearfully out their windows." He said that he was convinced that the "overwhelming majority of those who live in the Harlem community neither participated in, nor appreciated the violence or disorder." In what was essentially an appeal for law and order, the mayor said it was the obligation of local government to maintain law and order and he had a mandate to do so.[36]

He was trying to persuade the residents of Harlem not to go back out in the streets to take part in violent confrontations, for the reason that maintaining law and order was in the best interests of black Americans: "The Supreme Court decision of 1954 is law and order. What would civil rights be without that decision—without that law and order?" The just-passed Civil Rights Act of 1964 and the antidiscrimination laws passed during his mayoralty were other examples of how law and order helped black people, and without it "civil rights would be set back fifty years." Wagner argued that the "opposite of law and order is mob rule, and that is the way of the Ku Klux Klan and the night riders and the lynch mob."[37]

But if reasoning with African Americans proved not enough to keep them off the streets, Wagner also warned of dire consequences, declaring that "illegal acts—including defiance of, or attacks upon the police whose mission it is, to enforce law and order, will not be condoned or tolerated by me, at any time." Attacks against people, "property or police by individuals" and "groups of hoodlums, rowdies and troublemakers, bent on destruction, theft, and rioting, will be brought to a halt and the guilty will be punished to the full extent of the law." Attempting to balance a tough law and order stance by also embracing a liberal formula for solving crime, Wagner's statement tried to reassure the residents of Harlem, Bedford-Stuyvesant, South Jamaica, East Harlem, and other areas of high unemployment and slum housing that he would do his best to relieve those problems. Adding that he was aware of white citizens' prejudice and of the dangerous thinking that leads to the "perilous concept of inevitable conflict between black and white," he stressed that the city must do its best to "reduce inequality, and to remove all conditions and practices which are a source of resentment and recrimination among these fellow citizens of ours."[38]

Moving on to the issue of police brutality, the mayor again tried to strike a balanced tone, stressing that Commissioner Murphy had his "complete confidence," yet saying also that the "ultimate authority and responsibility for the police force rests in civilian hands, the mayor himself." Wagner would not admit to police brutality, but he did acknowledge that even though the NYPD had the best training rules and regulations in the world, at times, due to stress and danger, some officers "act as the individuals they are" and commit acts that were not part of the department's training. He insisted that disciplinary action had to be taken when the evidence of such violations was clear. However, that action would not come from outside the department: "There is, within the Police Department, a Civilian Review Board." He also noted Deputy Mayor Cavanagh's assignment to review existing procedures to see if changes were needed. Although Wagner's administration was reviewing civilian boards in other cities, he gave no sign that New York's police-controlled board might be anything other than permanent.[39]

Noting the measures Screvane had taken to improve relations between the police and minority communities by stationing more black cops in Harlem, Wagner ordered Murphy to move ahead with programs aimed at recruiting black police officers and providing NYPD training for a greater number of qualified young people from minority groups. He wanted New Yorkers to know both that district attorney Frank Hogan had given Gillian's case to a grand jury and that "perpetrators of violence against" people or "property of the innocent, or of the police" would be apprehended and turned "over to the courts of justice." He said he would also exercise his right to review and consider cases of police brutality and review the present measures within the NYPD. He promised to spend time in minority communities to talk to residents and meet with representatives from various groups concerning community problems. He would also encourage heads of city departments to do likewise. Wagner said he had directed Screvane and the Poverty Operations Board and Poverty Council to expedite their efforts to provide unemployed youths with work in anti-poverty programs, "constructive counseling," and job training. Striking a Cold War theme, he warned that the entire nation and the world were watching events in New York City: "We carry the deepest responsibility these hours and days of trouble."[40]

A Divided Leadership

The one issue that Mayor Wagner did not address in his July 21 statement was the matter of a civilian complaint review board. His avoidance of the topic did not endear him to local black leaders, nor did his decision in late July to invite Martin Luther King Jr. to New York to discuss the riots—indeed, it aroused considerable anger. Commenting on the riots in New York City and Rochester at a press conference in Atlanta on July 27, King had said that African Americans should receive justice in their communities and that justice included an end to ghetto housing, "discriminatory barriers to jobs, inferior and segregated schools and discriminatorily barriers to the right to vote." The ability of civil rights leaders to keep the movement nonviolent depended on the progress blacks could make in jobs, housing, and schools, he said, noting a *New York Times* article showing that 62 percent of blacks in that city felt that nonviolent means were a better way to achieve equality than was violence. Regarding the role of black leaders, King said, "We must condemn the violence and lawlessness of the Negro Community," but also must blame the white power structure "to give us some victories." Leaders had to be as concerned about the environmental causes of the riots as "we are in condemning the violence." He called for massive spending to end the social isolation and economic deprivation of blacks, for such action would do much to "cast a radiant light into the dark chambers of despair." He called on white and black citizens to continue to struggle to end racial oppression and not to allow this "noble cause" to face a setback and be "defeated by provocation both within and without our movement."[41]

In an attempt to confront accusations that he was meddling in the affairs of a city where a number of civil rights leaders and groups were based, King said that he was going to New York because Mayor Wagner had invited him there to discuss the riots, but he was also going to meet with leaders in Harlem and Brooklyn for conversations about the violence. He also told reporters at the Atlanta press conference that he was willing to go to New York on a "peace mission" because the violence was damaging to the movement. Thus, his message to Wagner and to civil rights leaders critical of his visit was that the riots were not just a local affair—because they could jeopardize the entire civil rights movement, it was his duty to try to help end the violence.[42]

Wagner had surmised that King's visit to New York would calm the situation there; instead, it set off a storm of criticism. Livingston L. Wingate of the Unity Council of Harlem Organizations held a press conference on July 27, the day King arrived in New York City, denouncing his visit and saying that Harlem leaders were "mad as hell at Mayor Wagner for importing Dr. King from Atlanta to discuss problems in Harlem."[43] Adam Clayton Powell Jr. accused King of letting himself be used by Wagner. In a sermon at Abyssinian Baptist Church, Powell said the mayor and King, who had already held their first meeting to discuss the unrest, should have asked him to join them and that "no leader outside of Harlem should come into this town and tell us what to do." Hurling insults at both King and Wagner, Powell declared that he had been organizing demonstrations when Martin Luther King was "still in diapers" and warned that his exclusion from the talks could have dire consequences and that the blame for any future rioting in the city should be place in the "lap of Bobby Wagner." Even a close supporter of King echoed Powell's claim that King was being manipulated. Kenneth Clark, professor of psychology at City College—who, along with his wife, Mamie Clark, conducted the doll test that was used as evidence of the negative impact of segregation in *Brown v. Board of Education*—warned King not to let Wagner use him.[44]

L. Joseph Overton of the Harlem Labor Council also expressed his resentment that King was discussing Harlem's problems with Wagner before he reached out to Harlem's leaders. The Reverend Alvin A. Childs, bishop of the Faith Temple Church of God in Christ—the fastest growing Pentecostal church in New York City, with three thousand members—acknowledged that he was upset that King did not bother to consult him: "I cannot envision Dr. King being able to speak on a local level for all Negro people everywhere. I feel the Mayor should have consulted myself and other community leaders if he was really interested in resolving the tense situation in the City."[45]

For his part, King told the press that he had called for a civilian review board and the suspension of Officer Gilligan.[46] He said that when he met with Wagner he had made it clear that City officials must talk to Harlem leaders and that he had not come to New York to subvert local black leaders.[47] This did not stop the criticism of King's presence in the city. Some of the harshest criticism came from Aminda Badeau Wilkins, the wife of NAACP leader Roy Wilkins. She telephoned Julius C. C. Edelstein, Wagner's executive assistant, to share with him the sentiments of her husband's "friends" regarding how black people felt about the mayor's conference with King. She claimed that her husband had received at least twenty calls accusing Wagner of showing contempt for the city's black population. One caller, identified as a "property owner," had asked if Wagner had used taxpayers' money to fly King from Atlanta to New York. Aminda Wilkins said it was a "well known fact that he charges [a] fee for appearances and consultations" and that if that was the case, she was "going to protest on this basis." The most critical reaction, she told Edelstein, had come from those asking her to sign a letter to President Johnson objecting to Wagner's role in bringing King to New York: "This is a letter signed by fifty prominent people which will be sent to President Johnson."[48]

Aminda Wilkins's criticism was not aimed just at King but also at other national civil rights leaders who became involved in New York City affairs. She complained about Bayard Rustin, a close adviser to King, having been asked to play a role: "Although Rustin is a smart man, good organizer, he has [a] terrible reputation—former communist, known homosexual, etc.—doesn't make any Negro feel good to have this kind of man speaking for Negroes." She claimed that the NAACP was the only civil rights organization that had a "real constituency" in the city, with "thirteen bona fide chapters," whereas King had no organizational presence. And while CORE did have a presence in the city, "Farmer has an organization of 'kooks.'" She went on to say that callers to the NAACP "have resented very much the fact that the mayor did not call Whitney Young, Mr. Wilkins, and other responsible Negro leaders here in the City before taking the drastic step of calling King."[49]

To add to the division within the civil rights community, Jesse Gray, leader of the Community Council for Housing, which in 1963 had conducted a rent strike by tenants in a fifteen-block section of Harlem protesting slum conditions, and William Epton, head of the Harlem Defense Council, affiliated with the Maoist Progressive Labor Movement (PL), planned to conduct a march in Harlem on July 25 denouncing police brutality. Although Commissioner Murphy had banned demonstrations in Harlem, Gray and Epton said they would defy his order. This increased Wilkins and Rustin's fears that violent confrontation might ensue, and they sent a letter to Wagner asking him to rescind Murphy's ban; some also tried to convince Gray and Epton to call off their demonstration.[50] Wilkins, showing his concern about what a violent confrontation would produce, told the heads of other civil rights organizations in a telegram, "The promise of the Civil Rights Act of 1964 could well be diminished or nullified and a decade of increasingly violent and futile disorder ushered in if we do not play our hand coolly and intelligently." However, Epton insisted that the march would go on.[51]

To stop the march, the City Corporation Counsel got a temporary court injunction naming Epton, Jesse Gray, and PL head Milton Rosen.

On July 25 Epton launched the march from the headquarters of the Harlem Defense Council on Sixteenth Street and Lenox Avenue, which was also the headquarters of PL. At 4:20 p.m. the thirty-two-year-old Epton linked arms with the fifty-five-year-old civil rights attorney Conrad Lynn and began to urge supporters to join them. But police soon moved in, arresting both Epton and Lynn.[52] In response to Epton and others insisting that the demonstrations had to be continued, Wilkins called together leaders of top civil rights organizations on July 29 for a meeting that resulted in a call for a moratorium on demonstrations.

The admonitions of King, together with Gray and Epton's determination to go ahead with their July 25 march despite the pleas of Wilkins and others, brought to the surface what some saw as a disconnect between the leaders of nationally established civil rights organizations and ordinary people. Attorney Clarence Jones, for example, told the *Times* in late July that in his opinion, established civil rights leaders did not speak for the poor. Jones was part of a group of artists and intellectuals that had come together to discuss the meaning of the Harlem and Bedford-Stuyvesant riots, including writer John Oliver Killens, actor Ossie Davis, actress Ruby Dee, painter Mel Williamson, and Martin Luther King Jr. They all agreed that the riots were symptomatic of the larger problems poor blacks faced. Jones told the press that Harlem's young people had witnessed too much police corruption to have any respect for the law and that Farmer, King, Rustin, and other prominent leaders could not go into New York's streets and expect those who were rioting to listen to them. White authorities were wrong in thinking that established black leaders spoke for poor black people, Jones insisted, for they had no contact with the poor. The "white power structure itself," he went on, "diminished the influence of the Negro leaders by refusing to make the necessary concessions" they had requested.[53]

A Protest Moratorium?

The Harlem and Bedford-Stuyvesant riots not only revealed a divide between King and New York City civil rights leaders over who had the right to speak for black New Yorkers, but also brought to light the deep ideological fissures within the national movement regarding the question of whether civil rights organizations should continue protest demonstrations or call for a moratorium on them. The question had taken on a great deal of importance because the nation was in the midst of an election campaign in which Lyndon B. Johnson was seeking to retain the office that he, as vice president, had assumed when president John F. Kennedy was assassinated the previous year. Johnson's strong support of Kennedy's Civil Rights Act and his own efforts to eradicate poverty and racism had won him the support of civil rights groups. In his January 8, 1964, State of the Union speech, Johnson called on Congress to "do more for civil rights than the last hundred sessions combined" and announced that "this administration today here and now declares unconditional war on poverty in America."[54]

Johnson's Republican opponent, senator Barry Goldwater, was seen as civil rights' nemesis. He publicly opposed and voted against the Civil Rights Act, arguing that the federal government had no right to dictate to states that they must integrate schools. He called a public accommodations bill unconstitutional because it tampered with the "right of assembly, the freedom of speech, the freedom of religion, and the freedom of property." Civil rights leaders spoke vehemently against Goldwater. King called his position on civil rights "politically and socially suicide, and while the Republican candidate was not a racist, he articulated a philosophy that gave aid to racists."[55] Responding to a May 12, 1964, campaign speech by Goldwater at Madison Square Garden, in which he said that the problem of integration was one of the heart, Roy Wilkins sent the senator a letter arguing that leaving civil rights to the states would grant immunity for the "use of cattle prods and shotguns by Alabama state troopers, the armored tank and dogs and fire hoses of Birmingham police, the Bomb murderers of little children in church in Alabama, and the assassins in Mississippi."[56]

One faction of the civil rights community argued strongly that the riots around the country only increased Goldwater's chances of victory, because the violence would lead to a white backlash that could harm Johnson's chances.[57] Urging civil rights leaders not to do anything to assist the Goldwater campaign, Wilkins called for a meeting of the top civil rights groups to discuss how to keep the riots in Harlem and Brooklyn from damaging the civil rights movement.[58] On July 29 he, Bayard Rustin, national director of the NAACP Legal Defense Fund Jack Greenberg, head of the National Urban League Whitney Young, James Farmer,

Martin Luther King Jr., head of the Negro American Labor Council A. Philip Randolph, SNCC chairman John Lewis, and Courtney Cox, also of SNCC, met at the NAACP headquarters in Manhattan to see if they could decide on a uniform response to the riots. Some at the meeting wanted a "broad curtailment if not total moratorium" on demonstrations. Wilkins, King, Young, and Randolph signed a statement warning that the riots posed a "serious threat to the implementation of the Civil Rights Act." Reflecting their concern about Goldwater, they recommended a "voluntary temporary alteration in strategy and procedure." Simply put, they wanted a halt to demonstrations until after the November elections. Wilkins, King, Young, and Randolph said Goldwater's position on civil rights was "clear enough language for any Negro American," but Farmer's and Lewis's signatures were not on the group's final statement calling for a moratorium on demonstrations. Wilkins explained the absence by saying that the two men first had to clear it with their organizations, but this was not exactly a forthright explanation of the missing signatures.[59]

Farmer did not sign because he had already left the meeting when Wilkins presented the statement. And although John Lewis was present, he said he did not speak out against the statement in order to maintain unity but later told the Associated Press he thought demonstrations must continue in order to put pressure on those in power. During the meeting, he said, there had been no discussion about continued demonstrations. Instead, he thought emphasis should have been placed on voter registration. A spokesperson for Farmer later said that as far as CORE was concerned there was no moratorium, but the issue would be put on the agenda of CORE's National Action Council on August 8. Lincoln Lynch, head of the CORE Long Island branch, said he did not see giving up the one tool civil rights groups possessed. Herbert Callender, chair of the Bronx branch of CORE, vowed that as long as there was injustice, they would demonstrate.[60]

The split between CORE and SNCC on the one side and SCLC, the NAACP, the Urban League, and Randolph's Negro American Labor Council on the other was in part ideological, but it was also a matter of timing. Wilkins and the NAACP and Whitney Young's Urban League were, for the most part, opposed to using demonstrations as a means of achieving civil rights and preferred the tools of legislation and lobbying. Young was a powerbroker who had strong contacts with influential people in government and in the corporate world. He believed that the way to win concessions from those in power was by cultivating trust and friendship and not through demonstrations. In a 1964 interview he characterized the Urban League as the "professional arm" of the movement, made up of people who tried to implement policy with the "highest echelons of the corporate community, . . . the highest echelons of the governmental community," and at the "local, state and federal level." Thus Wilkins and Young's support of a moratorium was not surprising.[61]

More to the left, CORE and SNCC militants contended that lobbying and cultivating strong relationships with those in power were not enough to end racial inequality. Nonviolent resistance was a central element of both CORE and SNCC's philosophy, and the groups' grassroots activists and organizations contended that organized demonstrations using such tactics were necessary to force those in powers to act and make concessions. Hence, many in both these organizations believed that any suspension of mass protest would weaken the movement's position.

King, Randolph, and Rustin were for the moratorium. Although they had a long history of supporting nonviolent resistance, Randolph and Rustin felt that at this special moment, when the national government was supportive of taking action against racial discrimination and economic inequality, a moratorium was the right thing. It was Randolph who had convinced John Lewis and the young SNCC activists to drop Lewis's plan to criticize the Kennedy administration in his speech at the March on Washington because it could jeopardize the unity of the event. More important, any criticism of the administration could also jeopardize support for a civil rights bill. Randolph saw Johnson as a strong ally on the issue (Johnson had even reached out to him the previous November to ask for his support) and did not want to take any steps to jeopardize his goodwill.[62]

At the July 29 meeting, Rustin gave his reasons for supporting the moratorium. "Leadership often has to do what is right, whether or not people like it," he said. He called the action "politically sound" and said the civil rights "leaders have taken a very courageous stand." He announced that he would travel around the country to convince people of the "soundness of the position."[63] A year later Rustin would call for an end to street protest and ask African Americans to embrace more

serious political and economic agendas. Blacks had ended legal discrimination, now they needed to address economic disparity and social
isolation. Coalition politics, he felt, would win programs to improve the
economic plight of working-class Americans. Indeed, since the Democratic Party supported ending poverty and racism, it made sense for
black Americans to embrace the party along with labor.[64]

King's position is harder to decipher. He was a strong believer in nonviolent protest and had discussed its power on several occasions. For
instance, in his 1963 "Letter from a Birmingham Jail" he made a moral
case for nonviolent resistance: "Nonviolent direct action seeks to create
such a crisis and establish such creative tension that a community that
consistently refused to negotiate is forced to confront the issue. It seeks
so to dramatize the issue that it can no longer be ignored." King argued
that action was necessary in order to gain freedom: "We know through
painful experience that freedom is never voluntarily given by the op-
pressor; it must be demanded by the oppressed."[65]

King most likely agreed to the call for a moratorium because he did
not want strife within the movement, especially among its leading figures. Despite King's willingness to challenge white segregationists, he
was less willing to challenge Roy Wilkins, who had criticized King's
campaigns in conversations with other civil rights leaders. In addition,
King had already concluded that a Goldwater presidency would be a
danger to the movement and called the Republican Party's nomination
of him "unfortunate and disastrous."[66]

Of the two national civil rights organizations that opposed a moratorium on demonstrations, CORE had the larger presence in New York
City, where its national headquarters and over a dozen chapters were
located: Brooklyn, the Bronx, and Staten Island each had a chapter, two
were in Queens, and four in Manhattan, including Harlem, Downtown,
and East River. In addition, New York University, Columbia University,
and Queens College each had chapters, and neighboring Long Island
had one of the most active. By 1963 most of the chapters had conducted
significant protests in the city. The Bronx chapter had led protests against
the White Castle fast-food restaurants demanding that 25 percent of
the jobs go to blacks and Puerto Ricans. At Downstate Medical Center,
Brooklyn CORE conducted one of the largest civil rights campaigns in
New York during the 1960s. The chapter teamed up with pastors of the

borough's largest churches to demand that a quarter of the jobs at the center's construction site be provided to blacks and Puerto Ricans, and over seven hundred people were arrested for protesting at the site. It was no surprise that the national CORE organization announced it would ignore the moratorium and continue direct action.[67]

Roy Wilkins made his case for a moratorium in his *New York Times* piece titled "What Now!" He agreed with the more militant wing of the movement on the systemic causes of the riots—the relegation of black children to segregated schools, high unemployment and underemployment rates among blacks, housing discrimination that forced many into slums, and other social evils. Aiming his message at more militant factions, he insisted, however, that any program to eradicate inequality must also win the support of white America, and that rioting and the destruction of property would not convince it to support civil rights objectives. Riots hurt the nation more in 1964 than if they had taken place in 1924, because the "World Struggle" between "controlled and free societies" was at a crucial phase.[68] Thus, the riots had a detrimental impact in the competition between the United States and the Soviet Union for the loyalty of emerging nations in Asia, Africa, and Latin America. Rioting would lead to repression.

Although he was not supportive of nonviolent protest, Wilkins gave credit to King for leading the 1955–56 Montgomery Bus Boycott but would not credit it with ending segregation on the transit system. He was willing to acknowledge, however, that the protest was not violent and had raised the national consciousness. He was not so kind when referencing the Brooklyn chapter of CORE's New York World's Fair "stall-in." In April, when the fair opened, members and supporters of Brooklyn CORE attempted to stop motorists going to the event by stalling their cars and creating traffic jams. Proponents of the "stall-in" hoped their action would pressure Governor Rockefeller and Mayor Wagner to pay attention to the horrible conditions in black and Latino slums.[69] Although this protest was nonviolent, it was aimed at people who did not have any power to end poor housing or employment discrimination in the building trades and had just led to resentment by ordinary citizens of the "shotgun technique."[70]

Black people in the North, Wilkins pointed out, had a weapon for gaining civil rights that southern black people lacked: the franchise. "Violence, however, had to be ruled out" as a viable option. "It seems clear that the outbreaks in New York State and New Jersey have hurt the Negro's cause and that more of the same will injure it still further." He also visited the topic of how rioting could lead to the election of Goldwater, a man so far to the right that he was "supported by the John Birch Society and endorsed by the Georgia Ku Klux Klan" and who so exploited the fears of white voters that "racial violence will be rampant." Thus "nothing could be more important at the moment in the Negro civil rights struggle than refraining from any action that aids Goldwaterism. The response to the moratorium plea will be the measure of the maturity of the Negro Community."[71]

CORE made good on Farmer's promise to continue demonstrations, the first of which would be in August at the Democratic National Convention in Atlantic City in support of seating delegates from the Mississippi Freedom Democratic Party. Farmer announced that CORE "will throw the full weight of our organization into demonstrations if the delegation is not seated" and that SNCC would join CORE at the convention. Farmer was unconvinced by the argument that demonstrations would lead to resentment among white citizens and insisted that "white backlashers" were going to vote for Goldwater anyway.[72]

Farmer maintained two years later in his book *Freedom When?* that organized demonstrations were a positive course of action because there was little violence when they were carried out; rather, it was when there was a lack of organization that violence erupts. Nonviolent protest was a CORE stock in trade, and Farmer insisted that a demonstration was not a riot; instead, demonstrations tended to help by providing an alternative to violence. To support this claim, Farmer compared the 1963 demonstrations CORE conducted at construction sites throughout New York City, where there were no cases of people "throwing bottles and bricks," to the situation in 1964 when CORE did not conduct organized protests and there was violence.

In the telling, Farmer omitted the fact that the July 18 riot in Harlem had followed a demonstration organized by CORE chapters. Farmer pointed to the police when arguing about responsibility for the Harlem and Bedford-Stuyvesant riots. Lieutenant Gilligan's shooting of Powell, a "slight, fifteen-year-old Negro," near a school housing hundreds of students was a formula for disaster, Farmer wrote. The students were "furious, many of them literally choking with rage at such wanton injustice."

CORE intervened to organize "hundreds of Powell's schoolmates" to march two days later to the police precinct to demand Gilligan's suspension and a "civilian investigation." "That demonstration, all agree, was a model of peaceful protest" and a key factor in "sublimating the anger of the youngsters."[73]

While Farmer took credit for the students' nonviolence on their march and near their school, it was a different story in Harlem. "If legitimate mass demonstrations" had been allowed by the NYPD, and "if the police had not acted so unwisely—the Harlem riots could have been averted," Farmer wrote, accusing the police of arresting CORE leaders on July 18 even as members of the force were putting up a barricade near the precinct. He accused an Inspector Pendergast of making the fateful decision to crack down on the protests and allegedly saying "I've had enough of this. Get them niggers"—words, Farmer wrote, that were "suicidal" in Harlem. The demonstrators "went crazy and began throwing the bottles and bricks." Officers came out of the station and began pushing the crowd back; the Tactical Patrol (which Farmer labeled the "shock troops") appeared and charged into the crowd. "The police could not have acted more foolishly that evening had they tried," Farmer wrote; they were "thirsting for action." But the police were not the only ones at fault. Farmer wrote that he had consistently asked Mayor Wagner for a civilian complaint review board, and had such existed, there would not have been rioting. Instead, people would have been waiting for the board to act. In addition, had there been a jobs program for youths, they would have been at work instead of taking to the streets.[74]

Farmer's positions aligned him with the militant wing of the civil rights movement, and even twenty years after the riots he had not changed his view on who bore responsibility. In his 1985 autobiography he called the Powell shooting a "classic case of police brutality" and said he doubted that the teen had charged at Gilligan with a knife. Black police officers, he claimed, had told him that the police often carried knives in order to plant them on suspects. Indeed, CORE's investigation at the time of the incident had called it an "unnecessary killing," and Farmer acknowledged at a press conference shortly after the shooting that he had said the "policeman should be tried for murder."[75]

Notwithstanding his consistent support of nonviolence as the means of achieving racial equality, Farmer paid a heavy price in the press for his position on the Harlem and Bedford-Stuyvesant riots. Woody Klein of the *New York World-Telegram and Sun* accused him of inflaming racial tension in Harlem with his alarming remarks, pointing to Farmer's claim that he had personally seen a woman "shot in the groin" by a police officer when she had asked for assistance. He later admitted that he had not seen the incident. When Klein questioned Farmer about his having called the police "our enemies" at a rally in a church, Farmer responded that the people in the church were in no mood for a speech on nonviolence and he had been booed and jeered when he was introduced. He wanted to let them know he was on their side.[76]

Not only the press and Roy and Aminda Wilkins but also some who identified themselves as supporters of CORE singled Farmer out for criticism. A number of people sent Farmer letters claiming that they admired Farmer's balanced leadership but also expressing disappointment with his role in the Harlem riot. One Fred Howard wrote on July 23 that he was sympathetic "with the controlled militancy of your movement" and had supported CORE's earlier boycotts and demonstrations. He considered Farmer a national leader for whites as well as blacks and identified himself as a white man who had "been kicked around more than you" and "suffered more brutality than you." He urged Famer to "temper your remarks" and begged him not to "inflame and not to fight demagoguery with emotional outbursts" and not to accept as fact unsubstantiated rumors. He also asked Farmer not to condemn an entire police department. Inflamed emotion, Howard wrote, was a form of "violence," and while he did not deny incidents of police brutality, should the actions of one officer or for that matter the actions of looters condemn all police or an entire community? "Mr. Farmer, your cause is just. White backlash thrives on irrational and irresponsible action, and leadership. If we both take issue with Barry Goldwater's statement of extremism, I respectfully suggest and urge that we all conduct ourselves accordingly and that you, as a leader, protect only the best of us."[77] Another correspondent, Ronald Freund, wrote on July 21 that he thought Farmer had been "one of the few who has demonstrated both the ability and responsibility for leadership in the civil rights area," but his actions over the last few days had caused him to "question either your responsibility or your judgment." He claimed that "irresponsible demonstrations and riots" and Farmer's actions have served only to incite rather than to discourage this "unfortunate behavior," and urged Farmer to "exert the kind of rational leadership of which you are capable and not allow yourself to be led by the unreasoned emotionalism of mob psychology."[78] Blaine Lotz, who claimed to be a supporter of CORE, wrote that he would no longer contribute financially to the organization because "whatever good it might have served in registering new Democratic voters in Mississippi has been lost by your riots," which would only create more votes for Goldwater.[79]

A majority of the letters Farmer received in response to his statements on the riots expressed similar anger. Milton Ellenbogen, writing the day after the July 18 riot, agreed that CORE had the right to hold a rally but argued that the problem was timing. "But the actions of CORE in holding that rally this past Saturday evening" in a "mob of impassioned people whose emotions have clouded their rational thinking and good common sense, represents to me a failure of your organization in seeking justice in a civilized society." Using the courts or peaceful demonstrations were appropriate actions, Ellenbogen wrote, "but not violence or speeches that incite violence." He accused Farmer of adopting the philosophy that the "ends justify the means." His only "consolation" was that the "Negro people still have a very splendid organization championing their cause—the NAACP."[80] Perry S. Samuels was even more critical of Farmer's role. He declared that the most tragic aspect of the Harlem riot was the "attitude of James Farmer" whose remarks were "contradictory and inflammatory." His example of the latter was Farmer's statement about the woman who was "shot in the groin": "If ever there was a time when calm, objective leadership is needed, this is it."[81] One letter writer went so far as to blame Farmer for the disturbances: "Your attitude only encourages those that are hoodlums to keep it up with all your answers to everything."[82]

While some of the letters to CORE targeted Farmer, others leveled criticism at various black people involved in the civil rights struggle. Justin G. Ferguson, who expressed sympathy for the "plight of the Negro," nevertheless was "appalled by the actions of new leaders (especially CORE)." He accused black leaders of supporting retaliatory action against the New York police in the forms of demonstrations and group marches because of alleged "police brutality." Ferguson wrote that he was "opposed wholeheartedly to mob demonstrations" because "by virtue of their being retaliatory [they] inevitably lead to violence." Scolding black leaders, Ferguson claimed that "any consequences which may arise out of mass demonstrations of this sort are your sole responsibility" and asked how they could expect whites to embrace their cause when they were responsible for mob violence in Harlem. The events in Harlem showed that CORE had a "disregard for basic democratic principles." The writer denied that he was a "so-called Southern bigot. I have lived in Massachusetts for 22 of my 23 years."[83]

Many of those who criticized the actions of Farmer and other civil rights leaders and activists seemed unable to see police brutality as an issue or to link it with the civil rights struggle. Many letters to Farmer defended the police and blamed black people for the violence. Herbert B. Geist, for example, blamed Farmer "for setting the civil rights movement back ten years." He wrote in disgust that after witnessing the "rabble rousing performance of you and the other negro demagogues during the recent New York riots, I find that the principle [sic] difference between you and your kind and Governor Wallace is color and direction." Calling the New York riots "mass violence" and "unbridled savagery" he asked Farmer how he could equate the killing of Powell with the civil rights struggle, and added that he was going to disassociate himself from the those "who brought shame in the Negro leadership."[84] Louis Schata characterized Powell as a "punk" Farmer had elevated to martyrdom: "Does Negro leadership have any good tactical reason to refuse to admit Negro shortcomings and continue to sweep these glittering deficiencies under the rug?"[85] Joanne Ferrera called the recent actions of CORE "absolutely disgusting and your demand for a murder charge against Lt. Gilligan is ridiculous." Courageous police officers like Gilligan, she claimed, were needed and "only an idiot would condemn a man for enforcing the law, much less for saving his own life."[86] Anne C. Jordan congratulated Farmer for selling his "people down the river faster, better and more permanently than any group of segregationists" or "white racists could do in several years." He had proven "what the White Southerners have been stating: Give the black man a finger and he'll take both hands . . . Boy you are clever." She demanded that Farmer stop blaming the New York City police for the mistakes of black people and justifying the actions of an "emotionally crazed people" by crying police brutality.[87]

These and many other such attacks on Farmer and other civil rights leaders reflected the growing discontent in both the nation and New York City with the civil rights campaigns.[88]

Conclusion

Although the major national civil rights organizations and their leaders turned their attention to the issue of police brutality in New York City during and after the Harlem and Bedford-Stuyvesant riots, they came up short when it came to making any gains. The lack of any meaningful changes following the riots demonstrated how extremely difficult an issue police brutality was to solve and how much more work it would take to effect change.

One major impediment to solving police brutality issues was the intransience of mayor Robert Wagner. He refused to adopt any serious proposal that would make him seem as if he were an adversary of the police. Despite his liberal reputation and his advocacy of civil rights, Wagner had built a strong alliance with municipal labor unions, including the police, and was unwilling to risk jeopardizing it. In addition, his political instinct informed him that challenging institutions such as the police would not be a popular move.

A September 1964 *New York Times* survey showed that most white New Yorkers felt the struggle for civil rights for American blacks "had gone too far." While denying that they were prejudiced, a large percentage of white New Yorkers claimed that blacks got "everything on a silver platter" and that whites faced "reverse discrimination." Over a quarter of those surveyed said they had become opposed to the objectives of black people. Even though 68 percent of whites surveyed said that they would vote for Johnson, 54 percent said that the civil rights movement was moving too quickly. An impressive 93 percent contended that the summer riots had hurt blacks, while 55 percent said that Commissioner Murphy had handled the violence in Harlem and Bedford-Stuyvesant well.[89]

The *New York Times* survey revealed that while civil rights leaders argued that police brutality was a civil rights concern, they had a hard time convincing white Americans that this was the case. The issues of crime, race, and policing have never been easy to untangle. Many white

New Yorkers, as the *Times* survey noted, were not persuaded that blacks were victims of police abuse, or if police officers used excessive force, they believed it was in response to violent resistance by blacks who were breaking the law. In a letter to CORE, Thomas Hudson McKee epitomized this view. Describing himself as an opponent of "the institution of racial segregation" who had sent a check to CORE, he wrote forcefully about how disturbed he was by "Farmer's attacks on New York City police officers and the CORE leader's accusation that a police officer murdered Powell." Admitting that he was not familiar with the details of the case, he still seriously doubted that "any policeman in New York City or even Jackson, Mississippi, would murder any fifteen-year-old in cold blood without very substantial provocation." He insisted that "CORE people" should support the police and other law enforcement officers because they were risking their lives in stopping "Negro riots."[90]

The rebellions in Harlem and Bedford-Stuyvesant did help police brutality become a national civil rights issue, but efforts to make the city and the NYPD take steps to end the killing and beating of black New Yorkers continued to face resistance throughout Mayor Wagner's administration. The mayor and the NYPD ignored proposals for change, but some elected officials, sensing that the atmosphere continued to be explosive, came forward with their own approaches to ending police brutality.

6

John Lindsay, Racial Politics, and the
Civilian Complaint Review Board

The failure of Roy Wilkins, Martin Luther King Jr., James Farmer, and other prominent civil rights leaders to get the Wagner administration to take serious action to stop police brutality revealed how very difficult it was to even begin to influence policy on the issue. After the 1964 riots, local civil rights and grassroots organizations, civil liberties groups, and some New York political figures continued battling to curtail police power and calling for an independent civilian complaint review board. However, Mayor Wagner would not agree to such a board or take any steps that would end the practice of the police investigating the police. Wagner had a year and a half more in office after the riots, and it seemed that the hope for an independent review board was doomed: the City Council decided to table a motion made by council member Theodore Weiss in April 1964 to establish an all-civilian nine-person review board to be appointed by the mayor; Wagner and Police Commissioner Murphy vigorously opposed an independent board; and the Patrolmen's Benevolent Association waged a vigorous campaign against it. Even though Murphy resigned in 1965, Wagner's opposition remained unchanged.[1] Then, in January 1966, John Lindsay was sworn in as mayor.

In May 1966, just five months into his term, Mayor Lindsay created a civilian complaint review board on which only three of the seven members were from the NYPD. This created an opportunity to mitigate the immense power that the police had over New Yorkers by providing citizens the opportunity to submit complaints to a board on which the majority of members were not NYPD employees. The new board's power was limited; it could recommend to the commissioner the actions it felt were appropriate to take against police officers found guilty of violating the law or infringing on department regulations, but it could not mandate them. However, the board could conduct investigations and hold hearings, and in the eyes of many New Yorkers this alteration in the balance of power had the potential to seriously address issues of police brutality. The Patrolmen's Benevolent Association, members of the law enforcement community, conservative columnist William F. Buckley, and the New York Conservative Party all opposed the new CCRB and put as many hurdles as they could in its way, particularly by exploiting racial fear.

John Lindsay

John V. Lindsay, a Republican member of the U.S. House of Representatives, declared his candidacy for mayor in the spring of 1965, and boldly announced at the annual meeting of the New York County Lawyers Association that if elected he would create a civilian-controlled complaint review board comprising four civilians and three police officers. For Lindsay, the purpose of government was to serve those who needed help. He claimed that while he was in Congress from 1959 to 1965, more than twenty-five thousand constituents had approached his New York City office for assistance. He had created a team of volunteers to address their needs, but felt that big government was not fulfilling its role with respect to its citizens. As mayor he wanted to "break down the barriers" and make the relationship between citizen and government more "human" and more "workable." There must, he said, "be due process in the workings of bureaucracy" including "law enforcement."[2]

Early in his political career Lindsay was attracted to the more progressive wing of the Republican Party. He grew up in an elite eastern Protestant household of forward-thinking Republicans in the tradition of Theodore Roosevelt, one attribute of which was a commitment to public service. According to Lindsay biographer Geoffrey Kabaservice, Lindsay cultivated these values while attending school at Buckley, St. Paul's, and Yale University.[3] Before running for Congress, Lindsay served as an executive assistant in the Justice Department under President Eisenhower's attorney general Herbert Brownell (1952–57). As the president's main counselor on civil rights, Brownell successfully advocated that judges nominated for federal posts in the South be pro–civil rights and willing to carry out the Supreme Court's 1954 *Brown* decision.[4] Lindsay became Brownell's ally and helped to draft the Civil Rights Act of 1957, a bill for which Brownell pushed and which Eisenhower signed. That act created a Civil Rights Commission to investigate, among other things, allegations that people were being denied the right to vote due to race, color, national origin, or religion. Among other provisions, the commission was to "study and collect information concerning legal developments constituting a denial of equal protection of the laws under the Constitution and appraise the laws and policies of the Federal Government with respect to equal protection of the laws under the Constitution."[5]

After joining the House in January 1959, Lindsay remained an outspoken champion for civil rights. In an attempt to pressure President Kennedy to keep his promise to introduce a civil rights bill, Lindsay joined with Republican representatives William McCulloch from Ohio and Charles Mathias from Maryland to introduce their own civil rights bill. However, Kennedy opposed their bill because he did not think it could pass in the House.[6]

Kennedy did eventually introduce his own bill, which Lindsay supported. However, Lindsay faced a lobbying effort against that bill by fellow Republicans and the public, which sent voluminous mail in opposition. Lindsay stood firm, however, and publicly criticized the misinformation campaign being waged by anti–civil rights forces. He noted that supporters of civil rights "climbed a very high mountain on this bill in the House, myself included. We went through the fires holding this bill together and getting it through intact." In both the 1957 and 1960 Civil Rights Acts, the Senate cut key provisions that had been adopted by the House. However, Lindsay warned that the House would not accept a 1964 bill if the Senate watered it down. Speaking on a radio program in May of that year, he said that the Senate could "filibuster until the cows come home," but if the American people were faced with accepting a compromise bill or having no bill at all, he would find that a difficult decision.[7] His public warning against modifying the 1964 Civil Rights Act is a good illustration of the depth of Lindsay's commitment to civil rights. It was also evident at the 1964 Republican National Convention, where he joined Nelson Rockefeller and other pro–civil rights Republicans to advocate that the Platform Committee adopt a pledge in support of the 1964 Civil Rights Act. More and more the party maverick, Lindsay publicly announced in the summer of 1964 that he would not support his party's nominee, Barry Goldwater, for president.[8]

In his May 1965 speech to the New York County Lawyers Association, Lindsay contended that the resignation of Police Commissioner Murphy was an illustration of the bad relationship between citizens and the City. This, he felt, was an "urban problem of all cities across the nation," though New York was the "first city" and must "show the way. Our city must deal with the problem of crime realistically, intelligently, and energetically." For Lindsay, the core problem was a lack of trust: "So long as we have large numbers of our population who believe that society cares nothing for them, we cannot hope to be successful." But there was also, he said, a need to "protect all our citizens from the few who will not respect the right of citizens to go safely about their business." This meant that the city should provide an adequate number of police officers to safeguard citizens as well as their property; however, for the NYPD to successfully fight crime, it must have "law abiding people on its side." Thus the NYPD's lack of such success was due to what Lindsay called the "unfortunate breakdown in the relationship between the police and a substantial part of the people of our city." He characterized the current situation by saying that too many New Yorkers had come to see the police "as an enemy rather than a friend," and acknowledged that the police might have reacted antagonistically on occasion. There was "a running war which goes on day after day with no sign of improvement," leading to resentment and misunderstanding, which in turn made the police officers' jobs much more difficult and dangerous. It was time, Lindsay said, to change "this sensitive area of human relationships.[9] At the heart of Lindsay's argument was his conviction that improving relations between the police and community was necessary for effective policing.

This change would not happen until all citizens felt they were being treated fairly and their complaints were being heard. In proposing the creation of a CCRB during his speech to the Lawyers Association, Lindsay said, "It is time for independent review to be joined with professional police knowledge" and suggested that four civilians be added to the current board. The civilian members would be selected by the mayor from a list of names provided by a "committee made up of men and women of unquestionable stature," such as the presiding justices of the First and Second Judicial Districts and the chancellor of the City University of New York. Lindsay's proposal, however, left the primary responsibility for taking disciplinary action with the police department.[10] His proposal offered a middle of the road solution that attempted to appeal to those who were calling for an all-civilian board and those who feared that such a body would be detrimental to the police. The mayor's plan was similar to the one advocated by a committee of the New York County Lawyers Association.[11]

City comptroller and Democratic candidate for mayor Abraham Beame supported civilian representation in the review process but seemed noncommittal about creating a CCRB and did not publicly endorse any form of civilian control.[12] In a not particularly bold move, Beame sent a telegram to all the mayoral candidates, asking them to meet him at his office on July 23 to work out an agreement on a CCRB in order to take the issue out of politics. Lindsay declined the offer, arguing that he believed in civilian participation in the board.[13]

The PBA's Appeal to Racist Sentiments

If Lindsay thought his plan would appeal to all proponents of a civilian complaint review board, he was wrong. Civil rights leaders dismissed it, claiming that the plan did not go far enough. James Farmer told the *New York Times* he did not see a need to have any police officers on a civilian complaint review board.[14] A. Philip Randolph, president of the Brotherhood of Sleeping Car Porters, and Bayard Rustin convened a meeting in Manhattan of various civil rights and grassroots community and religious organizations on May 26, 1965. Randolph told the 125 attendees that he did not think the Lindsay plan provided citizens with enough power to monitor police behavior; instead, Randolph called for an all-civilian complaint review board, arguing that it would serve the interests of the public. Randolph acknowledged that Lindsay's plan protected the police against false accusations but insisted that the board had to be "representative of the total New York community, including minority groups." Without a diverse representation, the board would not gain the confidence of "those who most deeply feel the need for redress of improper police behavior." He proposed that the mayor consult with community leaders before appointing members to a CCRB; with the exception of this proposal, his plan was identical to the one proposed by Councilman Weiss in April 1964.[15]

But the strongest criticism of Lindsay's proposal during his campaign came not from civil rights leaders but from political conservatives such as his Conservative Party opponent William F. Buckley and from law enforcement. To no one's surprise, John Cassese, head of the Patrolmen's Benevolent Association, accused the candidate of using the police department as a "political football." Interviewed on radio station WINS's *News Conference*, Cassese said he was satisfied with the existing board made up of three deputy commissioners and saw no reason to add four civilians to it, since no "pattern of police brutality" had been proven. In a sarcastic dig at Lindsay, Cassese suggested that the mayor sit down with civil rights leaders and let them know that "the policeman is their friend."[16]

In late June 1965, the PBA led a demonstration at City Hall denouncing the City Council's ongoing hearings on Weiss's bill proposing a civilian-dominated review board. Asking for public support, they marched in silence carrying placards, one of which read "Pressure Groups Want Control of the Police Department," a euphemism for the claim that blacks wanted to dominant the NYPD.[17] An FBI informant who attended the event noted that the well-organized demonstration had begun promptly at 10:00 a.m., that the demonstrators wore armbands, and that they acted in full cooperation with on-duty uniformed police officers. By 11:30 there were an estimated six thousand demonstrators, including a number of women, whom the informant assumed were the wives of police officers. Children also participated and carried signs. The FBI informant noted that in a television interview the day of the demonstration Cassese said "these people" wouldn't be satisfied until the city created an all "Negro and Puerto Rican" review board.[18]

Fifty members of CORE held a counter-demonstration, marching between police barricades on the other side of a park close to City Hall. Although the FBI informant reported that there were no disturbances or hostility where CORE demonstrated, some of the police demonstrators had gone over to the CORE protesters and "hurled uncomplimentary remarks at the group." He reported that later there were a "number of outbursts in the police line of demonstrators. They abused some people who were distributing leaflets and indulged in name calling etc. They chanted remarks against James Farmer." The informant also heard some police officers calling the CORE demonstrators "niggers" and "rat-packs" as well as other derogatory terms: "Some police officers soliciting signatures in support of their protest against the civilian re-view board were quite outspoken in regard to their attitude and feelings against Negroes and other minority groups. They used this in urging a number of people to sign their petitions. They talked openly in an un-complimentary manner about Harlem and other areas where minority groups lived." Many of the police officers carried "William F. Buckley for Mayor" signs, Buckley being one of Lindsay's two opponents. The agent also pointed out that some of the police demonstrators had ap-proached the young people from CORE, taken their literature, and then tossed it on the ground.[19]

The next day, the Reverend Gardner C. Taylor, pastor of Concord Baptist Church, one of the largest black churches in New York City, asked mayor Robert F. Wagner, City Council president Paul Screvane, and police commissioner Vincent L. Broderick for an immediate in-vestigation into "racism" in the NYPD and specifically into the racist behavior exhibited by police officers at the City Hall demonstration. The New York Times quoted Reverend Taylor's accusation that the police screamed racist insults. The officers' actions, he said, raised doubts about their willingness to protect the rights of minorities. James Farmer joined Taylor in calling for an investigation into the police demonstration.[20]

Cassese and the PBA did not simply express irrational racial fears; rather, they adopted a strategy of political racism, using racism for political gains, and they were impervious to criticism. With a larger goal of stopping any effort to infringe on their power, Cassese and crew were aware that stopping a civilian review board required stoking the fears of white citizens. They did this by arguing that the objective of black New Yorkers was to weaken the police so that black criminals would not be punished. In Cassese's rhetoric, if black New Yorkers and their liberal supporters had their way, it would have a devastating impact on white citizens.

Cassese's racist comments and the PBA's political position divided the police force along racial lines. On June 1, 1965, even before the City Hall demonstration, the Guardian Society, which represented 1,320 black police officers, voted in favor of an independent review board. In response, Cassese said that the Guardians had voted as "Negroes and not as police officers."[21]

William F. Buckley

William F. Buckley Jr., arguably the most influential conservative political thinker at the time, was one of Lindsay's two opponents in the mayoral race. Born in 1925 in New York, Buckley graduated from Yale University in 1950 and the next year gained notoriety with the publication of his book *God and Man at Yale*, which lambasted the university and the liberal and secular bias among its faulty. Arguing that academic freedom did not exist at Yale, he called for an uprising of conservatives to challenge the collectivist economic thinking he had encountered there.[22]

In 1955 Buckley continued to further the cause of political conservatism by founding the *National Review*, arguably the premier magazine of political conservatism in modern history. Buckley attracted some of the leading conservative thinkers of the postwar era, including Russell Kirk, author of *The Conservative Mind* and former Communist turned informer, and Whittaker Chambers, the author of *Witness*, a seminal work warning Americans of the dangers of Communism.[23]

Buckley was not well-known outside the circles of the intellectual elite and politically informed, but his decision to take on both Republican John Lindsay and Democrat Abraham Beame in the mayoral race brought him and the New York City Conservative Party fame among review board opponents, New Yorkers who were in support of "law and order," and those who believed that dysfunctional black and Latino communities were a major cause of the deterioration of life in the city. On the other hand, Buckley's political positions and outspoken opinions on welfare, crime, and the civilian complaint review board brought him infamy among civil rights leaders and liberals, who painted him as a racist.

In an August 4 campaign speech before the National Press Club, Buckley said he decided to run for mayor because "New York is a city in crisis, and all the candidates agree it is a city in crisis. But no other candidate proposes to do anything about that crisis." He accused the other candidates of appealing to various ethnic, racial, religious, and economic groups or "voting blocs" by promising to address their concerns instead of solving New York's most pressing problems. He defined those problems as crime, welfare, economic stagnation, and the lack of an opportunity "to be educated without weekly litmus tests administered by Milton Galamison, leader of the campaign to integrate New York City public schools, to determine whether the composite color of every school is exactly the right shade of brown."[24] Buckley elected to run on the Conservative Party ticket rather than challenge Lindsay in a Republican primary because, he told the National Press Club, in "New York the Republican Party is dominated by the Liberal Party," and so he saw no difference between them and the Democrats. Moreover, if he lost to Lindsay in the Republican primary he would have to support him in the general election as the candidate of his party—and he claimed he couldn't support a person who was "engaged in devitalizing the Republican Party."[25]

His stance regarding a civilian complaint review board drew support from certain political circles and many NYPD officers. In July 1965 Buckley denounced the review board concept before the City Council, saying that the "problem in New York is that there is too much crime—not that there is too much police brutality. And yet as the crime rate rises, the hue and cry in certain quarters is, of all things, for establishing machinery to harass not criminals, but policemen." For Buckley, the real victims were the police. The data, he noted, showed that crime was increasing and yet there was "not any documented rise in the instances of police brutality." The data also revealed that a "disproportionate percentage of the crimes being committed is by members of a minority group, namely New York's Negro population." He accused those who professed to speak for the entire black population of wanting to "encumber the Police," and said they had "succeeded in getting endorsements from men who mistakenly believe that to endorse a civilian review board is to do a service to Negroes and Puerto Ricans." At a time when there was "intense concern for life, limb, and property," to devote so much time to "one or two or three extra cases per year of possible undue force used by a policeman at the risk of the demoralization of the entire force" constituted a "diversionary act." Instead, the police should be encouraged "to detect one thousand, two thousand, twenty thousand murderers, rapists, muggers, junkies and thieves." But he also noted to the City Council that it was "relevant to remind us that the most numerous victims of lawlessness are the Negroes themselves." Black "demagogic leaders," Buckley went on, "are flogging the Negro population in an attempt to make them

believe that they are, as a race, the specially selected victims of a con-
certed police brutality."[26]

In addressing the City Council, Buckley tried to be careful not to
point his finger at black New Yorkers for holding anti-police sentiments,
but he did blame black leaders for creating the animosity between the
police and New York City's black population. It was not just that the
police would suffer under a civilian review board, he claimed: "If the
police find that yet another encumbrance is put in the way of duty, all of
us will suffer who live within the reach of the criminal." Buckley tried to
convince blacks that a review board would be detrimental to their communities, that they would "suffer most who live in areas where lawlessness is most active; most tragically, in those areas in which there is the
heaviest concentration of Negroes."[27]

Social and economic problems, Buckley went on to claim, should not
be overlooked; however, it was not the duty of police officers to act as
social workers. The main task of a police officer was to prevent criminal
acts against innocent citizens. "That is the function of policemen. That
and only that." Others should create ways of discharging the "debt we
have to the Negro people." But those making the decision to pay the
debt should not succumb to "pressure, generated by the frequent ex-
aggerations of a few misled leaders, to render more difficult the job of
the policemen." Indirectly lecturing black leaders while speaking to the
City Council, Buckley insisted that they should stress "racial pride" that
encouraged black people to embrace "hope, the hunger for knowledge,
the appetite for industry, an excited concern for the rights of others."
Accusing black leaders of "berating the police," he said they should instead encourage police officers to arrest and "isolate the criminals in
their midst." He went on to urge city officials not to dilute the "authority
of the police to manage their own affairs" but instead rely on the existing
apparatus that consisted of the mayor, the commissioner, the courts, and
"the established review board to which any victim of police brutality has
access."[28] Later, Buckley would argue in his position paper on crime and
law enforcement that the "proposed Civilian Review Board is nothing
less than an agreement to elevate the campaign to discredit the police to
official City policy."[29]

Buckley's public condemnation of Lindsay's proposed review board
and his focus on black crime did indeed fuel the predicted white back-

lash. Despite his attempt to qualify his stance by noting the existence of "law abiding black people" or those making "justified progress," the message that stood out for thousands of New Yorkers was contained in his rants about black and Latino criminals who, he claimed, committed 80 percent of crimes. By calling black leaders racist and accusing them of convincing blacks that, "as a race," they were targeted by the police, Buckley marked black people's grievances against the police as illegitimate. When he warned the City Council not to "submit to synthetic pressures to cure an imaginary evil [police brutality] at the risk of undermining the pursuit of a demonstrated evil [crime]," he both portrayed black charges of police brutality as fraudulent and argued that blacks were the major reason for New York City falling into "barbarism."[30]

The New Civilian Complaint Review Board and Its Challengers

John Lindsay won the mayoral election by a narrow margin, with 45 percent of the vote (1,149,109) compared to Abraham Beame's 41 percent (1,046,699). The 13 percent of the vote (341,226) that went to Buckley was a considerable surprise, because the New York Conservative Party had only been established four years earlier, and its candidates in earlier state and city elections had never obtained more than 5 percent of the vote.[31]

Lindsay's win was a triumph for the moderate wing over the conservative wing of the Republican Party, but the vote for Buckley indicated the growing strength of conservatives[32] and reflected the power of white resentment and anger spurred by the rioting in Harlem and Bedford-Stuyvesant and the numerous civil rights demonstrations throughout the city. It was also an indication of New York City's growing racial divide. Nonetheless, the Lindsay/Beame totals also indicated that in 1965 New Yorkers maintained enough faith in liberal principles, including advancing civil rights, to provide the proponents of a civilian complaint review board with their best chance to achieve their objective. With the Weiss bill tabled and other such proposals needing unlikely legislative approval, as mayor, Lindsay had the power to implement his plan for a complaint review board comprising four civilians and three police officers.

At the same time, Lindsay appointed a Law Enforcement Task Force headed by former judge Lawrence E. Walsh to make recommendations for modernizing the NYPD. In its February 1966 report the task force advocated the creation of a civilian-controlled board to review complaints against police. It also called for appointing a special assistant to the mayor who would coordinate the work of all law enforcement agencies, the consolidation of the five district attorneys' offices, the revision of the courts and probation services, and better collaboration between the NYPD, transit, and housing police agencies. The eight-member task force also recommended adding four civilians to the current review board.[33]

Soon after these recommendations were issued, Vincent Broderick, who served as commissioner from 1965 to 1966, launched an extremely critical attack on Lindsay, urging him to "renounce political expediency." In a seven-page letter to the mayor, the commissioner accused the task force of putting out a report that was hastily prepared, contained erroneous ideas, and did not mention that the NYPD "should be cleared of political interference." The recommendations, he felt, were nothing more than an invitation for Lindsay to take over the police force by implementing them "as soon as possible." Broderick asked:

> Is it not time for you as Mayor to say that you know that a civilian review board is a shadow and not substance; that you realize the establishment of an independent board to review complaints against police officers will not solve problems and may create new problems? Is it not time, Mr. Mayor for you to say that you renounce political expediency; that you realize that the principal effect of an independent civilian review board will be to depress the morale of your police department and hence to impair its capacity to prevent crime?[34]

Broderick's letter, which he made public, went on to accuse the board of "drain[ing] off energies which should be dealing realistically with basic problems of human relations and more deeply with the underlying problems of poverty, discrimination, slums, inadequate schooling, and unemployment which beset our deprived communities today." Pointing out that there were no police officials on the eight-person panel, he said that the task force's decision to issue its proposals without consulting the NYPD indicated its haste in preparing the report.[35] Lindsay would later blame Broderick for their dispute: "I did everything in my power to work with Broderick. I could not control the decision on his part and others to make a public war."[36]

Though civil rights leaders had been critical of Lindsay's plan for a civilian complaint review board, he gained their support when he selected Howard R. Leary as the new police commissioner. Leary had worked well with Philadelphia's civilian review board when he was police commissioner there, and the NAACP, the Urban League, and CORE all praised Lindsay for his choice. John A. Morsell, assistant to NAACP executive secretary Roy Wilkins, said Leary had the "experience of running a police department in a city which has a civilian review board. This experience should serve a constructive purpose here." The Urban League's Whitney Young said Leary's selection "opens a new chapter in police–community relations." Lindsay, Young declared, "has taken a significant first step." Expressing optimism about Leary's selection, CORE issued a statement asserting that Leary would "convince the mayor that an entirely civilian board as exists in Philadelphia is superior to the mayor's proposal." Leary also drew praise from Roy Wilkins, who gave him credit for walking the streets of Philadelphia to calm people during its riot. Bronx borough president Herman Badillo, a Democrat, said he hoped that Leary would expedite the creation of a civilian review board.[37] In a letter to the *New York Times*, Thomas R. Farrell, former president of the Bronx chapter of the Catholic Interracial Council, said he was gratified that Mayor Lindsay had appointed a police commissioner who recognized the necessity of civilian control of the police department and declared that the police department "should be responsive to the needs and the rights of the entire community. It cannot be regarded, as it is by all too many Negro and Puerto Rican citizens, as an occupying army maintained to protect one class of citizens against another." However, Farrell was critical of Lindsay's plan to add four civilian members to the existing board. Rather, he backed Ted Weiss's plan and called for an all-civilian review board with its own staff to investigate complaints.[38]

Lindsay announced the creation of the civilian review board on May 2, 1966, telling New Yorkers that the widespread suspicion of it by law enforcement was unhealthy for police work, and that it was the public's fear that police brutality cases were not being addressed to the satisfaction of victims that had led him to act.[39]

In order to address the legal challenge filed by the PBA and the Conservative Party claiming that a CCRB was in violation of the City Charter because the matter of disciplining police personnel was to remain in the hands of the commissioner, Lindsay bypassed relying on the City Council to pass his proposal and instead created it via an executive order by the police commissioner. Commissioner Leary himself issued General Order No. 14 creating the review board on May 17. He noted that it was the responsibility of the NYPD to "maintain desired standards of conduct by its officers" and that it was to their advantage to have an "impartial forum for the review" of accusations of improper actions to determine if they were justified or false. To this end, the department's existing civilian complaint review board procedures were revised to include seven members: three police officers chosen by the commissioner and four civilians selected by the mayor to serve a two-year term. The mayor would also designate a chairman from among the seven members. The CCRB was given the authority to review complaints of "abuse of authority, unnecessary or excessive use of force, discourtesy, abusive or insulting language, or conduct or behavior which is derogatory of a person's race, creed or national origin." An investigating unit was assigned to assist the board; staff would include an executive director to supervise the administration of complaints, a deputy director responsible for the "scope and content of investigations," and an assistant director to supervise the board's conciliation process. All three would be appointed upon the recommendation of the mayor. Civilian hearing officers would hold all the hearings. Both the complainant and the officer could be represented by legal counsel at hearings. The board would provide financial assistance to those unable to afford to hire a lawyer. Parties and their attorneys would have the right to cross-examine witnesses.[40]

Lindsay created a panel of eleven prominent New Yorkers, under the chairmanship of former U.S. attorney general Herbert Brownell, a close political ally, charged with recommending to him candidates to fill the board's four civilian slots. The panel included three African Americans and one Puerto Rican, and the mayor remarked that for selecting civilian members of the CCRB, "No group surpasses the achievements of the individual members" of the panel.[41]

Conclusion

The *New York Times* praised Lindsay for creating a civilian complaint review board: "Undeterred by bitter opposition inside and outside the police department, Mayor Lindsay has taken a constructive step in establishing a civilian complaint review board to pass upon charges of police brutality. This courageous fulfillment of a pledge originally made during his election campaign deserves the sympathetic support and cooperation of all citizens—and of the police force." The *Times* agreed with the administration that the "assurance that a board with a civilian majority will review complaints of abuse of authority by police officers should prove of major benefit in overcoming fear in slum areas that the rights of suspects are sometimes trampled upon."[42]

The praise that Lindsay received from civil rights leaders for his selection of Leary and his creation of a new review board opened the door for healing the relationship between the police and black and Latino citizens of the City. However, John Cassese, the PBA, and the New York Conservative Party's relentless, ongoing racial campaign against civilians on the review board would all but destroy any chance of healing that relationship and establishing trust.

7

The Triumph of a False Narrative

On May 4, 1966, a spokesperson for PBA president John Cassese released a statement to the press declaring that "we do not accept a review board that is being established as a political payoff, and which caters to the demands of minority groups because they have brought pressure against the city government to further their own causes."[1]

Foes of the new Civilian Complaint Review Board (CCRB) proposed by Mayor Lindsay embarked on a racist campaign to defeat it, and the Patrolmen's Benevolent Association used civil disobedience and propaganda as well as legal and political actions to consolidate a great deal of political power during this time.

While the police and their supporters opposed any alteration, however slight, of the power advantage that law enforcement enjoyed, civil rights and civil liberties proponents generally welcomed the proposed addition of four mayor-appointed civilian members to the board, though some said it didn't go far enough. It would, they felt, alter the police–citizen balance of power by providing those with legitimate grievances a forum in which to hold the police responsible for abuses such as verbal abuse, disrespect, physical assault, and other forms of misconduct. A review board by and large unaffiliated with the NYPD had the potential to determine how police should conduct themselves in communities of color—police would be more reluctant to step outside the law and to disrespect communities where complaints of police abuse were already widespread. Norman Dorsen, professor of law at New York University Law School, was quoted in the *New York Times* saying that defeat of the CCRB would bestow on the police "an exemption from public surveillance, which would be intolerable in a democratic society."[2] Lindsay's version of a review board would be capable of curtailing the police power that, for many, was tantamount to a form of state terror, and would give citizens a voice in governing the police and making law enforcement accountable to communities, thus changing the power dynamics between police and citizen. This was a change that review board supporters insisted would not only benefit those claiming abuse but the police department and its officers as well, because investigations conducted by a board whose majority was independent of the NYPD would not be subject to claims of a police department cover up. Just as important, proponents claimed, a review board would improve police–community relations, because impartial oversight would protect those officers who were unfairly accused of wrongdoing.

Although prominent liberals praised Lindsay's CCRB announcement, a few civil rights leaders expressed their disappointment. Robert L. Carter, the NAACP's general counsel, argued that Lindsay's proposal had "serious inadequacies" that would result in "suspicion and hostility of minority group communities toward police justice and policemen." The new board, Carter argued, would not be independent of the police: the civilian director would be on the police payroll; the police would control practically all the investigative process; and hearings would not be open to the public.[3] Floyd B. McKissick, the new national director of CORE, requested an "immediate conference" with Mayor Lindsay so that he could explain his objections to the proposed board. The *New York Times* carried his criticism of the eleven-member screening panel for not including Harlem and Bedford-Stuyvesant representatives or anyone from a civil rights organization. He called the panel a "political gimmick" and insisted that it be broadened to include representatives of the missing groups. He also declared that the CCRB should be completely independent rather than a unit of the NYPD.[4] James Farmer, who had stepped down as the head of CORE, said the proposed board was "right but not right enough, unfortunately," and insisted that Lindsay create a "board outside the Police Department entirely." After all, if the police had "nothing to hide, why should they hesitate to go before a review board?"[5] For some black leaders, Lindsay's hybrid board appeared to be a way to appease the black community but not give them an effective means of countering the police.

Such criticisms were mild, however, compared to the response from the Patrolmen's Benevolent Association and the New York State Conservative Party. Speaking to the press in early May 1966, PBA head John Cassese said that the CCRB proposal was both improper and illegal and stressed that the PBA would make sure the board would not be established.[6] To that end, the PBA, the New York Conservative Party, and its 1965 mayoral candidate, William F. Buckley, launched a campaign to derail the proposed board, pushing their ongoing racial narrative that such a board would tie the hands of the police and give what would later be referred to as the "black super-predator" an opportunity to prey on the innocent. Opponents also maintained that implementing Lindsay's proposal would make the police reluctant to stop black criminals out of fear that the board would unfairly accuse them of using excessive force and brutality.

The PBA's Campaign

The PBA's campaign to defeat the CCRB took a multipronged approach. It initiated legal maneuvers, such as seeking injunctions and filing lawsuits; lobbied the New York State Assembly and New York City Council to pass measures outlawing such a board; committed civil disobedience at demonstrations and rallies in order to win public support; and launched an advertising campaign using both overtly racist rhetoric and coded language to paint blacks as dangerous criminals in an effort to galvanize white voters to defeat the review board at the polls.

As early as February 1966, Cassese began to threaten legal action to fight the creation of a CCRB.[7] Then, on May 8, he announced that the PBA planned to sue the city in order to abolish the revised board before it could be implemented. The suit would be just one part of the PBA's campaign, Cassese claimed. Other tactics would include seeking passage of a bill in the State Assembly to bar civilian members from the CCRB and getting a city referendum on the ballot that would allow voters to determine whether such a board should exist.[8]

To assure the success of its legal campaign, the PBA hired the law firm of Phillips Nizer Benjamin Krim and Ballon. Charles Ballon's first move was to ask the New York State Supreme Court for a show-cause order against the mayor and the police commissioner, which would force City Hall to explain to the court why the mayor was reconstructing the review board.[9] This tactic was a long shot, but a legal ruling would make it unnecessary to push for a referendum and would save the PBA money.

On May 10 New York State Supreme Court justice Margaret M. J. Mangar handed the PBA a victory and ordered the Lindsay administration to explain why it was revamping the board. Then the PBA received more good news when former mayor Robert Wagner publicly expressed his support for the PBA's position in a radio interview on WOR, saying that if the "majority of the people" had the "opportunity to vote, [they] would probably be against the civilian review board." Using the PBA's own argument, he even claimed that a civilian-dominated board would increase the chances that the police might allow race riots to get out of control: "If you got a riot, you got to put your hands on somebody, you can't just blow a whistle and say, everybody stand at attention." The former mayor assured listeners that police officers were going to be less efficient if a civilian-dominated board were allowed to exist.[10]

After the Lindsay administration was issued the show-cause order, the PBA filed a class action suit for a permanent injunction restraining Mayor Lindsay and Police Commissioner Leary from "implementing and enforcing General Order No. 14." The PBA claimed that the creation of a CCRB and the procedures established for processing complaints by civilians against police officers were "invalid and illegal."[11] Ballon argued the PBA's case before justice Francis T. Murphy Jr., saying that the CCRB would make decisions denying the rights of police officers and that officers would be reluctant to do their jobs effectively: "If a policeman sees a violent labor dispute, will he intervene to keep order if he knows that the Civilian Review Board includes a labor leader? . . . It is becoming more and more common for the problems of society to be blamed on the man on the beat. He did not create the slums, or the breakdown of the educational system, nor unemployment. But he is the nearest and must vulnerable representative of the Establishment."[12]

The PBA also focused on winning public support. It had launched a campaign to do so almost a year earlier in its opposition to the Weiss proposal, promoting racial animosity and fear of black people. Cassese's ongoing racist rhetoric did not take the form of irrational diatribes but was a calculated attempt to appeal to white New Yorkers who resented both the national and local civil rights movements. He portrayed himself as a person willing to draw a line in the sand and stand up for white New Yorkers. He constructed an image of anti-cop blacks with no respect for law enforcement whose real objective in supporting a CCRB was to make the NYPD ineffective. "These people," the head of the PBA insisted, "would never be satisfied unless there are seven Negroes and Puerto Ricans on the board and every policeman who goes in front of it is found guilty."[13] By portraying the proposed civilian review board as an agency that would endanger the lives of hardworking Americans by tying the hands of the police, Cassese hoped white voters would rally to the cause of the survival of white people in New York and vote for the referendum.[14]

The PBA enjoyed broad support among police officers and claimed to represent them all. However, the Guardians, an organization representing 1,300 black New York City police officers, backed the proposed new board and emphasized that the PBA did not speak for them. Instead of addressing the Guardian's concerns, Cassese accused the group of betraying their professional duty as law enforcement officers in the interest of racial solidarity. He claimed that "they put their color ahead of their duty as police officers."[15]

When speaking on June 2 to three hundred PBA delegates about the organization's efforts to derail the CCRB, the *Times* reported that Cassese was met with cheers of "Atta boy Johnny!" that revealed deep rank and file support for the PBA leader and encouraged him to continue playing the politics of race. Portraying black people as a danger not only to New York but also to the entire nation, he told the delegates, "What will happen in New York City will be a barometer for cities throughout the country." In an interview with the *Times* later that day, he reiterated that there was no need for a civilian complaint review board: "Notwithstanding the cries of various minority groups, there is no set pattern of police brutality." Going beyond simply outlining the flaws of such a scheme when it came to policing, he continuously invoked the notion that blacks were out to destroy effective policing, thereby giving the upper hand to criminals and thugs who threatened the lives of white citizens.[16]

The Referendum and the Effort to Defeat It

In early June the PBA announced the launch of its most important effort to defeat the CCRB: the campaign to convince New York voters to reject the review board by referendum. Cassese pledged that the PBA would gather enough signatures to have the referendum placed on the November ballot.[17]

While the PBA's political efforts were moving forward, by late June its actions on the legal front were falling apart. On June 23 the State Supreme Court upheld the city's proposed CCRB. Justice Murphy noted in his opinion that civilian complaints against the police "reached a high pitch during the summer of 1964 when riots erupted in the Harlem and Bedford-Stuyvesant areas of the city." Since those riots, there had been a barrage of criticism leveled at the existing review board that comprised only three deputy police commissioners. Justice Murphy noted that the most "consistent source of discontent" voiced by critics was that the review board members were employees of the police department. Minority communities in particular were disturbed that such a board was "overly protective toward their cohorts," he noted, and went on to observe that the police were "servants of the people" and that those who upheld their duty had nothing to fear from a civilian-controlled board. The justice also rejected the PBA's arguments that a civilian-dominated board would deter police from doing their jobs and that General Order No. 14 usurped the state legislature's role, since the legislature was the only body with the authority to create a civilian review board. He also rejected the PRB's argument that the order violated sections 431, 434, and 1103 of the New York City Charter, or sections of the City Service Law of New York, or the Fourteenth Amendment of the United States Constitution.[18]

Justice Murphy pointed out that it was not the mayor but the police commissioner himself who issued the general order, so the court's only concern was whether the commissioner had the power to do so. "The Police Commissioner should be permitted to operate this most critical City agency with sufficient aid, if required and requested," the court ruled. With respect to the mayor appointing four civilians to the review board, that provision of the general order was ruled valid as it was in line with subdivisions a and b of section 434 of the New York City Charter, which provided to the police commissioner "cognizance and control of the government, administration, disposition and discipline of the department." The commissioner possessed the power to punish members of the NYPD: "The unambiguous language contained in the above statutory provisions effectively rests broad administrative power in the Police Commissioner." Judge Murphy noted that Commissioner Leary had decided that the appropriate "control and administration of the Police Department may best be effectuated by resort to a civilian advisory board." The court noted that there was no legal obstacle barring the commissioner from exercising his discretion, nor were there devious motives in his action; rather, he wanted citizens to gain "confidence in the impartiality of the administrative machinery" that supervised the use of police power. In sum, the court ruled that "the Commissioner has apparently determined that the needs of the community mandate a change in the existing procedure to provide a review board dominated by civilians. The decision is his alone, by statute, and this Court may not sit in judgment upon that determination."[19] Judge Murphy's ruling ended the PBA's attempt to use the courts to destroy the new board.

Having known from the beginning that the legal strategy was a long shot, the twenty-thousand-member PBA had already focused on the referendum and mounted an ongoing campaign of fear. Sidney Zion of the *New York Times* noted that the police were relying on their "tried and true slogans" like "don't handcuff the police" and the "pendulum has swung too far."[20] Mayor Lindsay accused "highly organized, militant, right-wing groups" of leading the effort to kill his CCRB. At a City Hall press conference he promised to fight the referendum drive, saying that he "never kidded [himself] into believing that the review board was a popular idea around the City as a whole." He admitted that if it got on the ballot, it would be pretty hard going for the review board.[21]

Although the mayor "never kidded" himself, he really was unaware that the formation of a citizen-majority review board would result in a full-scale battle with the police. Jay Kriegel, who served as Lindsay's chief of staff and special counsel, said in an interview that they had never expected the opposition's fierce and virulent response to the CCRB, and he admitted that the administration was caught off guard by the effectiveness of the PBA's campaign.[22]

Apparently unable to combat the PBA's campaign, Lindsay simply moved ahead with forming a review board. After receiving the names of eight prominent New Yorkers from his review board selection committee, in July Lindsay chose the four he thought had the best experience in human rights, terrific reputations, and respect across racial and ethnic lines: Algernon D. Black, head of the New York Society for Ethical Culture and chair of the National Committee against Discrimination in Housing, to serve as board chair; Dr. Walter Murray, an African American who was a professor of education at Brooklyn College; Manuel Diaz, chief consultant and acting director of the Puerto Rican Community Development Project of New York City; and Thomas R. Farrell, also an African American, who was a trial attorney and former president of the Bronx chapter of the Catholic Interracial Council. Of the three police officers selected by Leary, one was Franklin A. Thomas, deputy commissioner in charge of legal matters and one of the highest-ranking African Americans on the force. The other two were Edward McCabe, deputy commissioner in charge of the Division of Licenses, and deputy inspector George P. Meagher.[23]

Cassese continued his race-based argument at a news conference on July 11 at the Warwick Hotel at which he implied that the new CCRB would be in the hands of civil rights leaders who opposed the police. "They're so pro-civil rights and so Lindsay-thinking, I think Lindsay went out of his way to get these four."[24] The head of the PBA also took the opportunity to deny the existence of police brutality once again: "You show me an accelerated pattern of police brutality, and we'll accept a review board but not a campaign promise by a politician."[25]

Civil liberties and civil rights groups attempted to counter Cassese's racial narrative by condemning him. The New York Civil Liberties Union joined others in accusing him of "injecting a thinly veiled racism" into the debate and demanded that he "desist from demagoguery." Roy Wilkins, head of the NAACP, called the PBA's criticism "irrational" and argued that the "police, like all other civil employees, are the servants of the citizens and thus subject to regulation by the citizenry and the law."[26]

By July it became clear that despite the board supporters' best efforts to refute the PBA's message, it had been quite effective—the PBA and the New York Conservative Party each submitted petitions with more than thirty thousand signatures calling for a referendum on the civilian complaint review board. The PBA's petition called for an amendment of the New York City Charter

to require that all members of any review board established to investigate and process civilian complaints against policemen be full-time members of the police department, thereby prohibiting establishment of a review board comprised in whole or part of civilian members. . . . Civilian complaints against members of the Police Department of the City of New

York shall be investigated and dealt with fully and fairly by the appropriate officials regularly charged with the governance and discipline of the Police Department without interference by any person or group of persons not regularly in police service.[27]

If the referendum passed, not even the mayor—the city's chief executive—would have a say in the disciplining and monitoring of police misbehavior, for it assured that the police would be able to act without civilian oversight. The Conservative Party submitted a similar petition, which would amend the City Charter "in relation to the disciplinary procedures of the New York City Police Department, prohibiting the creation or maintenance of a civilian complaint review board composed of members who are not deputy police commissioners."[28]

In September the PBA launched its most ambitious effort to date to win public support: it placed an advertisement in New York's daily newspapers depicting a young white woman leaving a subway station alone at night with a caption that read, "Her life . . . your life may depend on it." It went on to claim that the CCRB could "hamper a conscientious policeman's decision to act. . . . With a civilian review board, it may be the police officer who hesitates, not the criminal."[29] The coded message targeted white New Yorkers: the CCRB would endanger wives and daughters because it would give black and Latino criminals the green light to prey on them. Well aware of the subtext in this message, Lindsay blamed the PBA for conducting an "offensive" against the CCRB and referred to its racist advertisement.[30]

The racist appeal of the campaign was so deeply concerning to the New York Civil Liberties Union, the Guardians, and other groups that they created the Federated Associations for Impartial Review (FAIR), a group that worked to defeat the referendum by countering the false narrative of the review board's foes. U.S. senators Jacob Javits and Robert F. Kennedy were honorary co-chairs of FAIR, and practically every civil rights organization appeared on its masthead. The group planned an educational campaign in which lawyers would speak to the public, businesses, and civic groups in order to convince them to vote against the referendum. In addition to educating voters on the true work of the CCRB, FAIR also revisited the 1964 presidential campaign in which liberal groups had labeled Republican presidential candidate Barry Goldwater a racist in an attempt persuade people not to vote for him; the strategy was to shame New Yorkers into voting against the referendum. As a FAIR spokesman said, "It will be like the Goldwater thing all over again."[31]

Proponents of the review board had good reason to be concerned. Six weeks before the referendum, a FAIR-commissioned public opinion poll showed that two-thirds of those surveyed saw street safety as a fundamental concern. An overwhelming 86 percent of those New Yorkers surveyed who identified as Irish American saw the CCRB as a threat to the police and said that they would vote against the review board. The American Jewish Committee maintained that Lindsay challenged the "historic Irish Catholic hegemony in New York's City Police Department" when he confronted the power of the police. His dispute with the police was a reason so many Irish Americans opposed the CCRB. Other white ethnic groups also expressed their disapproval of the review board. Among Italian Americans, 72 percent would also vote against the board, as would 50 percent of the Jewish New Yorkers polled. Groups more likely to have had a conflict with the police were more supportive of the CCRB—for instance, 30 percent of Puerto Ricans and only 10 percent of African Americans would vote against it.[32]

Although the future of the civilian review board seemed bleak, the mayor attempted to paint a positive picture. Speaking at a meeting of FAIR, Lindsay said that despite the attacks on the review board, "we are definitely on the upswing—I think we have a fighting chance." He then thanked Democratic gubernatorial candidate Frank D. O'Conner for promising to campaign for the review board; O'Connor's opponent, governor Nelson Rockefeller, remained silent on the issue.[33]

It was clear from the FAIR poll that the Lindsay administration had to do more to defeat the referendum. One step it took was to issue a paper titled "Myths about the Review Board." One of the "myths" it addressed was the argument that the review board would not be fair to the police. The Lindsay administration claimed that unlike under the old board, which placed all complaints on an officer's record, the "new procedures are fairer to the police" given that only complaints that the police commissioner concluded were "substantiated" would go on the officer's record. The paper also refuted the PBA's claim that the board would undermine police morale, citing the fact that since its start in July "there has been no incident of a policeman turning away from his duty." The PBA's assertion that the review board was "a give-away to the civil rights groups" was rebutted by the assertion that the CCRB had the support of Senators Javits and Kennedy, Mayor Lindsay, the City Council president, and over fifty civic groups such as the American Jewish Committee and the International Ladies Garment Workers Union.[34]

Chances that the PBA's referendum would pass increased by late September, when the New York State Supreme Court ruled that the Conservative Party could withdraw its petition calling for a referendum. The party had requested the withdrawal when it became clear that having two referenda on the November 8 ballot would confuse supporters and split their vote. The Lindsay administration understood that it would be advantageous for the Conservative Party's referendum to remain on the ballot and insisted in court that the withdrawal not be allowed. The court, however, agreed with the Conservative Party that removing the referendum would clarify the issue for voters.[35]

After that court ruling, Lindsay's sense of urgency was evident in his declaration that the vote on the PBA's referendum was the most important issue to be decided by New Yorkers in years. Attempting to appeal to New Yorkers' sense of fair play toward the city's blacks and Latinos, he declared at an October 3 press conference, "I'm terribly concerned about it and totally committed, because it is an issue that lies at the very root of American democracy." The new review board's survival was essential "if we are to give the people who live in the troubled neighborhoods a feeling that progress is being made in the area of police protection." The mayor also reached out to and received support from religious organizations, including the Episcopal Diocese of New York, the Protestant Council of New York, and the New York Board of Rabbis. He contended that the rabbis' support was vital because "there is a very large segment of the middle-class Jewish community who have been misled into believing that somehow the streets will be more dangerous if the [current] Review Board is retained." According to Lindsay, the new CCRB was as fundamental as a "civilian check on the country's armed forces." To counter the PBA's well-financed efforts to defeat the CCRB, the mayor turned to the entertainment industry for support. Henry Fonda, Eli Wallach, Anne Jackson, and other well-known stage and screen actors joined him at the press conference.[36]

Defeat

The *New York Times* reported in October that a poll conducted by an undisclosed group noted the review board was in trouble. It showed that 47 percent of New Yorkers polled were opposed to the CCRB, 40 percent supported it, and 11 percent were undecided.[37] The police and their supporters collected 51,832 signatures opposing the referendum, more than twenty-one thousand in excess of the number needed. When the council refused to hear that request for the measure to be passed, the PBA gathered an additional forty-five thousand signatures, though only fifteen thousand were needed to place a referendum on the ballot.[38] The PBA's signature-gathering prowess was a measure of the effectiveness of its campaign, which relied not only on advertising and legal maneuvers but also on thousands of volunteers who hit the streets. As early as June, Cassese had been able to inform the press that more than twenty thousand volunteers would gather signatures supporting the referendum.[39]

Of equal importance was that the PBA could tap into white New Yorkers' festering resentment of the local civil rights movement. This resentment was first revealed in the early 1960s, years before the fight over the civilian complaint review board. Parents and Taxpayers (PAT), a group of white New Yorkers primarily located in Queens; the Brooklyn Joint Council for Better Schools; and Parents and Citizens of the Bronx, another all-white parent organization, had waged an effective campaign to oppose school integration. In the summer of 1964, PAT submitted a 42,749-signature petition to the city requesting a referendum that would mandate neighborhood schools. City clerk Herman Katz rejected the petition, claiming that it sought legislation that was beyond the city's authority to enact. Among other reasons for Katz's rejection were that the proposed law was "vague and ambiguous in requiring the Board of Education to adhere to a so-called 'traditional concept of the neighborhood school' without defining the quoted terminology," and that 8,040 of the signatures on the petition were invalid. Thus the petition fell short of the thirty thousand required for a referendum.[40]

PAT accused Mayor Wagner of ignoring the concerns of the majority by saying that to the "wishes of any minority, he has been as weak and pliable as clay." Amazingly the organization was able to gather over forty-two thousand signatures in only eight days, an indication of the magnitude of white New Yorkers' resentment toward the objectives of civil rights groups.[41] In addition to submitting its petition, PAT, along with the Brooklyn Joint Council for Better Education, conducted a one-day boycott of the city's public schools in September 1964 to protest the Board of Education's plans to integrate some of the predominantly white schools in Queens and Brooklyn. Over 275,600 white children stayed out of school, and PAT and the Joint Council also led a demonstration of fifteen thousand protesters, mostly white parents, in front of City Hall, proving that many white New Yorkers rejected integrating the public schools, largely out of the belief that including black and Latino students would endanger white children's education and physical safety. The vote on the CCRB referendum would be yet another manifestation of New Yorkers' resentment of the city's civil rights community.[42]

This resentment reflected a national trend. The summer of 1964 witnessed riots in cities across the Northeast such as Philadelphia, Rochester, New York, Patterson, and Elizabeth.[43] A year later, one of the worse riots of the decade occurred in the Los Angeles community of Watts—over a thousand people were injured, thirty-five were killed, close to four thousand were arrested, and $40 million worth of property was destroyed. To quell the riot, two thousand National Guardsmen were dispatched.[44]

A 1963 Gallup poll found that 78 percent of whites would move out of their neighborhood if a black person moved in, and 60 percent of white respondents held an unfavorable view of Martin Luther King Jr. Shortly after the 1964 Harlem and Bedford-Stuyvesant riots, another Gallup poll found that 60 percent of Americans considered race to be America's major problem.[45] In October 1964, after several more riots, 73 percent of those surveyed agreed that blacks should stop demonstrating, even if some of their objectives had not been met. A July 1965 Gallup poll revealed that 49 percent of those surveyed expected that relations between blacks and whites would get worse.[46]

Such polls indicated that a substantial percentage of whites were demonstrably not sympathetic to the objectives of the civil rights movement. Many felt animosity toward King and the push for integration, and it should not have been surprising that many New Yorkers who held such views were also opposed to a civilian complaint review board—sentiments Cassese was likely well aware of. Thus, by linking the review board and its supporters to civil rights activists Cassese helped to mobilize support for the referendum.

On November 8 New Yorkers voted 3–1 to abolish the Civilian Complaint Review Board. To no one's surprise the heaviest vote in favor of the referendum came from white areas in Queens, Brooklyn, the Bronx, and Staten Island. Voters of Irish and Italian heritage voted overwhelmingly for the referendum. The final tally was 1,307,738 for the referendum to 768,492 against, with the heaviest no votes coming from Manhattan and the outer boroughs' black and Latino communities. Lindsay appeared at FAIR headquarters at the Grover Clinton Hotel after it was clear that the referendum had passed looking "glum." Speaking at Gracie Mansion at a midnight news conference, he blamed the defeat of the CCRB on "emotion, misunderstanding and fear." Asked by a reporter if he thought that voters had also repudiated him, Lindsay responded, "I don't know."[47]

Cassese was jubilant and declared victory while addressing three hundred supporters at the Sheraton Atlantic Hotel. "In every campaign there is a winner and a loser. I say tonight that there were eight million winners," he said. Invoking the argument that the review board was a danger to the welfare of New Yorkers, he added, "Thank God, we saved the city."[48] Cassese's presumption that he was speaking for all eight million New Yorkers once again highlighted his disregard for the large number of citizens who supported a civilian complaint review board and voted against the referendum.

Conclusion

Accessing why voters had rejected the CCRB, Thomas R. Brooks of the *New York Times* called the referendum a sign of white backlash and said the PBA's position originated in police resentment of the city's civil rights movement. According to Brooks, the police perspective was that once the CCRB went into operation, blacks would have "won another victory, an unjustified one based on unsubstantial claims of police brutality."[49]

Brooks's analysis was correct. Cassese's racist rhetoric and the PBA campaign, as well as William F. Buckley's attacks on black leaders, his defense of a "white backlash," and his blaming blacks and Latinos for rising crime rates in New York City all helped to foster a false narrative that the interests of black people were diametrically opposed to those of whites. Cassese, the PBA, and Buckley depicted black people as dismissive of criminal behavior and black leaders as wanting to gain control of the NYPD because the police stood in their way. Many white New Yorkers subscribed to the view that the CCRB would endanger their lives by handcuffing the police and providing criminals an opportunity to terrorize the city. The overwhelming opposition to the CCRB demonstrates that the PBA's narrative helped to delegitimize the grievances of black New Yorkers in the minds of whites by characterizing their complaints of police brutality as simply a means of stopping the police from doing their job. The narrative that civilians on the CCRB would give the green light to black criminals appealed to enough of the city's white electorate to help defeat the proposed board before it was implemented, thus ending in 1966 and for years to come the opportunity for residents to have a voice in determining how the police operated in their communities.

8

Mayor Rudolph Giuliani and Police Brutality

In 1986, twenty years after the defeat of Lindsay's civilian complaint review board, mayor Edward Koch (1977–89) publicly announced his support for a City Council bill that would create a twelve-member review board. Six would be "members of the public selected so that one resident from each of the five boroughs of the city and one citywide representative" would be seated. The mayor would appoint for two terms those representing the public in consultation with the City Council. The other six would be appointed by the police commissioner. Each of the members selected by the police was required to have served at least one year as a full-time administrative employee of the NYPD.[1]

Speaking before the City Council's Committee on Public Safety, Koch noted that the bill expanding the civilian complaint review board "will give more public credibility" to what he claimed was an "already effective board. The selection of six highly qualified civilians, whose approval will be subject to the advice and consent of the City Council, can only serve to strengthen the public's confidence in the police department." Koch said that this "moderate and reasonable proposal, should not be divisive or destabilizing" and now was the time to act on it, "because discussion will not be fueled by any particular incident of alleged police misconduct or review of an incident. To wait for the next incident, when tempers will be high, and willingness and ability to agree will be low, would only insure paralyzation of any reform proposal."[2]

For most of his tenure as mayor, Koch had opposed any effort to restructure the police-controlled civilian complaint review board. A major reason for his about-face had to have been the major scandal in the 106th Precinct in Queens, which involved a number of officers who were accused of torturing an eighteen-year-old black high school student with a stun gun in order to make him confess to the crime of selling small quantities of marijuana.[3] On April 17, Mark Davidson was arrested and accused of attempting to sell a ten-dollar bag of marijuana to an undercover police officer. Davidson said they took him to the precinct and assaulted him. After he accused the police, three other young men came forward and also claimed that they were tortured at the 106th by police who used a stun gun.[4] Koch was criticized for a number of police brutality cases, including the 1984 cases of twenty-one-year old graffiti artist Michael Stewart, who was beaten to death by New York City transit police, and the shooting of sixty-year-old Eleanor Bumpurs. The Stewart and Bumpurs cases, as well as other police assaults on people of color, led to citywide protest and condemnation of the mayor. Koch, who was seeking a third term in office, knew that if he did not take action against police misconduct he would lose the election.

Given Koch's support for restructuring the review board, it may seem that he had taken a position unfavorable to the police. This was not the case. His "moderate and reasonable" stance was designed to fend off attempts to create the kind of independent, all-civilian complaint review board that civil rights activists sought, which was anathema to the NYPD.[5] But by the early 1990s an all-civilian complaint review board would become a reality.

Early in his single term as the city's first black mayor, from 1990 to 1993, David Dinkins pledged to be tough on crime. To that end, he pushed a plan he called Safe Streets, Safe City, a form of community policing that would place more police officers on the streets in an effort to put more criminals behind bars. In 1990 the city hired more than six thousand additional police officers, bringing the force to over thirty-one thousand, making it the largest in New York's history. Dinkins's plan put some five thousand of them in neighborhoods in ten-member patrol teams and also deployed as many as 1,800 patrol cars a day. Safe City, Safe Streets also called for diversifying the police racially, hiring more probation officers and corrections officers, creating larger cell spaces for prisoners, and adding more after-school centers as a way of preventing crime. Both the transit and housing police forces were expanded and transit police officers rode the subways between the hours of 8:00 p.m. to 4:00 a.m.[6]

Safe Streets, Safe City saw positive results. Rape, murder, felony assault, and larceny rates all dropped, and by 1991 Dinkins was able to point out that the crime rate overall had dropped by 6 percent in just one year. This was good news for an administration that the year before had witnessed the highest number of murders in the city history (2,245). While accounting for just 2.9 percent of the nation's population, New York City experienced 9.6 percent of the nation's homicides.[7] Despite these improvements, by the fall of 1992 Dinkins was at war with New York City's police officers.[8]

On September 16, 1992, a PBA-sponsored protest drew an estimated ten thousand off-duty police officers to a demonstration against Mayor Dinkins. Many carried signs and wore T-shirts reading "Dinkins Must Go" and "No Justice, No Police," and others saying Dinkins was "on crack." Some police protesters also carried posters displaying racist images, such as one depicting Dinkins with a large Afro and big lips and another showing him as a washroom attendant. The police demonstrators jumped over barricades, climbed on top of automobiles, blocked traffic on the Brooklyn Bridge, and swarmed the steps of City Hall chanting "Dinkins must go!" What was the source of their anger? The mayor had decided to call for and support the formation of an all-civilian complaint review board.[9]

Rudolph Giuliani, who was expected to challenge Dinkins in the next election, encouraged the protesters' unruly behavior and their disrespect for the mayor by telling demonstrators at City Hall that the only reason morale among the police was so low was "David Dinkins." The three hundred on-duty police officers present did nothing to stop their off-duty colleagues from trampling cars and committing other criminal offenses. Furious, Dinkins blamed PBA head Philip Caruso and Giuliani for egging on the police behavior.[10]

Dinkins, who had close ties to the Harlem community, had campaigned on a platform of police reform and had promised New Yorkers an independent review board that would be citizen-controlled. Despite the vociferous protests of the police and PBA, with Dinkins's support the City Council eventually passed such a bill in 1993. But Dinkins lost his bid for reelection that year, ending any serious efforts to establish community policing and give citizens a voice in determining how police would function in their communities. The next administration would adopt more aggressive ways of policing, which not only led to a growing number of complaints of brutality but also limited the ways that black and Latino citizens could find redress.

Making the Civilian Complaint Review Board Ineffective

The 1993 version of the civilian complaint review board was intended to reflect the city's diversity. It was proposed to have thirteen members, all of whom had to be residents of New York City. The City Council designated five members, one from each of the five boroughs, and three were selected by the police commissioner. The final five were appointed by the mayor, who also selected the chair. The new CCRB had the power to receive, investigate, hear, and make findings public concerning complaints by members of the public against the police department that alleged misconduct involving excessive use of force, abuse of authority, discourtesy, and use of offensive language, including, but not limited to, slurs relating to race, ethnicity, religion, gender, sexual orientation, and disability. The CCRB could also recommend that certain disciplinary actions be taken against officers found guilty.[11]

But after winning the mayoral election in 1993, Giuliani's new direction regarding policing was soon evident in his administration's treatment of the CCRB. He refused to provide it with adequate funding to effectively perform its duty, reducing its budget by 17 percent. According to Giuliani, the city was facing a $2.3 billion deficit in the upcoming year's budget, and therefore he needed to implement a hiring freeze—to which the police department was not subject. In fact, Giuliani was planning to hire additional police. His administration would be characterized by special treatment for the police, while the agency created to grant citizens a means of taking action against police abuse would be marginalized.[12]

It was through the Vacancy Control Board, an agency created by Mayor Dinkins to oversee government costs, that the new mayor attempted to make the CCRB ineffective. Giuliani selected deputy mayor Peter Powers to head the board, and he hindered the CCRB by not allocating sufficient funds for it to hire an adequate number of investigators. The Vacancy Control Board held up the appointment of the eight additional CCRB investigators and did not fill the personnel director and budget director positions. The CCRD also could not hire a legal investigator and chief investigator, assuring that it could not operate effectively. By March 1994 the CCRB employed just forty people, twenty-two fewer than the previous review board that had been under the control of the police. Although the CCRB was expected to perform more effectively than the police-controlled board, the denial of adequate resources guaranteed it would be ineffective. Norman Siegel, head of the New York City Civil Liberties Union, complained to the City Council about the subpar training of investigators, inadequate funding and staffing, and the growing case backlog affecting the CCRB. Siegel also described a "bias arising from the large number of former police department employees on the investigative staff." The CCRB, he said, was "in crisis" and was failing both complainants and supporters of the new, independent board. He lay the blame for the failure at the feet of Giuliani, the City Council, the CCRB's board members, and its supervisory staff.[13]

The new CCRB's inability to hire new investigators meant that the existing investigatory staff was made up largely of "former police department investigators, a number of whom have been promoted to supervisory positions." The small number of new investigators hired from outside the police department filled entry-level positions and had little experience as investigators.[14]

Siegel maintained that the "wholesale transfer of investigators from the police department raises doubts about the independence and objectivity of the new CCRB." Moreover, he argued, there were "indications that complaints filed with the Board are not being resolved in a timely manner." As an example, he noted that a complainant who was being represented by the NYCLU was given an initial interview with a CCRB investigator on July 15, 1993, and as of January 1994 had not heard from the review board again. Siegel admitted that this could have been an aberration, but NYCLU's concern was that it "may be typical."[15]

By March 1995 the CCRB had reduced its docket of cases from 5,754 to 5,203. Testifying before the City Council at that time, David Zornow, the board's chairperson, maintained that the investigators were overburdened, and if the board was to continue to reduce its overall caseload, "we must redouble our efforts to continue reducing the backlog until we have reached the goal of completing our investigations and reaching determinations in a timely and expeditious manner." He called for funding the additional resources "necessary to meet our increased responsibilities."[16]

In a March letter to the City Council quoted in the *New York Times*, NYCLU head Siegel pointed out that Giuliani had refused to hire at least one-third of the CCRB investigators and a number of the administrators that had already been allocated for in the city's budget. He went on to accuse Giuliani of being in contempt of the law by withholding those funds. Some members of the City Council accused Giuliani of purposefully weakening the CCRB by refusing to fill positions. Reminding the city's budget officials of the already-budgeted funds, Sheldon S. Leffler, councilman from Queens, charged the Giuliani administration with "undermining the credibility" of the CCRB.[17]

Giuliani's hostility to the CCRB reflected his notion that any restraint on police officers carrying out a more forceful approach to fighting crime simply interfered with officers doing their job. The CCRB got in the way, and to make it ineffective, the administration improperly funded it. This effort of defunding the CCRB demonstrated that the issue of police brutality would take a back seat in Giuliani's more aggressive approach to crime fighting. And that aggressive approach signaled to black and Latino New Yorkers and others concerned about police abuse that they would have to intensify their pressure on the mayor, elected officials, and the NYPD to protect their civil rights.

Zero Tolerance

Giuliani selected William Bratton as the new police commissioner. Bratton had served as head of the New York City Transit Authority Police Department since 1990, gaining it national and state accreditation and building a force of 4,500 police and civilian employees, making it one of the largest departments in the country.

Together, Giuliani and Bratton moved away from Dinkins's community policing policy, which the new mayor complained was forcing police officers to provide social services instead of performing their primary task of preventing crime. At a news conference in January 1994 the mayor attempted to redefine policing: "Social service aspects that were kind of added on to community policing, some of that has to be done but can't become the primary focus of all the police aspects in the neighborhood. The police officer's there to make sure that the burglary doesn't take place, the robbery doesn't take place, a person can walk the street safely." Community policing, Giuliani argued, had become a "complex, convoluted academic science, training police officers in accessing social services." This was simply "inconsistent with the role of the police."[18]

Although he had been an early proponent of community policing, Bratton had a change of heart and would later note in his book *Turnaround: How America's Top Cop Reversed the Crime Epidemic* that community policing focused on the cop on the beat rather than on crime, and in particular it did not address the quality-of-life crimes that encouraged more serious offenses.[19] Testifying before the Committee on Public Safety of the New York City Council in May 1994, Bratton said that the Giuliani administration "hit the ground running with new comprehensive strategies to get guns off the streets, curb youth violence, drive out drug dealers and stem the tide of domestic violence." His goal was to reduce "fear, crime and disorder in every neighborhood in the five boroughs." In addition to cost-saving measures such as merging the NYPD with the Transit and Housing Police Departments, Bratton promised to implement "sweeping crime and disorder control strategies, as well as the new technology needed to support them." He acknowledged that the police department was exempt from the city's budget cuts but said it had adopting a number of measures to become more productive and efficient.[20]

Bratton served as commissioner of the NYPD from 1994 to 1996 and during that time Giuliani increased the police force by 35 percent. Speaking to Congress in 2000, Giuliani noted that he had added ten thousand officers to the force since taking office.[21] With an expanded police force, Giuliani and Bratton focused on fighting crime by adopting an official policy of "Zero Tolerance" that targeted those committing quality-of-life offenses such as begging, panhandling, graffiti, drug dealing, and prostitution. It was an effort, according to Giuliani, to reclaim the streets for those who obeyed the law.

Giuliani's Zero Tolerance policy was closely associated with the "broken windows" theory of political scientists George L. Kelling and James Q. Wilson, who contended that if quality-of-life crimes are not stopped, criminals would become bolder and commit more serious crimes, and neighborhoods could experience a "criminal invasion. Though it is not inevitable, it is more likely that here, rather than in places where people are confident they can regulate public behavior by informal controls, drugs will change hands, prostitutes will solicit, and cars will be stripped." Writing in *The Atlantic* in 1982, the sociologists argued that "the unchecked panhandler is, in effect, the first broken window. Muggers and robbers, whether opportunistic or professional, believe they reduce their chances of being caught or even identified if they operate on streets where potential victims are already intimidated by prevailing conditions. If the neighborhood cannot keep a bothersome panhandler from annoying passerby, the thief may reason, it is even less likely to call the police to identify a potential mugger or to interfere if the mugging actually takes place."[22]

Under Zero Tolerance, Giuliani, a strong supporter of the broken windows theory, moved from going after serious crimes to stopping low-level violations of the penal codes of New York City. Bratton began applying a broken windows policy in 1990 while he was still head of the transit police. Writing in 2015 he recalled, "We wouldn't ignore the little things. Fare evasion and graffiti would no longer be considered too petty to address. In fact we focused on them as vigorously as on the serious crimes like robberies, if not more so." Bratton's reason for focusing more on low-level offenses was that "serious crime occurred in a lawless environment and ubiquitous low-level disorder signaled lawlessness even more than serious crime, which was less common." Bratton asserted that the quality-of-life approach worked in the New York City transit system: from 1990 to 1991 crime fell by almost 36 percent.[23]

Bratton also introduced CompStat (short for computer statistics), a police department management tool that relies on the most recent data on crime in specific neighborhoods to deploy appropriate resources to those area. It examines tactics such as stop, question, and frisk along with broken windows, and constantly reviews and analyzes the outcomes. Using CompStat, data are gathered quickly and studied in order to understand crime trends in a community and take action to prevent further criminal actions. Police and resources are quickly deployed in the troubled areas and officers use tactics that have been proven effective. Under CompStat, commanders are responsible for knowing the crime data in their district and coming up with a scheme to reduce the crime rate. The program encourages a police department to share data internally and with other law enforcement agencies.[24] Instead of responding to crime, Bratton and Giuliani adopted CompStat as a means of crime prevention[25] and it became the heart and soul of Zero Tolerance.

There was no doubt that Zero Tolerance and CompStat dramatically reduced crime in the city. The mayor's management report noted that from 1993 to 1997 the number of felony complaints decreased by 44.3 percent, murders and non-negligent homicides by 60.2 percent, reports of rape by 12.4 percent, and robbery by nearly 50 percent. Undoubtedly, the quality of life improved throughout the city. One of the most apparent and welcome outcomes of Zero Tolerance was the disappearance of the so-called squeegee people, panhandlers who accosted drivers at red lights by wiping their windshield in order to receive a tip. Prostitution and drug trafficking in high-crime areas were also dramatically reduced because of Zero Tolerance. Under Bratton's leadership, police were said to be "reclaiming the streets."[26]

In a jointly authored article in 2015, Bratton and sociologist George Kelling argued that the broken windows policy required police to "address disorderly illegal behavior, such as public drinking and drug use, fights, public urination and other acts considered minor offences."[27] But while defenders of broken windows point to vulgar offenses that most people would agree should be stopped, they seldom publicize the many minor but less vulgar offenses that resulted in police issuing a summons—for example, selling loose cigarettes, jaywalking, spitting, walking on the streets with an open alcoholic beverage, or riding a bicycle on the sidewalk. The extremely broad list of Zero Tolerance crimes subjected large numbers of people to arrest and pulled them into the criminal justice system. The number of non-felony offenses increased from 86,000 in 1989 to 176,000 in 1998.[28] For example, there were 39,000 marijuana arrests made between 1987 to 1996. However, between 1997 and 2007 the number jumped to 362,000.

The number of B-misdemeanor arrests in 1998 was double the number in 1989 and outnumbered all other 1998 arrest categories. Among the B-misdemeanor categories are fortune-telling, possession of graffiti instruments, refusal to aid a peace or police officer, loitering, unlawful assembly, adultery, and possession of small amounts of marijuana.[29]

Blacks accounted for 50 percent of overall arrests in 1989, which did not change in 1998; Latino arrests went from 27 percent in 1989 to 32 percent in 1998. However, though the percentages remained the same or similar, the actual numbers went up. Among blacks, the 1989–98 number increased by forty-five thousand.[30] Bratton has argued that critics of broken windows ignore the fact that most of the victims of criminal activity were black and Latino, therefore those demographics benefit from the policy. African Americans and Latinos accounted for 53 percent of the city's population in 2013 and were the victims in 74 percent of the reported rapes and 71 percent of assaults. In that year, 83 percent of the murder victims were black or Latino.[31]

Judith Greene, a criminal justice policy analyst, maintains that while Bratton's reforms were innovative, "at the neighborhood level, his crime-fighting strategies were grounded in traditional law enforcement methods and in relentless crackdown campaigns to arrest and jail low-level drug offenders and other petty perpetrators." Greene accuses Bratton of taking the "handcuffs off the police department" and "unleashed patrol officers to stop and search citizens who were violating the most minor laws" on record. She points out that in a four-year period (1994–98) new civil rights suits against the police for abusive conduct increased by 75 percent and police brutality got worse under Giuliani. The percentage of "general patrol incidents," or ordinary police contacts with citizens with no arrest or "suspension of criminal activity," increased from 29 percent in 1993 to 58 percent during the Giuliani years. The vast majority of complaints came from black and Latino communities. The New York City public advocate during these years, Mark Green, is quoted as noting that over 50 percent of the complaints came from nine of the seventy-six precincts, and that all nine were in black and Latino communities.[32]

Fighting Police Reform: Giuliani's Response to the Mollen Commission

In July 1992 Mayor Dinkins had created both a Commission to Investigate Allegations of Police Corruption and the NYPD's Anti-corruption Procedures. He selected Milton Mollen, a former judge of the New York City Criminal Court and former deputy mayor, to head what became known as the Mollen Commission to investigate police corruption. The commission examined thousands of NYPD documents, held dozens of hearings, analyzed hundreds of personnel files, and interviewed current officers, private citizens, defense attorneys, victims of corruption, and police informants.[33] It shared in its official 1994 report that it found while the vast majority of police officers were honest, police corruption was a serious problem that extended far beyond the individual corrupt cop:

> It is a multi-faceted problem that has flourished in parts of our City not only because of opportunity and greed, but because of police culture that exalts loyalty over integrity; because of the silence of honest officers who fear the consequences of "ratting" on another cop no matter how grave the crime; because of willfully blind supervisors who fear the consequences of a corruption scandal more than corruption itself; because of the demise of the principle of accountability that makes all commanders responsible for fighting corruption in their commands; because of hostility and alienation between the police and the community in certain precincts which breeds an "Us versus Them" mentality; and because for years the New York Police abandoned its responsibility to insure the integrity of its members.[34]

The corruption uncovered by the Mollen Commission differed from the type described by the Knapp Commission as having occurred in the 1960s. According to the Mollen Commission, police officers were not only taking bribes from drug dealers but some became dealers themselves, and gangs of cops sold narcotics raided from drug dealers. To cover up their crimes, police officers falsified reports and committed perjury. The NYPD had "allowed its systems for fighting corruption to virtually collapse." Internal Affairs, the agency delegated to investigate corruption, did almost nothing to uncover such behavior: "Most Internal Affairs investigators and supervisors embraced a work ethic more dedicated to closing corruption cases than to investigating them. . . . Weak corruption controls reduced the chances of uncovering serious corruption and protected police commanders' careers."[35]

The Knapp Commission Report, issued in 1970, had investigated police corruption but ignored police brutality. Although most of the Mollen Report dealt with police corruption, it also included police brutality and contended that the two could not be separated: "We found that corruption and brutality are often linked in a variety of ways and should no longer be artificially separated by managers, corruption fighters and policy makers." It identified police brutality as the "implicit or explicit threat of physical harm or the actual infliction of physical injury or pain." Police brutality, according to the report, took place in crime-ridden areas of widespread corruption with a large black and Latino populations.[36]

An explanation for some instances of police brutality, the commission maintained, was the implementation of "officers' own brand of vigilante justice," though for others there seemed to be "no apparent reason at all." It found that brutality was a "means to accomplish corrupt ends and sometimes it was a gratuitous appendage to a corrupt act." Cops did not just become corrupt; they became "corrupt and violent." The commission asserted that the corruption it found "sometimes involved abuse of authority and unnecessary force, and the violence we found sometimes occurred to facilitate thefts of drugs and money." It also maintained that officers who are corrupt were "more likely to be brutal."[37]

According to the Mollen Commission, "brutality also occurred independently to show power, out of fear or hostility towards a person or the community that person represents, to vent frustrations and anger, or in a misplaced attempt to compel respect in the community." Officers who were interviewed by the commission told its members that it was not unusual "to see unnecessary force used to administer an officer's own brand of street justice: a nightstick in the ribs, a fist in the head, to demonstrate who was in charge of crime-ridden streets they patrolled."[38]

The Mollen Commission recognized that brutality was not limited to criminals: "Unlike serious corruption, which most cops outwardly tolerate but inwardly deplore and resent, officers seem fairly tolerant—both outwardly and inwardly—of occasional police brutality." Supervisors also tolerated police brutality: "This is because many supervisors share the perception that nothing is really wrong with a bit of unnecessary force and because they believe that is the only way to fight crime today." Supervisors did not question the stories reported by their officers.[39]

One factor the Mollen Commission did not take into consideration was racism. It placed the overall blame for police brutality on past commanders. Despite the Knapp Commission's report twenty years earlier, corruption had remained. Even though it was the CCRB that was responsible for investigating police brutality, that should not have taken commanders off the hook for taking action to prevent and eradicate abuse. In previous years, the NYPD had refused to see police brutality as a serious problem and to see its "link to corruption," and the commission maintained that the NYPD itself should be primarily responsible for both problems. However, if left entirely on its own, the report maintained, the NYPD would not be able to completely root out corruption, so it also called for a number of reforms. These included improving screening and recruitment, upgrading education for recruits, "attacking corruption and brutality tolerance," and "enhancing sanctions disincentives for corruption and brutality."[40] An external review would assure the success of these recommended measures.

One recommendation was that the "Police Academy and In-Service Integrity training . . . address issues of brutality and other civil rights violations, which have traditionally been ignored in integrity training." Also pertaining to brutality, the Commission recommended that "Internal Affairs should immediately establish a Civil Rights Investigations Unit dedicated to the investigations of brutality, perjury, false arrests, and other types of civil rights violations." This unit should also work along with the CCRB to investigate charges of brutality.[41] A further recommendation was that police officers must be required to live in the city. It was assumed that if officers lived in the community where they worked, they would have a better understanding of the people and their social conditions.[42]

The commission also recommended a number of changes in the laws that helped to shield police from prosecution, including amending "New York City Administrative Code, Section 13-246 to provide for a minimum of ninety days' notice to the Department before an officer is permitted to retire with full pension." The existing thirty-day requirement failed to allow sufficient time to complete a disciplinary investigation before an officer could retire in order to escape punishment. It also called for amending "Public Officers Law Section 30(e) to allow for the revocation of lifetime pension benefits for officers convicted of a felony or federal law equivalent committed while in the performance of their duties."[43] The commission further suggested increasing "the statute of limitations for Department disciplinary proceeding to three years from the current eighteen months." The statute of limitations had been reduced from five to three years in 1962 and from three years to eighteen months in 1982 due to pressure from the PBA and other state and municipal unions.[44]

In order to assure that the department was following through on the task of reforming itself, the Mollen Commission also recommended a dual-track strategy. The first track would strengthen the NYPD's anti-corruption apparatus and improve recruiting and training, thus improving supervision and internal investigation and advancing ways of preventing corruption and brutality. The second track would be to establish a permanent police commission independent of the NYPD. Its duties would include performing "continuous audits of the Department's systems for preventing, detecting and investigating corruption." It would also assist the NYPD to implement "programs and policies to eliminate the values and attitudes that nurture corruption." The proposed police commission would guarantee a "successful system of command accountability" and when necessary conduct "its own corruption investigations."[45]

In April 1994, just before the Mollen Commission issued its final report, Bratton, in a television interview, voiced his opposition to the recommendation for an outside agency to monitor corruption. While noting that the Mollen Commission did good work, the police department under Giuliani had already strengthened its Internal Affairs division, he said. Mayor Giuliani agreed with Bratton that there was no need for an outside agency or special prosecutor. He favored giving responsibility for investigating corruption to the City's Department of Investigation, headed by his close friend Howard Wilson, who had served under Giuliani when he was a U.S. attorney in Manhattan. Wilson had served as the chairman of the selection panel that recommended Bratton for police commissioner. By farming out the investigation of police corruption to the agency that investigated corruption in all other city agencies, the mayor was sending the message that police corruption was no different than other forms of corruption. Giuliani had no intention of placing the power to investigate police corruption in the hands of an outside agency with subpoena power.[46]

For its part, the City Council was concerned that once the publicity generated by the Mollen Commission died down the NYPD's commitment to rooting out corruption would diminish. It decided to act, and on November 23, 1994, it adopted legislation creating the Police Investigation and Audit Board, which would have the authority to explore and audit the NYPD's anti-corruption efforts and at the same time independently investigate corruption. It would also have subpoena power. To avoid duplication or interference with ongoing investigations, the Police Investigation and Audit Board would have to coordinate with the police commissioner, the CCRB, and district attorneys. The City Council, acting under Local Law 13, would appoint two members of the board, the mayor would appoint two members, and the fifth member would be appointed jointly by the mayor and City Council.[47]

Giuliani opposed the new board, arguing that it interfered with the power to appoint nonelected officers as granted to the mayor under City Charter section 6(a). On December 23 he vetoed the bill. On January 19 the council overrode his veto. Not giving up, Giuliani took the City Council to court in an effort to have the board declared illegal. In June 1995 the New York State Supreme Court ruled that creating the board under Local Law 13 was invalid, because the City Council did not have the power to appoint members of such a board. Only the mayor had the authority to appoint "officers of the City," according to the City Charter. The City Council appealed, but in January 1997 the First Department of the Supreme Court Appellate Division upheld the New York State Supreme Court's decision that Local Law 13 was invalid because it interfered with the mayor's appointment powers. Moreover, the New York State Court of Appeals refused to allow the City Council to appeal the Appellate Division's decision.[48]

While fighting the battle in court, Giuliani countered the efforts of the City Council by creating his own investigation board. On February 27, 1995, he issued an executive order establishing a Police Commission to combat law enforcement corruption. The mayor would appoint the five members tasked with monitoring for corruption within the police department and evaluating the NYPD's anti-corruption systems. Specific allegations of police corruption would continue to be investigated by the NYPD, with no interference from the Police Commission without permission from the mayor, the police commissioner, and the commissioner of the Department of Investigation.[49]

The City Council criticized the Police Commission because it was not independent of the mayor, who created it and appointed all its members. A further indication of its lack of independence was the executive order provision that allowed it to investigate specific allegations only with the permission of the mayor and the commissioner of the DOI, who is appointed by the mayor.[50]

Speaker of the City Council Peter Vallone remained committed to creating an independent Investigation and Audit Board, maintaining that such a body would be beneficial to the NYPD and would enhance public trust in the police. He offered an amendment to Local Law 13, Local Law 91, which gave the mayor power to appoint the Investigation and Audit Board's five members. However, two of those members would be "designated" by the City Council. Local Law 91 also declared that the mayor would also appoint the chair of the board, but only "after consultation with the Speaker of the Council."[51]

The amended bill still gave the independent board the power to "perform assessments and audits of the police department's internal systems for detecting, investigating and preventing corruption among uniformed and civilian members of the police department." But to further assure that the board would not interfere with the powers of the mayor, it could only "make recommendations to the police department in relation to the formulation and implementation of policies and programs to detect and eliminate corruption." Although it could undertake investigations of possible corruption within the NYPD at the request of the mayor or commissioner, it could also simply conduct investigations on its own accord. If during its investigation it believed it had uncovered corruption, the board had to report it to the police commissioner and the "appropriate prosecuting attorney." In addition, the amended bill granted the independent board subpoena power.[52]

Giuliani reacted as he had to Local Law 13. From his perspective, it ceded authority to a board that was not solely appointed by the mayor and infringed on the mayor's sole right, granted to him under City Charter section 8(a), to guarantee the efficiency of city government operations. It also infringed on the investigative and prosecutorial powers of the district attorney.[53]

The New York Supreme Court ruled that the mayor's complaints were unfounded. Local Law 91 did allow the mayor to appoint the five members of the board, thus it did not violate the New York State Constitution or the New York City Charter. The court did find that the independent board's subpoena power and other powers interfered with the mayor's power but not with the district attorney's, and according to the City Charter, the City Council had the legal right to delegate powers to an administrative agency in the executive branch. The court ordered Giuliani to implement Local Law 91.[54]

Conclusion

The defunding of the Civilian Complaint Review Board early in the Giuliani administration, the increasing number of police brutality complaints due to Zero Tolerance, and the fight between Giuliani and the City Council over the Investigation and Audit Board all demonstrated the mayor's determination to oppose any attempt to allow an independent body to investigate police corruption or brutality. In large part this was because he did not want to derail his objective of fighting and preventing crime. It was also due, however, to the fact that Giuliani did not think that police brutality was a serious issue.

The mayor's dismissal of the seriousness of police brutality was reflected in a speech he made before the U.S. House of Representatives in 1999 asserting that the number of police brutality cases was lower during his administration than during the Dinkins and Koch administrations. Noting that there had been 62 percent fewer shootings by police officers the previous year than during the final year of the Dinkins administration, he went on to claim, "In every single year of my administration the police officers have grown more restrained in their use of firearms, even as we have added 10,000 police officers and given them automatic weapons." Admitting that there were difficulties and a lot more that needed to be done, he expressed his sympathy not for the victims of police violence but for police officers: "I said to the 800 police officers [at graduation ceremonies] last week that what we expect of them is restraint, almost an inhuman ability to be restrained when they have to be."[55]

Giuliani's downplaying of the extent of police brutality during his administration revealed his refusal not only to see the issue as a serious problem but also to recognize that the victims of police abuse had a legitimate claim to redress. His determination to snub all who called for earnest measures to stop police brutality would lead to a number of sensational brutality cases that rocked his administration and all of New York City.

9

Abner Louima, Amadou Diallo, and the
Resistance to Giuliani

Asked by the *Washington Post* in a January 1997 interview to defend his
record when it came to black New Yorkers, Giuliani said sarcastically,
"They're alive, how about we start with that." The mayor was making
the argument that his policing policies were keeping black New Yorkers
safe,[1] but the remark pointed to his insensitivity to the growing problem
of police brutality during his terms. As we have seen, throughout his
tenure he defended cops accused of brutality, denied the Civilian Complaint Review Board the funding to properly investigate acts of police
brutality, and fought diligently against police reform efforts.

Giuliani's paramount goal was crime prevention, and he promoted
aggressive forms of policing, including Zero Tolerance, that targeted
low-level offensives but led to a dramatic increase in the number of unjustified police attacks on New Yorkers, especially blacks and Latinos.
Giuliani turned a blind eye to such attacks, sending a message to police
officers that they could assault people of color with impunity, and his
continued devotion to undermining efforts by city officials to address
the problem had tragic results. There was both a dramatic increase in
complaints filed by civilians alleging police brutality, and a number of
particularly brutal assaults, two of which would eventually horrify the
entire nation and lead to massive demonstrations. The brutality exposed
by press accounts of the police attacks on Amadou Diallo and Abner
Louima would expose on a global scale Giuliani's indifference to the
issue of police violence to black New Yorkers. Elected officials and grassroots activists alike organized street protests that put a spotlight not only
on police brutality but also on Giuliani's unrelenting efforts to protect
the police and denigrate those protesting police brutality. Eventually,
the effective organizing and protesting made it extremely difficult for
Giuliani to ignore or dismiss the existence of police brutality and its
devastating impact on black and Latino New Yorkers.

Brutal Cops

While many have claimed that Giuliani's major achievement was the dramatic decrease in violent crime, it is impossible to ignore the heavy price New Yorkers paid to achieve it. The number of police brutality complaints soared under Giuliani. A report by public advocate Mark Green submitted to the Public Safety Committee of the City Council in September 1997 noted that between 1992 and 1996 civilian complaints concerning police misconduct "increased from 3,437 complaints to 5,596 complaints." One reason for the almost 60 percent increase was the merger of the NYPD with the Housing and Transit police forces. Another reason was the hiring of an additional ten thousand police officers, with the result that 25 percent of the force had less than five years' experience. Moreover, more aggressive policing may have led to the increasing number of confrontations between citizens and the police, and the creation of an independent CCRB (Local Law 91) may have encouraged more people to come forward and file complaints. According to Green's report, the CCRB data showed "Brooklyn North and Queens have far out-paced increases across the City," with a 46.7 percent increase in Brooklyn North and a 61.4 percent increase in Queens. Manhattan South, the Bronx, and Staten Island also experienced increases in the number and percentages of complaints of police brutality.[2]

As we have seen, Giuliani's usual stance was to defend the police in brutality cases, including shootings, and express little sympathy for the victims. A case in point was the shooting death of sixteen-year-old Kevin Cedeno in early April 1997 by officer Anthony Pellegrini in Washington Heights, a neighborhood in northern Manhattan. The police said that Cedeno had a machete and was ready to confront the officer, who had no choice but to shoot him. However, witnesses said Cedeno was running away from the police, and it was later determined that Cedeno was shot in the back.[3] Giuliani declared that he would always support the police unless there was proof to the contrary. At a news conference about the Cedeno shooting he emphasized that officers would always have his support because they were sworn to protect the public. Asked if he thought that police brutality should be an issue in his reelection campaign, he said that teens running around in the streets at 3:00 a.m. carrying machetes should be the focus.[4] The officer eventually admitted that he was chasing Cedeno because he thought the boy had a gun, and Manhattan district attorney Robert Morgenthau ruled that Pellegrini did not act inappropriately when he shot the teen.[5]

Another Giuliani tactic when police were involved in killing people of color was simply to remain silent. For example, in the early morning of December 22, 1994, twenty-nine-year-old Anthony Baez was playing football with his three brothers when for the second time the football hit a parked police car. Officer Francis Livoti got out of the car, cursed at the brothers, told them to stop playing, and reentered the vehicle. The brothers continued throwing the football; Livoti again got out the car and began arguing with them. When David Baez, one of the brothers, began to verbally protest Livoti's behavior, the police officer arrested him. Anthony Baez protested his brother's arrest, Livoti attempted to arrest him, Anthony resisted, and Livoti placed him in a chokehold. The boys' father came down from his apartment begging the officer to let his son go. Livoti finally released Anthony, who fell to the ground and was handcuffed.[6]

According to an Amnesty International report, Anthony Baez "was left face-down on the ground in a prone position for around ten to fifteen minutes before being dragged into a police car, with no attempt made to resuscitated him." He was taken in the police car to a hospital, where he was pronounced dead about an hour later. The medical examiner concluded that he died of "asphyxia due to compression of the neck and chest," as well acute asthma, and classified the death as a homicide. Officer Livoti had fourteen prior complaints of brutality on his record yet remained on the force.[7] Giuliani remained silent, expressing no words of condolences to the Baez family and never apologizing to them for Anthony's death.[8]

Amnesty International

The growing number of police brutality cases in New York and the mayor's refusal to address the problem in any serious way led Amnesty International (AI) to investigate. AI's *Police Brutality and Excessive Force in the New York City Police Department* was one of the most critical reports issued on the topic. After an eighteen-month investigation, AI found the NYPD responsible for the "ill treatment, or excessive use of force" that resulted in "ill treatment or death" in ninety cases from the 1980s to early 1996. By that time, the NYPD employed over thirty-eight thousand officers, making it the largest police department in the nation: "The allegations include people being repeatedly struck with fists, batons, or other instruments, often after minor disputes with officers on the street; death in police custody; and shootings in apparent violation of the NYPD's own very stringent guidelines. The victims include men and women, juveniles and people from a variety of social, racial and ethnic backgrounds." But the report noted that "evidence suggests that the large majority of the victims of police abuse are racial minorities, particularly African-Americans and people of Latin American or Asian descent."[9]

AI was not able to draw conclusions about the accuracy of all the case reports because the events were in dispute and there was a "lack of public disclosure surrounding investigations into police misconduct. . . . However, the information gathered suggests that police brutality and unjustifiable force is nevertheless a widespread problem, with a pattern of similar abuses occurring over many years."[10]

The largest number of cases reviewed by AI involved accusations of excessive physical force being used during arrests, disputes, or other incidents on the streets: "The most common forms of ill-treatment alleged were repeated kicks or punches by officers using fists, batons, or other instruments such as police radios or flashlights, sometimes while the suspect was handcuffed or otherwise restrained. In most cases injuries were sustained which required medical treatment, and in at least a dozen cases the injuries were severe enough to require the victim to spend some time in the hospital." AI gathered information on ninety cases of alleged ill-treatment or death of citizens by the police. Its sample included fifteen cases in which the victim died "after being forcibly restrained." In some of these cases death was caused by asphyxia after pressure was applied to the person's neck or chest. AI also claimed that in "many of the cases examined, the alleged victims were not involved in or suspected of criminal activity prior to their contact with the police but were reportedly ill-treated after they questioned police authority or became involved in relatively minor disputes." Several victims were bystanders who were "allegedly brutalized after taking photographs or criticizing police treatment of others."[11]

It was also quite common for police who committed brutal acts to charge their victims with a crime as a way of justifying the use of force. Over two-thirds of the cases researched by AI involved African American and Latino citizens; most of the officers involved were white. The majority of victims killed were from minority groups. The Civilian Complaint Review Board's biannual reports note that minorities were disproportionately the victims of police brutality. From January to June 1995, 75.9 percent of those who filed complaints with the board were black and over 25 percent were Latino. A little more than 21 percent were white. Of the officers accused of brutality between January and June 1995, just over 69 percent were white, 17.5 percent were Latino, and 12.5 percent were black.[12]

The NYPD did not cooperate with AI, which turned to other sources, including the victims' attorneys, to learn that very few of the officers in their study were ever punished for their actions—in fact, many of them were later promoted. Rarely was a police officer accused of abuse indicted and even more rarely were those indicted found guilty. One reason was the "high threshold for proving criminal charges against police officers"; another was the "code of silence among police officers."[13]

Complaints of police brutality rose sharply in the first year of Giuliani's mayoralty, 1994, when the CCRB received 4,920 new complaints, up by 37.43 percent over 1993. Commissioner Bratton asserted that the CCRB figures did not take into account the merger of the NYPD with the Transit and Housing Authority Police, but AI noted that the mergers would only account for a small proportion of the increase. Police officials suggested that the sharp rise in complaints was because of the increase in "arrests and police activity during an intensive anti-crime drive in the city during the past two years." Thus the Zero Tolerance and broken windows policies were cited as a major reason for the increase in arrests.[14]

One of the most noted cases during the Giuliani period was the January 1995 police murder of nineteen-year-old Anthony Rosario Jr. and his cousin, twenty-two-year-old Hilton Vega, and the wounding of Freddie Bonilla Jr., all of whom were accused of attempting to rob the elderly occupants of a Bronx apartment. Expecting Rosario and Vega to show up, one of the apartment's occupants called the police. When Rosario, Vega, and Bonilla arrived, officers Patrick Brosnan and James Crowe were on hand and confronted them. The cops later claimed that Rosario reached for his gun, so they fired at them. A March 1995 grand jury did not indict the officers, although the CCRB found their story implausible because forensic evidence proved that Rosario and Vega had been shot in the back of the head, torso, back, and underarms, indicating that they had raised their hands to surrender. A pathologist hired by one of the families concluded that the victims had been lying on the floor when shot. The CCRB sent its report to Commissioner Bratton, who criticized the agency for conducting an investigation while a federal inquiry was in progress. The CCRB maintained that it had completed its investigation before the federal inquiry had gotten underway. AI examined the autopsy report of Hilton Vega and reported that he had been "shot in the back from two sides with different bullets, both coming from behind."[15]

The Justice Committee of the New York City chapter of the National Congress for Puerto Rican Rights reported that Officer Brosnan was a friend of Giuliani's and had headed his security team during his campaign for mayor. In February 1996, thirteen months after the Rosario and Vega murders, Brosnan was awarded a line of duty disability pension, having claimed that he experienced hearing loss after he and Crowe fired so many shots at Rosario, Vega, and Bonilla.[16]

The Amnesty International report noted that the CCRB received 3,961 complaints between January and June 1995 but only 1,285 (less than a third) proceeded to a full investigation, only 119 (less than a tenth) were substantiated, and three-quarters were "unsubstantiated" due to lack of sufficient evidence. For a case to be substantiated, there needs to be sufficient credible evidence that the officer was involved in misconduct.[17] AI expressed its concern that the CCRB lacked its full quota of investigators despite the increase in complaints—rather than the eighty-seven investigators it was required to receive in 1987, it had only fifty-one, thanks to Giuliani's cut in the board's budget. AI pointed out that the CCRB may not receive a number of complaints about brutality and other abuses that take place between midnight and 8:00 a.m. because even though CCRB officials met regularly with precinct commanders, most commanders were not on duty during that time period to take complaints. Also, AI pointed out, a number of people claiming police brutality just filed civilian complaints rather than complaints before the review board, indicating a lack of confidence in the agency.[18]

Moving on to the relationship between the NYPD and the CCRB, AI characterized it as "increasingly strained," noting that even as late as 1994 the NYPD might still have been "reluctant in practice to accept a completely independent police complaints machinery." In addition to its ongoing undermining of the CCRB, the NYPD specifically objected to the board's initiating of its own investigations in cases where there were concurrent investigations by the NYPD and Internal Affairs. While Internal Affairs wanted to conduct joint investigations with the CCRB, the CCRB wanted to remain completely independent of the police agency. As a consequence, Internal Affairs and the CCRB interviewed the same witnesses in any given case, causing confusion. Although the CCRB was willing to cooperate with Internal Affairs, it refused to share information with it, insisting that because its investigations had to remain independent the board was opposed to joint reports with any arm of the police department. Agreeing with the CCRB's stance, AI asserted that it "believes that it is important for the CCRB to be seen to retain its independence and that joint investigations and joint findings with the NYPD are not consistent with an independent investigative body."[19]

In addressing many misconduct complaints, the police department ignored the work of the CCRB. From July to December 1994, according to AI, the police commissioner resolved eighty police officer misconduct complaints that had been substantiated by the CCRB: an administrative trial was held for thirty-two cases; twenty-two cases had the charges dismissed; and in seven cases the accused officers were found innocent. Only in three cases were the officers found guilty.[20] AI noted the dramatic drop from the 1992 findings, in which 63 percent of the officers accused of misconduct were found guilty.

According to AI, the CCRB claimed that data for 1995 also indicated that the police commissioner dismissed a high percentage of cases. Under David Dinkins the commissioner had acted on 60 percent of the CCRB's recommendations for disciplinary action; Commissioner Bratton only acted on 19 percent of analogous recommendations for the period from January 1994 to June 1995. One reason AI gave for this decline was that the Office for Administrative Trials often moved to have cases dismissed because the statute of limitations had expired. However, a CCRB executive informed AI that there was no statute of limitations on police conduct that constituted a crime, so assaults and other offences considered criminal offenses "could still be tried administratively even if no criminal charges had been filed."[21] The CCRB, AI asserted, was quite limited when addressing police brutality because it could not investigate an act unless a formal complaint was filed. It was also restricted only to investigation and providing recommendations to the police commissioner.[22]

AI recommended, among other things, an "independent inquiry into allegations of police brutality and excessive force by the NYPD," and it also called on the city administration and the NYPD to support the CCRB as an independent investigative agency: "The CCRB should maintain its independence in its investigation of complaints by members of the public against the police." AI also agreed with the Mollen Commission's recommendation for the establishment of an independent oversight agency to monitor corruption and for a thorough review of police training policies and programs.[23]

Giuliani criticized AI's work as a "scattershot report" and not a "real analysis." And while the document grabbed headlines, it did not seem to hurt Giuliani's popularity. Crime was down dramatically and his poll numbers were up. In early November 1996 his overall approval rating was 54 percent. Among black voters, however, his disapproval rating was 58 percent.[24]

Despite the Amnesty International report and the CCRB's report noting the increase in complaints of police brutality, Giuliani did nothing to address the problem at a systemic level. Instead, the administration just threw money at it. Between 1990 and 1995, New York City spent $87 million to settle lawsuits concerning police brutality: $12 million in 1990, $24 million in 1994, and $9 million in the last three months of 1995 alone. According to the CCRB, there was a 37.4 percent increase in police brutality complaints in 1994 compared to 1993, and personal liability claims (rather than civil rights violations) against police officers increased 80 percent over the last decade. Between June 1996 and June 1997 the city settled in court 503 cases of brutality.[25] In most of those cases, police officers involved in the crimes were not punished. Giuliani's refusal to address either the skyrocketing number of police brutality cases or the financial impact on the city indicated that he was willing to accept that this was just the price of doing business. This approach would be sorely tested by the cases of Abner Louima in 1997 and Amadou Diallo in 1999.

The Torture of Abner Louima

In the early morning of August 9, 1997, police were called to a disturbance at the Club Rendez-Vous, a popular night spot on Flatbush Avenue between Farragut and Glenwood Roads. Several officers rushed to the scene where a crowd of about two hundred people stood outside of the club and two women were fighting. Haitian immigrant Abner Louima was among those in the crowd. According to Louima, he attempted to break up the fight but was confronted by officer Justin Volpe, who began arguing with him and eventually struck him. According to Volpe, Louima punched him, so he attempted to arrest him. Both Louima and eyewitnesses denied that he struck Volpe. Instead, Louima said, he was knocked to the ground and then hit by several cops, handcuffed, arrested, placed in a police vehicle, and taken to the Seventieth Precinct.[26] According to later court testimony, en route to the precinct the car stopped at a secluded section on Glenwood Road where police officers Tommy Wiese and Charles Schwarz, who were escorting Louima, began beating him. One of them even hit him in the head with a radio. Afterward they proceeded to another secluded area, where officers Volpe and Tom Bruder, who arrived in a separate police car, began beating him while also using offensive insults against his race and his Haitian origins. By the time he arrived at the police station, his face was covered in blood and he could not swallow. Louima claimed that while being booked the officers pulled down his pants and walked him through the station naked from the waist down.[27]

According to Louima, Volpe and other officers took him to a restroom, where Volpe called him a "fucking Haitian" and threw him to the ground. While Schwarz held Louima down and stepped on his mouth in order to stop him from screaming, Volpe penetrated his rectum with the handle of a toilet plunger. According to Louima, Volpe then removed the handle, which was covered in feces and blood, and forced it into his mouth. There were other officers in the area who heard him screaming, Louima said, but they did nothing to stop the torture or report the situation. In addition, Louima claimed that Volpe threatened to kill him and his family if he told anyone.[28]

Louima was then taken to a cell—in handcuffs and with his pants still down—where he remained for several hours before being taken in an ambulance to the emergency room at Coney Island Hospital. Although he told the EMS technicians what had taken place, they filed a false report that covered up the crimes committed by the police.[29] In the hospital, Louima was handcuffed and charged with disorderly conduct, resisting arrest, obstructing governmental administration, and third-degree assault.[30] Tests revealed that he had a torn sphincter, which resulted in the loss of bowel control, a punctured colon, and a torn bladder.

After learning that he had been arrested, members of Louima's family attempted to see him in the hospital but were denied access by the police. Eventually family members, along with lawyers who had been contacted, did manage to see him. Members of the Haitian American Alliance, a New York City–based organization that advocated for Haitian immigrants and Haitian Americans, as well as others familiar with the incident, called the local news channel NY1, the *New York Times*, the *New York Daily News*, and other media outlets that could make the public aware of what took place at the Seventieth Precinct on the night of August 9.

In his suit against the city, Louima accused the PBA of taking part in the cover-up of his torture by colluding with the four police officers who were charged with brutality. When PBA representatives received incriminating information about the four officers' criminal behavior, they did not bring it to light: "Instead of coming forward and promptly reporting this information as they are obligated to do as police officers, the PBA and its police officer agents suppressed it and instead, adopted and orchestrated an affirmative strategy of obstruction and falsification." Based on his "information and belief," Louima accused the four officers of meeting with a representative of the PBA on August 13 in the basement of the precinct station house to "devise a common story, inconsistent with the truth" of what took place. To bolster their chances that he would not press charges, they planned to publicly defame Louima by claiming he sustained his injuries in a homosexual affair at the Rendez-Vous. The PBA representative was also accused of asking other officers at the precinct not to come forward and to remain silent on the incident.[31]

Giuliani's Response to Louima

In an unusual move for him, Giuliani acknowledged the severity of the incident. The "charges are shocking to any decent human being," he said.

"These charges, if substantiated, should result in the severest penalties, including substantial terms of imprisonment and dismissal from the force." The mayor and police commissioner Howard Safir then organized a meeting with leaders of the Haitian community, civic groups, clergy, and elected officials in an attempt to defuse the situation. In addition to promising to arrest the culprits, Giuliani pledged to look at the management of the entire Seventieth Precinct to see why the Louima incident took place.[32] The commissioner reorganized the Seventieth Precinct in August by reassigning its top command, suspending the desk sergeant who was in charge on the night of the incident, and assigning a number of officers to desk duty. Giuliani asked police to put aside their allegiance to their fellow officers and come forward with any information concerning the Louima case: "If you really are a police officer of the City of New York, if you really understand what it means to be a police officer, if you really understand what it means to protect the lives of other people, then you will be among the most revulsed and repulsed by what happened here." Yet police at the Seventieth Precinct continued their efforts to cover up the incident—for instance, the plunger handle disappeared and therefore could not be used as evidence.[33]

Though Giuliani publicly acknowledged that a "horrible and terrible" crime had been committed and offered Louima the city's support and sympathy, community leaders, municipal officials, civil rights groups, and others criticized him for not doing enough to stop police brutality. In response, the mayor created a twenty-eight-member task force to explore police–community relations. Its members included City Council member Una Clark; Margaret Fung, executive director of the Asian American Legal Defense and Education Fund; Abraham H. Foxman, national director of the Anti-defamation League of B'nai B'rith; author Stanley Crouch; Christine Quinn of the New York City Anti-violence Project; Michael Meyers, executive director of the New York Civil Rights Coalition; and Norman Siegel, executive director of the New York Civil Liberties Union.[34]

While some of its members were hopeful that the task force could be productive, others were skeptical.[35] Giuliani requested they develop a curriculum for establishing a structured dialogue between the police and the community and also set up forums in various communities to give citizens the opportunity to meet members of the NYPD in order to improve police–citizen interactions. The strong civil rights advocates on the task force, including Siegel, Fung, and Meyers, insisted that the body also address the causes of police brutality and offer solutions. They challenged the mayor's push for the group to limit its scope to police–community relations "instead of urging us to investigate how police officers who have abused citizens were able to become cops in the first place, what kind of training they receive, why officials who are accused of excessive force are rarely disciplined, and what can be done to break the blue wall of silence."[36]

Giuliani did not take the work of the task force seriously; rather, it was a publicity maneuver to demonstrate to the public that he was taking action. He never provided it with the full-time staff or the $12 million to $15 million he promised. And although he promised to be involved in its work, between September 16, 1997, and January 20, 1998, he failed to attend any of its functions, including the five public hearings. Moreover, although he assured the members of the task force that the NYPD would be available to them to answer questions, that was never the case. Most alarmingly, he actually reprimanded the task force for not having a "more respectful attitude" toward the police and accused it of going after the NYPD, arguing that "cop bashing was analogous to racism and anti-Semitism."[37]

Giuliani finally attended a task force meeting on January 20, 1998, at which he told the members that they had sixty days to complete their work. Members were under the impression that they had a year to investigate and produce a report; Giuliani had limited them to seven months. Despite the obstacles, they did submit a final report. Some of its most significant suggestions included eliminating the rule that prohibited prosecutors from interrogating police officers accused of police brutality within the first forty-eight hours of the alleged event; adopting an affirmative action plan; establishing a residency requirement for police; creating a police–community relations training program; and increasing officers' pay.[38] Individuals and community groups concerned with reform would increasingly reiterate most of these recommendations.

Siegel, Meyers, and Fung did not think the task force recommendations went far enough, so they produced a minority report highlighting a number of recommendations that the majority members had refused to consider. These included the "establishment of a permanent special state prosecutor for police corruption and brutality," the formation of an independent body to "execute a top-down investigation of the practices of the NYPD Training Academy," the establishment of "elected police Advisory Boards," and greater cooperation between the Guardians, the organizations representing black police officers, and the Latino Officers Association. The authors of the minority report also accused the mayor of pushing a public relations stunt to center stage instead of addressing police brutality. What the authors meant by stunt was that Giuliani was trying to portray the real problem with police and communities of color as one of public relations. If his effort to focus attention away from brutality were successful, they wrote, it would "mask the pervasive lawlessness among a significant percentage of police officers. New Yorkers will be in danger from those sworn to serve and protect them from crime and from those who are obliged to uphold their constitutional liberties."[39]

Angered by the task force's final report, at a March 26 press conference Giuliani went on record as opposing some of its recommendations. Later, a spokesperson for Giuliani pointed to the residency requirement as an example. It was untenable because the state legislature would never approve it. The reality was that Giuliani had no interest in the work of the task force. He even took the opportunity at his news conference to call some of the members "police bashers" who did not bother to recognize that his administration had reduced the crime and murder rates. Una Clarke responded in the *New York Times* by asserting that she joined the task force because she thought Giuliani was serious about addressing the problem of the perception among some in the black and Latino communities that the police were an "occupying force rather than a friend." The mayor's criticism of the task force's hard work, she said, meant that now "everything is as it was before Louima."[40]

The City Council Responds

Una Clark overstated somewhat. Although Giuliani himself had no intention of addressing police brutality, Louima's torture moved others to act. The extensive media coverage and the protests triggered by the Louima case persuaded the City Council to form the Committee on Public Safety, which would hold public hearings in August and September

1997 in an attempt to not only get at the root of the problem but to seek solutions. The hearings attracted a wide spectrum of individuals and groups, including the Latino Officers Association, the Center for Law and Social Justice, attorney Colin A. Moore, the Coalition of Harmony, 100 Blacks in Law Enforcement Who Care, congressman Major Owens, the Legal Aid Society, New York City public advocate Mark Green, Manhattan borough president Ruth Messinger, the Fortune Society, and a representative of District Council 1707 of American Federation of State, County, and Municipal Employees (AFSCME), a labor union representing twenty-five thousand members working in day care, home care, the Head Start program, and private nonprofit agencies.[41]

Giuliani faced opposition from public advocate Mark Green. The public advocate is a citywide elected position that serves as a watchdog for citizens by making sure they receive the city services to which they are entitled. The advocate, who also assures that New Yorkers have a voice in shaping city policy, is an ex officio member of the City Council who can introduce legislation.[42] In his testimony before the committee, Green maintained that the "torture of Abner Louima is part of a pattern of police abuse, brutality and misconduct that is an unfortunate part of the history of our city." He pointed out that despite the growing number of incidents, the Giuliani administration had failed to address the problem and the NYPD had failed to "initiate disciplinary action against the majority of police officers who are the subjects of substantiated complaints, rendering the civilian complaint process a sham. In 1995, out of 196 substantiated complaints, 62 were not even prosecuted by the Police Department." Of the 247 police officers about whom the commissioner reached a final disposition, 135 (close to 60 percent) faced no charges.[43]

Green criticized Giuliani's broken promise to spend $12 million to $15 million for the task force, which he characterized as a purely investigative body that ended up having no clear mission. He was also critical of the mayor for not properly funding the CCRB. The absence of a role for the CCRB in Giuliani's response to the Louima incident was "striking," Greene said, and the fact that no CCRB member was on the mayor's task force demonstrated he was not going to deal seriously with police violence.[44]

Esmeralda Simmons, executive director of the Center for Law and Social Justice (CLSJ), was even more critical of Giuliani. The CLSJ, founded in 1985, is a department in the School of Continuing Education and External Programs at Medgar Evers College whose objective "is to meet an existing need within the borough of Brooklyn and the City of New York for a civil rights, social justice and legally oriented community based advocacy institution." From the start CLSJ addressed police brutality. In 1988 it created a Police and Racial Violence Project to provide free legal assistance to victims and help them file complaints with the CCRB. It also sponsors educational and training workshops on issues related to police brutality.[45]

Simmons emphasized that Louima's experience was no aberration, especially for New Yorkers of color, and that the reason for such attacks was that racism was pervasive in the NYPD. In a pointed criticism, Simmons blamed Giuliani for stoking racist sentiment among the police. The "mayor's behavior and its implications have not been lost on New York City police officers. If the commander in chief behaves in such a fashion, why shouldn't police officers feel that it's okay to have a violent and racist perspective towards New Yorkers of color? Why shouldn't they believe that racist, violent behavior is permissible?" In addition to noting the increase in brutality cases, she found it almost more alarming that the number of deaths of suspects killed by police also increased. While the number between 1992 and 1996 was 187, 115 were killed between January 1994 and December 1996; all happened under Giuliani's watch. "The Louima case and dozens of others like it underscores the urgent need to address racism in the NYPD as well as deficiencies in the hiring, training, supervisory and disciplinary practices."[46]

Simmons, too, called on the state to enact a residency law for all police officers, asserting that "police officers are public servants and, as such, should be subject to public scrutiny." Police, Simmons insisted, should be required to carry and show when requested "business-like identification cards, including a picture of the officer, a physical description of the officer," and the badge number. "I also called for cops to carry the number of their immediate supervisor and phone number of the CCRB," Simmons declared. Simmons's recommendations that police use several measures, including carry cards for identification, would become an essential component of the Right-to-Know Act (discussed in chapter 11). She also proposed that video cameras with audio and time codes should be installed in every precinct and in cars. Other recommendations included an independent, all-civilian complaint review board that was fully funded and staffed. To assure its independence, all civilians on that board should not be civilian NYPD employees or appointed by the mayor: "It also must have the power to determine the form of disciplinary action that should be taken." Cops who commit racist acts, including using racist slurs, should be "immediately subjected to disciplinary action, including suspension or dismissal." CLSJ called for the appointment of an independent special prosecutor to "investigate and prosecute criminality, incidents of police and racial violence." And it also called for the U.S. Department of Justice to monitor the NYPD because of "continuous unlawful violations of persons' civil rights, particularly people of color."[47]

The group 100 Blacks in Law Enforcement, established in 1995 and consisting of men and women throughout the field of law enforcement, also spoke to the City Council's committee on the torture of Louima and police brutality in New York. It claimed that police brutality was "rooted in the difficulty involved in controlling human behavior." Police departments recruit from a public that is "bombarded with negative stereotypes and racist views. Law enforcement had become more complex because of the difficulty of identifying those who harbor racist views: "Many of the citizens who possess these aggressive and racist views find themselves in a blue uniform with the responsibility of policing the same public they do not respect." A racist cop is not exposed until he commits an act of brutality. The problem cannot be addressed simply by discussing whether a sensitivity course should be required. The solution required a "successful marriage between community leaders and police personnel"—and police of color must be part of that endeavor.[48]

Among specific solutions, 100 Blacks in Law Enforcement called for identifying and monitoring precincts with high levels of police brutality allegations and officers who have a tendency toward abuse, and monitoring areas with a high percentage of arrests. The group also called for the creation of a specialized unit that would answer to the police commissioner and comprise high-ranking officers. The unit should have an investigatory component, including an Immediate Abuse Response Team that would maintain around the clock coverage. Further, the unit should keep a list of types of incidents that lead to complaints, respond to such incidents, and evaluate the climate at the scene. Each unit member should receive training in conflict resolution, community tensions, and precinct-level cultural concerns.

The Latino Officers Association, New York City, Inc. (LOA) also expressed its concerns to the City Council Committee. LOA represented 1,500 police officers, the majority of whom were Latino and African American. All police officers, the association said, should be required to "attend community meeting or events in the communities on a regular basis." This would permit police officers to "identify with the community they're providing services for and enable them to interact with the residents independent of peer pressure." The NYPD, LOA said, needed to allow officers to seek help for stress without penalizing them or destroying their careers. It should provide confidential services outside the department through a trust fund. Just as important, the NYPD "must move away from the traditional paramilitary approach and mentality." Police should adopt a "corporate, service-oriented approach to assist and provide services to our community residents."[49]

The LOA insisted that the department's racial makeup should reflect that of the city as a whole, yet 70 percent of the force was white while 60 percent of city residents were people of color: "A police force which is not reflective of the communities in which it serves resembles an 'army of occupation.'" The LOA also mentioned the issue of residency, saying that the NYPD should recruit officers from the city because nonresident cops "see themselves as having authority over the very lives of the people they are paid to protect and serve." Regarding the community, the group proposed allowing community "leaders input in assignment of police personnel," having an outside body to "investigate complaints with subpoena powers," and creating a hotline independent of the NYPD to take calls from the public.[50]

Labor also had a place at the table. Ray LaForest, staff representative for DC 1707 AFSCME, told the Public Safety Committee that the Abner Louima torture had sparked outrage and anguish among his union's members, the vast majority of whom were African American, Latino, and African Caribbean. He highlighted other cases of police assault against African Caribbean residents of Brooklyn: Haitian Clement Bien-Aime had his knee smashed so badly by a Seventieth Precinct cop that he was unable to walk; Patrick Antoine, also from Haiti, and who was arrested along with Louima, was beaten by the police as well; Shawn

Anderson Walters, of Trinidadian origins, claimed that on April 29 he was pulled over for not wearing a seatbelt by two cops who called him a "fucking nigger," then punched him in the eye, beat, and kicked him.[51]

Taking It to the Streets

In addition to sparking impassioned testimony before the Public Safety Committee, Abner Louima's torture helped to unleash a flurry of demonstrations. Few blacks had the opportunity to speak directly to the mayor or voice their outrage at City Council hearings, so they took to the streets in an attempt to pressure those with the power to effect change. For black activists, Abner Louima's fate was part of a long history of police abuse and violence against people of color—which they were well aware had intensified under Giuliani's more aggressive policing and indifference to the consequences. Louima's torture was simply additional proof that blacks and Latinos were under siege and that those in power were not going to take any serious action to halt police brutality. So people of African origins and Latinos joined with the religious community, labor groups, and others and organized to put pressure on the mayor and police department.

On August 17, just a week after Louima was arrested, Haitian activists in New York staged a massive demonstration in Brooklyn. Telling the press that they were "not satisfied with the way the mayor is handling the situation," John Alexis of Haitian Enforcement against Racism, a grassroots organization, marched with thousands of others from Club Rendez-Vous to the Seventieth Precinct on Lawrence Street.[52] Spectators along the route cheered the marchers who chanted, "Seven-oh, shut it down." Haitian demonstrators drew comparisons for the press between police repression in New York and in Haiti, where the Tonton Macoute, a special force created in 1959 by dictator François Duvalier, regularly captured and tortured people who opposed the leader.[53]

The Haitian American Alliance and the Haitian Enforcement against Racism also organized a protest at City Hall on August 29, with support from Haitian clergy and other groups.[54] A few days before that demonstration, Giuliani sent his only black deputy mayor, Rudy Washington, to the organizing committee in an effort to convince them to call it off. Speaking to the press after the demonstration, Tatiana Wah, chairperson of the Haitian American Alliance, accused Giuliani of ignoring the Haitian community.[55] Like so many other groups, the Haitian American Alliance—made up of about eighty professionals, including doctors, lawyers, accountants, and teachers—demanded that the mayor make the CCRB more effective by hiring additional investigators and staff, and granting it subpoena power and the right to hold officers in contempt. In addition, officers found guilty of brutality should be dismissed, denied their pensions, and not transferred to desk duty or simply denied vacation pay.[56]

Wah was among a group of younger leaders of New York's Haitian and Haitian American communities who were more invested in American politics and distinguished themselves from older, Haitian-born community leaders who were both more closely drawn to events in their native country. Wah and her peers advocated for an independent course for their community, and instead of turning for leadership to conventional organizations such as the NAACP or well-known protest leaders such as the Reverend Al Sharpton they insisted that people of Haitian decent were capable of articulating their own grievances and should, therefore, lead their own struggle.[57]

The August 29 "Day of Outrage" protestors gathered at Grand Army Plaza, near the main branch of the Brooklyn Public Library, and marched through downtown Flatbush and across the Brooklyn Bridge to City Hall to meet up with throngs of other protesters. The press reported that the demonstrators were overwhelmingly Haitian Americans, but flags from Trinidad and Tobago, Jamaica, and the Dominican Republic were also in evidence. Ten thousand protesters, the largest demonstration the city had seen in years, carried signs targeting the mayor—one read simply "Brutaliani"—and chanted, "Shame on you," among other things, to the police officers assigned to monitor the crowd. Many demonstrators carried toilet plungers as symbols of Louima's torture. While it was mostly a peaceful event, a number of demonstrators taunted and scuffled with the police and some blocked traffic. The NYPD reported arresting 110 people, some of whom claimed that officers had physically and verbally abused them. One protester told the press that the "police have too much authority" and were "overusing it."[58]

Giuliani was upset by the Day of Outrage, claiming that while he agreed with the call for justice, the demonstration sent another message that was "nasty and vicious."[59] At a press conference at City Hall, his focus was on praising the 2,500 officers assigned to the march "for their exceptional work": "They were in fact at various times provoked, and they didn't take the bait in any way, shape or form."[60]

Almost two years after Louima's arrest and torture, in late May 1999 Officer Volpe, age twenty-seven, pled guilty in federal district court to sodomizing Louima with a stick from a toilet plunger.[61] In December he was sentenced to thirty years and ordered to pay Louima $277,499 in restitution.[62] On June 8, 1999, Officer Schwarz was found guilty of violating Louima's civil rights. On March 6, 2000, Officers Weise and Bruder were convicted in federal court of conspiring to obstruct a federal investigation into the assault of Louima.[63] Schwarz, Weise, and Bruder appealed their sentences, and in February 2002 a federal appeals court overturned their convictions on the grounds that there was no evidence that they obstructed justice.[64] The only police officer who was punished for the Louima torture was Volpe.

After Schwarz's conviction, Giuliani praised the NYPD for "breaking down the appearance that there is some kind of reluctance on the part of police officers to testify against other police officers when they have knowledge of serious criminal conduct." The mayor was referring to detective Eric Turetzky and officer Mark Schofield, who testified during Schwarz's trial that they saw Schwarz walk Louima, handcuffed and with his pants down, into the restroom.[65] Giuliani's choice of words indicated that he remained in denial regarding the pervasiveness of police brutality, and his subsequent nonaction proved that he planned to do nothing to change his policies of over-policing black people.

Amadou Diallo

The ghastliest police brutality case during the Giuliani years took place in December 1999, and it would finally leave Giuliani no choice but to act to address police violence. Twenty-two-year-old West African immigrant Amadou Diallo was a Guinea national who was born in Sinoe County, Liberia, in 1975 and came to the United States in 1996 seeking a better life. Like many other African immigrants, he eked out a living as a street peddler in Lower Manhattan, selling items as diverse as videos, socks, gloves, and umbrellas. His goal was to earn a college degree and climb the ladder of economic success. However, on February 4, 1999, at about 12:40 a.m. he encountered four members of the NYPD's Street Crimes Unit (SCU).

Diallo had entered the vestibule of his Bronx apartment after a long workday and a late-night dinner when SCU officers Edward McMellon, Sean Carroll, Kenneth Boss, and Richard Murphy pulled up in a Ford Taurus. Giuliani had created the 138-officer SCU as a component of his Zero Tolerance policy, and its mission was to confiscate illegally held guns from New Yorkers. The SCU slogan, "We own the night," carried the message that the most dangerous individuals on the streets were not those breaking the law but members of the unit.[66]

The four officers who spotted Diallo in the vestibule claimed during their trial in February 2000 that he resembled a serial rapist they had been seeking for over a year and said they had identified themselves as police officers and demanded he put his hands in the air. When he reached into his pocket and pulled out what they thought was a gun, they fired forty-one shots, striking him nineteen times and killing him. During his opening statement, the attorney representing Officer Murphy said that when his client "looked into that vestibule and saw Mr. Diallo standing . . . with his left hand up and in his right hand . . . a black object, which he saw to be a gun, which he believed to be a gun, which he perceived to be a gun, he had that sick feeling in his stomach that he was about to be shot. And he reacted. He fired four times."[67] However, an eyewitness said that the cops did not identify themselves but simply opened fire. A police investigation found that Diallo did not have a gun and had simply pulled out his wallet. The four SCU officers took advantage of the controversial forty-eight-hour rule and refused to come forward and give their version of events. They were put on desk duty and not suspended. Soon thereafter a Bronx district attorney announced he would convene a grand jury.[68]

Giuliani asked the outraged public to be patient until he could uncover the facts.[69] He also claimed, falsely, that all four officers had "good records," failing to mention that three of them had previous complaints lodged against them. McMellon, Boss, and Carroll had shot suspects, and Boss had shot and killed an unarmed man in October 1997.[70]

Despite the mayor's plea for patience, protests erupted throughout the city. There was one on February 7 outside the murder scene where over one thousand protested, but the most intense demonstrations took place at the NYPD headquarters at 1 Police Plaza. The latter began in early March and were organized by the Reverend Al Sharpton, a long-time political activist from Brooklyn who has been in the forefront of a number of campaigns against police brutality. Sharpton declared on March 12 that "5 to 12" people a day were going to be arrested in front of 1 Police Plaza "because we want the world to see the city is willing to arrest nonviolent protesters but not willing to arrest police that would shoot an unarmed man 41 times."[71]

Sharpton managed to mobilize people across racial, class, and ideological lines to lead the largest protest in New York City history. The Diallo demonstrations started in early March with fifty protesters led by Sharpton; twelve were arrested, and Sharpton promised daily protests until the officers who shot Diallo were themselves arrested.[72] By mid-March, an average of two hundred demonstrators a day were arrested in front of 1 Police Plaza. By the twelfth day of the protest, 820 people had been arrested, far surpassing the previous record for civil disobedience arrests (seventy protesters during the two-week Downstate Medical Center campaign in 1963). By the last day of the Diallo demonstrations 1,200 people had been arrested.

Sharpton was able to articulate the collective outrage at the rain of police terror falling on New York City, and he was a primary reason for the success of the Diallo demonstrations. He characterized the city administration as uncaring, even when it was evident that the police had committed murder. He masterfully orchestrated events by placing high-profile celebrities and political figures in the front lines, fully aware that the arrest of notables such as actors Susan Sarandon, Ruby Dee, and Ossie Davis along with the Reverend Jesse Jackson would draw massive media attention.[73]

Sharpton and the National Action Network's success was largely due to their efforts to build a broad coalition across racial lines. Sharpton had created NAN in 1991 as a way to move from strictly street demonstrations to broader-based work that included lobbying, coalition building, and electoral politics. Claiming to be in the tradition of Martin Luther King in that it uses nonviolent methods, NAN asserts that it has brought into a national discussion on racial profiling "the continued battle for police accountability, coalescing Black and Brown to fight for immigrant rights and education and labor reform." The organization insists that it maintains strong platforms when it comes to law enforcement, election reform, prisoner rights, workers' rights, and a host of other social justice issues, but its biggest issue is police brutality. It was not unusual during the Diallo protest to see political figures and representatives from black, Latino, Asian American, and white communities together at a National Action Network meeting.[74]

Labor played a significant role in the Diallo protests. Dennis Rivera, president of the 150,000-member Local 1199, United Healthcare Workers East of Service Employees International Union, said many of his members were victims of police brutality in their communities. Members of the union made signs for the demonstrations and phoned their fellow asking them to join the demonstrations; the union also donated over $100,000 to the campaign.[75] Other unions and union leaders joining Local 1199 included the National Health and Human Services Workers / SEIU; Anna Burger of the SEIU International executive board; Lee Saunders, administrator of AFSSCME District 37; and the Association of Legal Aid Attorneys / UAW Local 2325.[76]

Students and faculty from the City University of New York (CUNY) also joined the movement, carrying signs that read "Books Not Bullets" and shouting "CUNY against police brutality!" One professor told the Baruch College student newspaper, "The Diallo case is a catalyst for change in city policy." Another faculty member called for the firing of police commissioner Howard Safir, and a third said Diallo could have been any typical CUNY student—a young, hardworking immigrant who was an avid reader.[77] Columbia University's Black Student Union, along with other Columbia student groups, held a memorial service for Diallo.[78]

One effect of the Diallo protests was to catapult Sharpton into a leadership position in the broader civil rights movement. In 1999 Sharpton met with president Bill Clinton and attorney general Janet Reno to discuss police brutality. That meeting would eventually lead to a presidential order instructing federal law enforcement agencies to gather data on the race, ethnicity, and gender of the people they question and arrest.[79]

After the Diallo killing and the wave of protests, Giuliani announced that from February 4 to March 24, 1999, the number of arrests by the Street Crimes Unit fell dramatically to 291 arrests, down from 705 during the same period a year earlier and 735 in 1996. Moreover, the number of stop, question, and frisk reports fell from 27,061 in 1998 to 3,502 in the ten weeks after the killing of Amadou Diallo.[80]

Under pressure from the protests, the NYPD decided to highlight its cultural sensitivity training for rookies, which had been in place before the Diallo killing. "Streetwise: Language, Culture, and Police Work in New York City," funded by the U.S. Department of Justice, provided new police officers with a manual that included common expressions in Spanish, Haitian Creole, Russian, and several Chinese dialects in an attempt to help them become more familiar with the city's diverse population.[81] The course, one of twenty-seven such courses nationwide, offered training in community-oriented policing and cultural diversity.[82]

Despite Giuliani's post-Louima task force and the NYPD's post-Diallo efforts at sensitivity training, the mayor took a beating in public opinion. Only 26 percent of those polled by the *Daily News* thought the mayor dealt fairly with blacks and Latinos.[83] According to the *New York Post*, in February 1998 the mayor's approval rating was 74 percent. However, fourteen months later a Quinnipiac University Poll noted that his approval rating had dropped to 40 percent. Although 89 percent of blacks disapproved of how Giuliani handled the Diallo incident, only 52 percent of white New Yorkers shared that feeling.[84]

The Dorismond Shooting

The Louima and Diallo incidents drew into sharper focus the mayor's intransigent position that police brutality was not a problem in the NYPD. The protests organized around those two cases raised awareness of the police tactics promoted by Giuliani's policies and the complaints from blacks and Latinos of the violence they faced at the hands of the police. But even though the Louima and Diallo cases wounded Giuliani politically, he still refused to back away from his aggressive policing campaign. The Patrick Dorismond case is a case in point.

On March 15, 2000, at about 12:30 a.m., twenty-six-year-old Patrick Dorismond, a security guard for a business improvement district at Pennsylvania Station and Madison Square Garden, was waiting for a cab in front of the Wakamba Lounge on Eighth Avenue near Thirty-Seventh Street in Manhattan when an undercover police officer attempted to engage him in a drug transaction. According to the cop, who was part of a drug crackdown effort that led to over eighteen thousand arrests, Dorismond was outraged by the attempt and attacked the officer. Anthony Vasquez, a twenty-nine-year-old detective who was also on the scene, came to the rescue of the undercover officer being beaten. According to Vasquez's attorney, when Dorismond attempted to go for his client's gun it went off, hitting Dorismond in the chest and killing the unarmed man.[85]

Dorismond's was the third shooting of an unarmed black man by the police in thirteen months, following Amadou Diallo in February 1999 and twenty-five-year old Malcolm Ferguson, shot in the Bronx while fleeing from police earlier in March 2000. Dorismond's death sparked citywide condemnation. His funeral at Holy Cross Catholic Church in Brooklyn drew a crowd of thousands that came out to pay homage and protest his killing. Giuliani and the NYPD claimed that a number of those in attendance were disruptive, and twenty-seven people were arrested. Eyewitnesses, including media sources, asserted that the police were beating people without provocation while yelling for the crowd to "leave the area or you will be subject to arrest." One of the people beaten was Errol Maitland, technical director and producer at New York's WBAI Radio. He was thrown to the ground, beaten, and arrested despite his attempts to let the police know he was a reporter on the scene. He audiotaped the arrest as it was happening, and on the recording one can hear him reporting that the police were saying "Fuck him up." Maitland was taken to the Coronary Care Unit at Kings County Hospital in serious condition.[86]

The mayor did not send his condolences to Dorismond's family. Instead, in an unprecedented and illegal move, he ordered the release of Dorismond's sealed juvenile arrest record. In an interview on the conservative news program *Fox News Sunday*, the mayor said, "People do act in conformity very often with their prior behavior." The media "would not want a picture presented of an altar boy, when in fact, maybe it isn't an altar boy, it's some other situation that may justify, more closely, what the police officer did."[87]

Dorismond's juvenile record showed that he had been arrested on charges of robbery, attempted robbery, assault in a driving dispute, and criminal possession of a weapon. Mark Green, public advocate and mayoral candidate in the 2001 election, petitioned the New York County Supreme Court requesting a summary judicial inquiry into the mayor's statements to the press and his decision to release Dorismond's juvenile records. Green claimed that the mayor violated section 1109 of the City Charter:

> A summary inquiry into any alleged violation or neglect of duty in rela-
> tion to the property, government, or affairs of the City may be conducted
> under an order to be made by any justice of the supreme court in the
> first, second, or eleventh judicial district on application of the mayor, the
> comptroller, the public advocate, any five council members the commis-
> sioner of investigation, or any five citizens who are taxpayers supported
> by affidavit to the effort that one or more officers employees or other per-
> sons therein named have knowledge or information concerning such al-
> leged violation or neglect of duty.[88]

Dorismond's juvenile's criminal record had been sealed pursuant to the criminal procedure law and the Family Court Act, and the mayor, Green asserted, did not have the legal authority to release it. The inquiry that Green sought would reveal how Giuliani got a hold of the sealed record, how he illegally released it to the public, and how the release was in violation of sections 166 and 375-1 of the Family Court Act and section 1109 of the City Charter.[89]

Giuliani did not bother to submit an affidavit responding to the allegations in Green's petition. Instead, he sought dismissal of Green's petition, arguing that the sealing requirement of juvenile records under the Family Court Act and criminal procedure law did not apply to deceased persons. He also claimed that an inquiry went beyond the scope of section 1109 because that law only dealt with corruption and misapplication of city funds. However, writing the opinion of the court, judge Louise Gruner Gans asserted that section 1109 did not just apply to misapplication of funds and corruption but also gave a number of city officials, including the public advocate, the right to seek a summary inquiry into "any violation of the provisions of law."

Green was not on a freewheeling expedition. He wanted to know whether, for each "disclosure, was the information obtained from records of the New York City Family Court, the New York Criminal Court, the New York City Police Department, the New York City Probation Department and/or files of the State Division of Criminal Justice Services?" If so, had these records been sealed by court order or by operation of statute or both? Just as important, was the "Mayor's disclosure of information from sealed records a violation of court orders and/or statutes?" The court granted Green his application for a summary inquiry.[90]

In the summer of 2000, a Manhattan grand jury refused to indict officer Anthony Vasquez, declaring that Dorismond's shooting was an accident.[91] In the early spring of 2003, the city settled a wrongful death lawsuit with Dorismond's family for $2.25 million. However, the city's attorneys refused to admit guilt in his death, saying that "the City continues to feel deep sympathy for the Dorismond family on the accidental death of their son and father."[92]

Even in his last year in office, Giuliani refused to address police brutality in any serious way. The mayor's management report for fiscal year 2001 did not indicate any change of direction when it came to policing. When discussing the NYPD, Giuliani's report declared that the "Police Department's mission is to reduce crime, disorder, and the fear that these problems generate throughout the City." Under the category of police goals and objectives, the report listed the following: "Reduce the occurrence of felony crimes, murder, rape, robbery, burglary, felonious assault, grand larceny, and grand larceny motor vehicle"; "enforcement against felony and misdemeanor drug crimes and quality of life offenses"; reducing illegal gang activity; and reducing crime in schools.[93]

Conclusion

Despite the mayor's continued emphasis on fighting crime, the massive social protest movement that erupted after the Louima, Diallo, and Dorismond atrocities eventually forced him and the NYPD to take action. Even as early as 1997 Giuliani had begun to increase the CCRB's budget.[94] By 2000 the protests forced him to take steps to reduce the tension between the police and the city's black and brown people. Under the heading "Courtesy, Professionalism, Respect, Strategy," the mayor's management report noted that the State Regional Community Policing Institute's "Streetwise" program had expanded cultural diversity training for recent New York City police academy graduates and field training supervisors. Although there was no detailed description, the report claimed that they had developed a curriculum that covered Chinese, Spanish, Russian, Haitian, African, and African Caribbean cultures. It soon would add Indian, Bangladeshi, and other South Asian cultures to the mix. According to the mayor's report, "Between October 23 and November and 17, 2000, over 2,300 police officers from the March and October 2000 police academy classes received 'Streetwise' training."[95]

To help promote such measures, the NYPD received in the summer of 2000 a Cultural Awareness and Diversity Training Program grant from the Bureau of Justice Assistance. Moreover, the police department was working with the Citizens Committee for New York City to develop interactive workshops for youth and police officers: "A Police/Youth Team Building Workshop was piloted in Washington Heights in Manhattan between October and December 2000, involving officers from the local precincts and neighborhood youth group, the Fresh Youth Initiative." The purpose of the program was to foster good relationships between the police and young people. In February and March of 2001 the program was expanded to include the Crown Heights Youth Collective and officers from the Seventy-First Precinct.[96]

By 2001 the Giuliani administration had made commanding officers responsible for "establishing and maintaining positive relationships with the community they serve." To this end, commanders had to be involved in outreach efforts and communications with "members of the community." Also by 2001, as part of the CompStat process, to assure accountability all commanding officers had to submit reports on their efforts to improve community relations. That same year, the NYPD also developed its Community Relations Protocol to improve information sharing between the police and community leaders and organizations, requiring the police share such information in a timely matter.[97]

These attempts at improving relationships with the black and Latino communities on the part of Giuliani and the NYPD demonstrated the impact of the mass demonstrations, but they fell short of addressing police brutality. In fact, police brutality was not even mentioned in the mayor's management report. At the heart of Giuliani's efforts to improve police and community relations was better crime fighting. This is not to say that making officers more aware of the cultures of the racially, ethically, religiously, and sexually diverse communities they served was not beneficial to the police and those communities. Better understanding and improved communication are valid steps in a campaign to better relations between the police and black and Latino communities. But these efforts alone fell short of addressing a police culture that tolerated, maybe even promoted, violent physical attacks on citizens.

10

The Campaign to End Stop, Question, and Frisk

Four years before Mayor Giuliani made even token efforts in the direction of improving police–community relations, public advocate Mark Green made several well-thought-out recommendations on that and other matters pertaining to police misconduct in his September 11, 1997, testimony before the Public Safety Committee of the City Council, which was exploring solutions to police violence. Green strongly recommended that the CCRB create a subcommittee to hold community forums at which the community and police officers could meet to discuss how to get along. According to Green, the mayor and NYPD could empower precinct councils and community-based organizations to gather the participants together, and "every officer in the precinct—not just the commander or the community affairs officers—would be required to attend one or more of these meetings a year." Green maintained that such a meeting would be a form of community policing that allowed police and communities to work in a partnership. He also pointed out that Giuliani had abandoned community policing, labeling it "social work."[1]

Giuliani's 2001 effort to promote better police–community relations required only commanders to participate in any meaningful way. Green's plan required that all officers in the community to take part. Although attending a meeting a minimum of once a year, as Green suggested, was not substantive enough to lead to any change in attitude, it did provide members of communities throughout the city an opportunity to have direct contact with those who patrolled their neighborhoods so they could express their grievances and concerns about how these individuals were functioning in their communities. Moreover, Green's proposal could provide community leaders and organizations an opportunity to help set the agenda at community meetings.

Green also recommended that the NYPD should track civilian complaint trends, in order to help identify police officers who needed "retraining or should be dismissed." If tracking had been implemented, he said, officer Francis Livoti, the killer of Anthony Baez (discussed in chapter 11), would have been off the force. He also informed the council that state law might have to be changed in order to allow the NYPD to discipline those who have a pattern of abusive action, "even if some of those activities may have occurred beyond the [contractual] 18-month statute of limitations."[2]

Calling for "swift and certain punishment" of police who take part in acts of misconduct, Green said, "The potential sanctions for abusive or brutal police officers must be expanded and clearly set forth in the City Administration Code. The police need to have clear sentencing guidelines for misconduct." In addition, he called for reforming the CCRB or creating a new civilian oversight body, one that "should have jurisdiction over all forms of police abuse, including both brutality and corruption." It must be independent in order to ensure public confidence, and "it should be structured and staffed so that its recommendations, both as to individual cases and recommendations for systemic change, are highly likely to be adopted."[3]

Implementing Green's far-reaching recommendations would have been an important step toward providing citizens with some power to curtail police abuse; but there was no hope for that plan under Giuliani. The mayor's successor, Michael Bloomberg, was far more interested than Giuliani was in easing racial tension in the city, but he embraced a "stop, question, and frisk" policy that targeted mainly blacks and Latinos, which did nothing to improve relations between the police and citizens of color. The NYPD's ongoing racial targeting of blacks and Latinos led to a fierce community-based campaign to end the stop, question, and frisk policy. Organized by civil rights and civil liberties organizations, community activists, and victims of the policy, the campaign led to one of the greatest victories in the struggle to end police abuse of people of color.

Stop, Question, and Frisk

In January 2002 the newly elected mayor, Michael Bloomberg, selected Raymond Kelly as his police commissioner, a post Kelly had held under mayor David Dinkins as well. In April 2002 Kelly announced that he was dismantling the Street Crimes Unit and that four hundred officers would be transferred to either precinct detective squads or plainclothes anti-crime teams. Even before Giuliani left office in January 2002, he had cut the Street Crimes Unit by half in response to the Diallo killing. Although Kelly insisted that disbanding the SCU was not due to any particular case, an attorney for the Diallo family, which had filed a $1 million wrongful death suit against the NYPD, called it an admission that the SCU disproportionally targeted blacks and Latinos. Attorney Anthony Gair, who had also filed an $81 million wrongful death suit against the city, told the *New York Daily News* that the Diallo shooting "constitutes an admission on the part of the New York City Police Department that the street crime unit was out of control and was stopping individuals, predominantly African Americans, with nothing even approaching reasonable suspicion."[4] The unit had become notorious for stopping innocent young black men—in December 1999, for example, for every sixteen African Americans stopped there was one arrest.[5] As a result, the Center for Constitutional Rights filed a class action lawsuit against the SCU in 1999.[6]

Kelly's dismantling of the SCU signaled a new direction in policing in the city and, by extension, a new direction in community relations. He and Bloomberg even reversed Giuliani's policy of not meeting with the Reverend Al Sharpton at City Hall (Giuliani had claimed that doing so would signal recognition of Sharpton as a legitimate civil rights leader). Bloomberg said he was willing to meet with "anybody" who was a community leader. In 2002 he spoke at the Harlem headquarters of Sharpton's National Action Network during the Reverend Martin Luther King Jr. Day celebration—an event sponsored by Sharpton's organization which Giuliani had never attended.[7]

Bloomberg's response when police officers unleashed a hail of bullets at Sean Bell on his wedding day, killing the twenty-six-year-old as he and two friends sat in their car, also set him apart from Giuliani. Bloomberg publicly stated that it seemed to him that that "excessive force was used." Bloomberg told a group of black ministers and black elected officials at a City Hall meeting he organized to quell racial tensions, "I can tell you that it is to me unacceptable or inexplicable how you can have 50-odd shots fired."[8] In response, the right-wing publication *American Spectator* accused the mayor of "going out of his way to condemn the cops."[9]

Despite attempts to improve race relations in the city, the Civilian Complaint Review Board noted a disturbing trend in its annual report for January–December 2002: 50 percent of the substantiated complaints concerned young black men, even though blacks made up just 25 percent of the city's population. The disproportionate number of verified complaints made by blacks was unique; by way of contrast, 26 percent of substantiated complaints were filed by Latinos, which reflected their overall population ratio.[10] In the CCRB status report for 2003, its chair, Hector Gonzalez, pointed out that the agency had not been able to keep up with the growing number of complaints, and it had no explanation for the 36 percent increase in complaints since 2002. The "dramatic complaint increase" was a disturbing trend, Gonzalez declared, and noted that through the "first third of 2004, complaints rose 18 percent in comparison to the same period in 2003." Despite the increases, "the number of investigators the CCRB is authorized to hire has remained static."[11]

By the end of 2005, the CCRB had witnessed five consecutive years of increasing numbers of complaints. One explanation was that beginning in 2001 people could call in a complaint by dialing 311. In particular, the number of complaints resulting from police abuse of Stop, Question, and Frisk program had "risen at rates higher than complaints in which force, discourtesy, or offensive language allegations are lodged." It is difficult to pinpoint a date when New York City began the policy of stopping and questioning people they suspected of crime. However, retired police captain Ernie Naspretto recalled that it was not until the 1990s, with the creation of CompStat, that Stop, Question, and Frisk was extensively used by the NYPD. The police department "also began to keep meticulous track of such stops through paperwork that was alien to us back in the day. Although the procedure had been on the books since the beginning of time, it was now embraced like a child holding a new toy on Christmas morning."[12] In 2005, abuse of authority allegations made up more than half of all allegations lodged with the CCRB.[13] So, despite Bloomberg's public stance, which was far less hostile than Giuliani's, and despite the fact that he sought collaboration with civil rights leaders like Al Sharpton, his advocacy of stop, question, and frisk opened a new door for widespread police abuse of blacks and Latinos.

By the late 1960s stop, question, and frisk had become one of the techniques used in large cities to fight crime. It was challenged all the way up to the Supreme Court, which ruled in 1968, in *Terry v. Ohio*, that a police offer has the right to stop, question, and frisk a suspect if the officer has reason to suspect the person is or has been involved in a criminal offense—that is, if there is a "reasonable suspicion of criminality." Stop, question, and frisk was not a violation of the Fourth Amendment, the court ruled, because stopping is not an arrest and frisking is not a search.[14] When he was head of the New York City Transit Police, William Bratton was already using stop and frisk tactics. When Giuliani picked him as police commissioner, Bratton noted that under CompStat, precinct commanders use a number of strategies to fight the various types of crime affecting their area, including stop, question, and frisk, and on a number of occasions Bratton would refer to the policy as an essential crime-fighting tool.[15]

But under Bloomberg and Commissioner Kelly, both of whom served from 2002 to 2013, stop, question, and frisk was elevated from being one of many tactics to the city's primary approach. The New York Civil Liberties Union analyzed 2002–11 data gathered by the NYPD on the number of stops officers made. In 2002, 97,296 people were stopped, questioned, and frisked. Nearly 82 percent (80,176) were innocent of any crime. The following year the number jumped to 160,851, 87 percent (140,442) of whom were innocent of any crime. In 2004, there were 313,523 individuals stopped, 89 percent (278,033) of whom were innocent; and in 2005, 398,191 were stopped and 352,348, or 89 percent, were innocent. The peak was reached in 2011 with 685,724 stops, 88 percent of which turned up innocent citizens.[16]

Both black and Latino communities were targeted by the NYPD under stop, question, and frisk, and therefore made up the great majority of those stopped. In 2004, 54 percent (77,704) of those stopped were black and 31 percent (44,581) were Latino. Only 12 percent (17,638) were white. The overwhelming majority (83,937) were between the ages of fourteen and twenty-five. The racial percentages were similar for other years. From 2004 to 2015, 53 to 55 percent of those stopped were black, and the percentage of Latinos stopped ranged from 27 percent to 34 percent. From 2003 to 2015 the percentage of whites stopped ranged from 9 percent to 12 percent.[17]

Under this policy, officers could stop anyone walking on the street, then interrogate and search them based simply on an officer's suspicion that they might be in violation of the law. The targeted citizens had no recourse, especially given Commissioner Kelly's insistence that officers were not racially profiling. Speaking before the City Council on January 24, 2007, Kelly asserted, "Officers are stopping people they reasonably suspect of committing a crime, based on descriptions and circumstances and not on personal bias."[18]

Soon after the Amadou Diallo incident, and years before the NYCLU compiled its statistics on the practice, state attorney general Eliot Spitzer launched an investigation into New York City's use of stop, question, and frisk in response to "concerns about the . . . tactics upon minority communities and individuals in New York City." At a hearing in January 1999, most of the complaints the attorney general heard were not about the sensational cases of police brutality but "revolved around lower-level police involvement in the everyday lives of minority residents." The investigation looked at 175,000 UF-250 forms, which officers were required to complete for every stop, filed between January 1, 1998, and March 31, 1999. The forms revealed figures that stayed relatively static into the next decade. Whites made up 43.4 percent of the population and accounted for 12.9 percent of the stops. The figures for the Street Crimes Unit, however, were more dramatic: "Blacks comprised 62.7 percent of all persons 'stopped' by the NYPD's Street Crime Unit."[19]

The attorney general's investigation also revealed that in neighborhoods where blacks and Latinos made up less than 10 percent of the population, blacks accounted for 30 percent and Latinos 23 percent of those stopped. Blacks "were 'stopped' 2.1 times more than whites on suspicion of committing a violent crime and 2.4 times more often than whites on suspicion of carrying a weapon." Latinos "were 'stopped' 1.7 times more often than whites on suspicion of committing a violent crime and 2.0 times more often than whites on suspicion of carrying a weapon."[20]

Building a Movement: Richie Pérez and the National Congress for Puerto Rican Rights

One of the fiercest challenges to police brutality and stop, question, and frisk emerged when Richie Pérez of the National Congress of Puerto Rican Rights contacted the Center for Constitutional Rights. Pérez was born in the South Bronx, where he attended the public schools and then earned a bachelor's degree from the City University of New York and a master's degree in business economics from New York University. He also completed course work for a PhD in bilingual education. Pérez taught at Monroe High School and at Hunter College, Brooklyn College, and the College of New Rochelle, where he offered courses on the civil rights and labor movements, the Puerto Rican urban experience, and social policy. He became politically active during the "community control" struggle of the late 1960s when he joined the Young Lords, a revolutionary group of mainly Puerto Ricans who modeled themselves after the Black Panther Party.[21]

Pérez was also a key member of the Black and Latino Coalition against Police Brutality, formed in Brooklyn after the killing of twenty-nine-year-old Luis Baez by police in August 1979. The police claimed that Baez, who was mentally disturbed, lunged at them with a pair of scissors so they had no choice but to shoot him twenty-one times. Demonstrations erupted in Brooklyn to demand the arrest of the five officers involved in the shooting, but a grand jury decided not to bring charges. After that decision, the Rev. Herbert Daughtry of the Black United Front joined with Latino activists from Brooklyn College to form the Black and Latino Coalition. Its goal was to educate black and Latino communities on police brutality and "to build a mechanism against this rising brutality." The coalition organized demonstrations in Bedford-Stuyvesant and set up a hotline for people to report police brutality cases.[22]

Pérez was also a founding member of the National Congress for Puerto Rican Rights (NCPRR), a "mass base" civil rights organization attempting to end racial discrimination against Puerto Ricans by employing several strategies, including direct action and electoral politics. The NCPRR's goal was to pull people of different political bents under one umbrella; as Pérez put it, "Everyone has something to contribute to the liberation movement." To keep from alienating moderates and thus help to build a broader movement, issues such as independence for Puerto Rico, which is in the group's platform, were not highlighted. Since the NCPRR's founding, Pérez's focus remained on the issues of police brutality and racially motivated violence against blacks and Latinos.[23] The New York City chapter of the NCPPR formed a Justice Committee in the late 1980s with the objectives of documenting police brutality incidents, giving support to victims and their families, and establishing a network of private lawyers to provide free or discounted legal assistance.[24]

The Anthony Baez incident of 1994 provides an example of the organizing skills Pérez and the NCPRR employed to address police brutality against people of color. They reached out to Iris Baez, Anthony's mother, to offer support, and when she realized that no help would come from conventional sources to obtain justice for her son's death, she and the Baez family turned to Pérez and the NCPPR, which put them in contact with other families that had similarly lost loved ones so they would not feel isolated. The Justice Committee then built a coalition movement in which Iris Baez became a champion against police brutality. Her outspokenness attracted others to the campaign, and the Justice Committee's coalition eventually comprised groups as diverse as Latino youth gang / youth group members who had been harassed by police officers along with construction workers from East Harlem.[25]

In March 1995 officer Francis Livoti was indicted by a grand jury on charges of criminally negligent homicide in the death of Anthony Baez. In a 1996 speech, Pérez characterized the indictment as a major victory because cops are so rarely indicted for killing blacks and Latinos. In an effort to ensure Livoti's conviction, the NCPPR reached out to community organizations to "pressure the criminal justice system into responding with a guilty verdict." One NCPRR tactic was what it labeled "Adopt a Day in Court," which urged schools to send at least five teachers and guardians with at least fifteen students to observe the court sessions. The thinking was that since students were the major victims of the quality of life measures, they would be more than willing to go to court to show their support for the Baez family and, just as important, demonstrate their outrage at police brutality.[26]

However, in September 1995, before the court could convene, acting justice Gerald Sheindlin of the New York State Supreme Court division in the Bronx dismissed the case on the grounds that the district attorney's office had submitted papers with the wrong charges.[27] The Baez family then organized the Committee to Remember Anthony Baez to continue the legal battle.[28] The NCPPR led a sit-in demonstration at the Bronx district attorney's office to pressure on him to reindict Livoti and invited a number of journalists to record the civil disobedience campaign, which involved twelve people, including Iris Baez and other mothers who had lost children to the police. Apparently deciding that images of Iris Baez in handcuffs protesting his office's clerical error would be bad PR, the DA reindicted Livoti in December 1995. His trial got underway in September 1996 in New York State Criminal Court in the Bronx.[29]

Staying true to its mission, the NCPPR kept the community informed by launching a "Justice for Anthony Baez" campaign and publishing *Justicia*, a daily report providing a detailed account of the actions of both the prosecution and the defense, including opening statements, motions, and the testimony and examination of witnesses.[30] Judge Gerald Sheindlin acquitted Livoti, who had waived his right to a jury trial, ruling that the prosecution had not proved its case. Mayor Giuliani's response was to say that although he sympathized with the family, the verdict was a "well-thought-out, legally reasoned opinion."[31]

Not giving up hope, the Baez family and their lawyers pressed for the federal government to hear the case,[32] which it did nearly two years later, in the summer of 1998, bringing charges against Livoti for violating the civil rights of Anthony Baez. In a two-week trial in the U.S. Court of Appeal of the Southern District of New York, Livoti was convicted[33] and later sentenced by judge Shira Scheindlin of the U.S. Circuit Court of the Southern District of New York to seven and a half years in prison.[34]

Pérez maintained that the Anthony Baez case had to be seen in the context of Giuliani's policing policies. It was connected to Zero Tolerance, under which, "anything goes, the police . . . will be supported . . . no matter what attitude." Giuliani's policies were criminalizing even children of color, he stressed, "and now we had to worry about police officers who view our kids as criminals." The community's reaction to the killings of Anthony Baez and other people of color was due in large part, Pérez maintained, to the daily humiliation they faced at being stopped, questioned, and frisked, and the black and Latino communities could not "have the stopping and frisking of everyone, because that's against the law."[35] The killing of Amadou Diallo triggered a burst of activism and mass actions that Pérez felt strongly would increase policy makers' willingness to address the grievances of the black and Latino communities, and soon the NCPPR advanced the next phase of its struggle by suing the City, accusing the Street Crimes Unit of widespread racial profiling when it came to stop, question, and frisk.[36]

Pérez and the NCPRR convinced the Center for Constitutional Rights (CCR) to take on the legal challenge. Founded in 1966 by lawyers who represented civil rights activists and organizations in the South, the center is dedicated to protecting both rights guaranteed by the U.S. Constitution and those listed in the UN Declaration of Human Rights. Some its goals include "litigation, education, and advocacy" to "empower poor communities and communities of color" and "to guarantee the rights of those with the fewest protections and least access to legal resources and to strengthen the broader movement for social justice."[37]

In 1999 the CCR filed suit in the United States District Court, Second Circuit, on behalf of Kelvin Daniels, Poseidon Baskin, Djibril Toure, Hector Rivera, Raymond Ramirez, Kahil Shkymba, Bryan Stair, Tiara Bonner, Theron McConneyhead, and Horace Rogers. The plaintiffs accused all the members of the Street Crimes Unit, Mayor Giuliani, and Police Commissioner Safir of violating the Fourth Amendment of the U.S. Constitution, which protects against unreasonable search and seizure, and the Equal Protection Clause of the Fourteenth Amendment, which outlaws racial discrimination, when they were stopped and frisked by the SCU. They sought damages and a judgment asserting that the SCU's operation was unconstitutional.[38]

The city attempted to have the case dismissed, claiming that the plaintiffs lacked standing to sue for equitable relief unless they claimed they faced threat of future inquiry from stop, question, and frisk. However, the district court denied the motion and also refused to dismiss the plaintiffs' claim that their right to equal treatment under the Fourteenth Amendment had been violated. The court ruled that the SCU had a policy of stopping, questioning, and frisking individuals "solely based on [their] race." The NYPD decided to disband the SCU while the case was being litigated. After reviewing thousands of cases and completing depositions by a number of high-ranking NYPD officials, the CCR eventually forced the city to settle.[39] Judge Shira Scheindlin, who was overseeing the case, approved the settlement agreement in December 2003.

Under the agreement, the city was required to maintain an anti–racial profiling policy that complied with the United States and New York State constitutions. The city also had to audit all cops who carried out the stop, question, and frisk policy and their supervisors in order to determine if the stops were based on reasonable suspicion and to what extent they were being documented. The results of the audits were to be provided to the CCR quarterly. The NYPD also had to take part in educating the public by holding public meetings on its racial profiling policy and operating workshops at fifty city high schools on the legal rights of those stopped, questioned, and frisked. It also had to create informational handouts on stop, question, and frisk to be distributed at the workshop and other events.[40]

Not only did the city ignore the terms of the settlement in the *Daniels et al.* case, it dramatically increased the number of stop, question, and frisk incidents. In response, on January 31, 2008, the Center for Constitutional Rights filed a second federal class action lawsuit, again accusing the city and NYPD of racial profiling. The plaintiffs—David Floyd, David Ourlicht, Latit Clarkson, and Deon Dennis—were representing the "thousands of primarily Black and Latino New Yorkers who have been stopped without any cause on the way to work or home from school, in front of their house, or just walking down the street."[41]

In addition to *Floyd et al. v. City of New York et al.*, in January 2010 the City also faced a suit filed by the NAACP Legal Defense Fund on behalf of residents of and visitors to New York City housing developments who were stopped, questioned, and frisked and charged with criminal trespass without ample evidence for the arrests. *Davis et al. v. the City of New York et al.*, a class action suit against the city, the New York City Housing Authority, and the NYPD, charged that the police were racially profiling because a disproportionate number of arrests were of blacks and Latinos. According to the suit, the NYPD used a "vertical patrol" to sweep the hallways, stairways, rooftops, and elevators and "indiscriminately stop and question every person they observe, without objective individualized suspicion of a crime, and unlawfully arrest individuals for trespass without probable cause." The number of arrests dramatically increased because of these practices, which the lawsuit alleged that the city and housing authority "implement and apply . . . in an intentionally and discriminatory and race-based manner by focusing the patrols and trespass arrest practices entirely on communities of color, such as NYCHA residences, where historically entrenched racial segregation ensures that African Americans and Latinos will bear the brunt of Defendants' unlawful actions."[42]

All thirty-six plaintiffs were African Americans and Latinos who either lived in New York City Housing Authority buildings and were arrested or subjected to unlawful stops and searches, or were visitors or guests subjected to the same treatment. For example, after plaintiff William Turner left the apartment of his friend, plaintiff Kelson Davis, he was approached by four officers when exiting the elevator. They told him to produce identification and state why he was in the building. He complied but was still arrested for trespassing. None of the officers contacted Davis to verify Turner's story.[43] In another example, plaintiffs Roman Jackson and Kirstin Johnson, who were friends, were approached outside of Jackson's apartment by the police, who asked their purpose for being there and demanded identification. Johnson produced her identification, and Jackson asked the police to allow him to go to his apartment to retrieve some form of ID. The police refused and arrested both Jackson and Johnson.[44]

An additional challenge to the stop, question, and frisk policy came in March 2012, when the New York Civil Liberties Union represented twelve African American and Latino New Yorkers in a class action suit in the United States District Court of the Southern District of New York against New York City, Commissioner Kelly, and a number of NYPD officers. *Jaenean Ligon et al. v. the City of New York et al.* accused the NYPD of violating the Fourth Amendment by stopping, frisking, and arresting citizens for trespassing near buildings that had been enrolled by their landlords in the Trespass Affidavit Program (TAP). TAP, formerly known as Operation Clean Halls, was launched by the city in an attempt to fight crime in and around residential buildings. However, residents complained that the police were targeting blacks and Latinos for TAP stops: "Each year this program results in thousands of illegal stops, searches, summonses, and arrests of those buildings' residents and their invited guests without cause."[45]

The NYCLU argued that residents leaving their apartments experienced stops, interrogations, and searches by cops in vestibules, stairways, hallways, lobbies, and exterior courtyards as well as on public sidewalks outside their building. In some cases, the stops led to summonses or arrests if the person could not justify his or her presence in the building to the satisfaction of the police. To avoid arrest, residents were forced to carry identification when exiting their apartments, as they were "frequently stopped and forced to produce identification while engaged in completely innocuous activities like checking their mail or taking out their garbage." The NYCLU suit also accused the NYPD of conducting hundreds of thousands of vertical patrols annually. "Residents of some Clean Halls Buildings," the NYCLU claimed, "are stopped, questioned, and searched by NYPD officers on a regular basis—sometimes multiple times a week. For many young men of color in particular, being searched and seized by NYPD officers in and around their homes has become normalized and is simply a routine part of their lives."[46]

The buildings in the Operation Clean Halls program housed residents of many races, but blacks and Latinos were the targets of the stops, the suit charged. The NYPD did not bother to determine if a building in the program had "substantial or sustained criminal activity," and the ACLU claimed the police could not justify the disproportionate number of stops of blacks and Latinos.[47]

Jaenean Ligon, the lead plaintiff, was a forty-year-old African American women who argued that she and her three sons were frequently stopped, questioned, and searched in or near her residence without cause. She described one terrifying incident when her son was returning from the store after purchasing a bottle of ketchup and was stopped by four police officers. Even though he told them he lived in the building and produced identification, the cops insisted that his mother come to the vestibule to identify her son. When she arrived and saw her son surrounded by four cops, she collapsed. One cop responded by laughing. Other plaintiffs also provided the court with numerous similar stories of unconstitutional stops, searches, and arrests.[48]

On September 24, 2013, the plaintiffs filed a motion requesting a preliminary injunction to halt trespass stops at enrolled buildings in the Bronx.[49] U.S. Circuit Court judge Shira Scheindlin, who heard the case, argued that the "plaintiffs offered more than enough evidence at the hearing to support the conclusion that they have shown a clear likelihood of proving at trial that the NYPD has a practice of making of unlawful trespass stops outside of TAP buildings in the Bronx." Scheindlin ordered the NYPD to stop conducting trespass stops at that site and also to "develop and adopt a formal written policy specifying the limited circumstances in which it is legally permissible to stop a person outside a TAP building on a suspicion of trespass." Such stops must not violate the Fourth Amendment of the U.S. Constitution. A draft of the written policy had to be submitted to Judge Scheindlin. Moreover, she ordered the city to assure that UF-250 forms were completed for every trespass stop and to implement a review system.[50] The NYPD was required to set up a training program and issue training materials to conform to the court's opinion. The city agreed to be observed by a court-appointed monitor.[51] These court orders were what the plaintiffs had hoped for when filing for the injunction in the first place.

While *Ligon et al.* was narrowly focused on TAP, *Floyd et al.* directly addressed stop, question, and frisk, and on August 12, 2013, the U.S. District Court of the Southern District of New York issued its findings in that latter case: the NYPD did practice racial profiling, and the practice was unconstitutional. Judge Shira Scheindlin, writing for the court, noted that between January 2004 and June 2012, the NYPD had stopped 4.4 million people, over 80 percent of whom were black or Latino: "In each of these stops a person's life was interrupted. The person was detained and questioned, often on a public street. More than half of the time the police subjected the person to a frisk." One of the most important pieces of evidence that targeted blacks was the fact that between 2004 and 2009, 30 percent more blacks were arrested than whites who were suspected of having committed the same crimes. In her opinion, Judge Scheindlin wrote that her duty was not to judge stop, question, and frisk's effectiveness as a police tool; her job was to rule on its constitutionality. The plaintiffs in *Floyd et al.* claimed that they were stopped by police without reasonable cause, violating the Fourth Amendment, and also because of their race, violating the Fourteenth Amendment. According to the judge, "Each stop is a demeaning and humiliating experience. No one should live in fear of being stopped whenever he leaves his home to go about the daily activities of daily life. Those who are routinely subjected to stops are overwhelmingly people of color, and they are justifiably troubled to be singled out when many of them have done nothing to attract the unwarranted attention."[52]

A major rationale for the stop, question, and frisk policy was that it removed illegal guns from the streets. But Judge Scheindlin noted that in the 4.4 million stops between 2004 and 2012, a "weapon was found after 1.5 percent of those frisks." Only 6 percent of those stops led to an arrest, and 6 percent resulted in a summons; 88 percent of the 4.4 million people stopped were innocent. Almost a quarter of the stops of blacks (23 percent) and Latinos (24 percent) resulted in the use of force. Between 2004 and 2009, incidents in which the officer failed to note a specific suspected crime that triggered the stop increased from 1 percent to 36 percent.[53]

The judge rejected the city's argument that the number of blacks and Latinos stopped was high because it was proportional to the number of blacks and Latinos who commit crimes. The judge characterized that reasoning as "flawed because the stopped population was overwhelmingly innocent—not criminal. There is no basis for assuming that an innocent population shares the same characteristics as the criminal suspect population in the same area."[54]

Judge Scheindlin concluded that the "City is liable for violating plaintiffs' Fourth and Fourteenth Amendment rights. The City acted with deliberate indifference toward the NYPD's practice of making unconstitutional stops and conducting unconstitutional frisks." She also ruled that the city "adopted a policy of indirect racial profiling by targeting racially defined groups for stops based on local crime suspect data. This has resulted in the disproportionate and discriminatory stopping of blacks and Hispanics in violation of the Equal Protection Clause." In addition, the "City's highest officials turned a blind eye to the evidence that officers are conducting stops in a racially discriminatory manner." City officials were so convinced that the policy was effective, they were willing to ignore "overwhelming proof that the policy" of targeting who they thought were the "right people" was racially discriminatory and a violation of the Constitution.[55]

The court ruled that a stop can only be made when there is "reasonable suspicion that criminal activity may be afoot," in compliance with the Fourth Amendment. A stop cannot be made on a hunch; rather, the police must be able to "point to specific and articulable facts which, taken together with rational inferences from those facts, reasonably warrant intrusion" on a person's constitutional rights. The court maintained that a "reasonable suspicion standard" was objective and not based on a police officer's subjective intentions. According to the judge, "There is no exception for stops of pedestrians for the general purpose of controlling crime."[56]

Scheindlin also accused city officials of ignoring the fact that they were violating the Fourth Amendment despite their having been made aware of the violation as early as 1999. Instead of addressing the problem, the city had escalated "policies and practices" that led to a greater number of arrests. It also hindered the collection of the necessary data concerning the constitutionality of the stops.[57] Furthermore, the NYPD leadership ignored the fact that better training was needed for those conducting stops. The NYPD's practice of targeting the "right people" to stop constituted "indirect racial profiling," the judge ruled, because "officers are directed, sometimes expressly, to target certain racially defined groups for stops"—a clear violation of the Fourteenth Amendment. The department directed cops to carry out stops in predominantly black and Latino neighborhoods because those groups were heavily represented in the crime suspect data, but the city went beyond the law in using race as a determining reason for the stops.[58]

In a separate ruling, Judge Scheindlin ordered a number of remedies for the city's stop, question, and frisk program. The remedies included creating a monitoring program to ensure that the NYPD did not violate the Constitution when carrying out stop, question, and frisk, and the revision of policies and training materials used for the program to prevent racial profiling. She ordered that the UF-250 form officers were required to complete for every stop be revised to include a detailed explanation of why the stop was made and why a frisk was done. A new tear-off portion of the form should be provided to the person who was stopped stating the reason for the stop and including an improved check-box system noting common reasons for stops. In addition, officers in each precinct of the five boroughs would start wearing a body camera to monitor how stops and frisks are executed.[59]

Soon after a decision was made in the *Floyd et al.*, a settlement was reached in the Davis case as well. On January 7, 2015, the NAACP Legal Defense Fund signed an accord with the city and the New York Housing Authority agreeing to a number of stipulations, including that the NYPD change its Patrol Guide, the manual that contains the rules that city police must follow when carrying out their officials duties, to instruct police on how to conduct vertical patrols lawfully and with respect for the rights of tenants and their guests. Those conducting the vertical patrols had to complete a trespass crime fact sheet after the arrest of a suspect.

All police patrolling city housing had to be involved in the monitoring process ordered under *Floyd*.[60]

Clearly upset that the judge in Floyd called stop, question, and frisk "indirect racial profiling," Bloomberg attempted to make his case to the general public. In a 2013 opinion piece in the *Washington Post* he attacked the judge for being "ideologically driven" and having a "history of ruling against the police." The mayor made the claim that "if New York City had the murder rate of Washington, D.C., 761 more New Yorkers would have been killed last year. If our murder rate had mirrored the District's over the course of my time as mayor, 21,651 more people would have been killed." Stop, question, and frisk, he insisted, was keeping New York City safe. He included black and Latino lives among those saved: "We know that more than 90 percent of those 21,651 individuals would have been black and Hispanic. Some of them would have been children." He took the judge to task for not mentioning the lives that police officers saved by stop, question, and frisk and for demonstrating a "disdain for our police officers and the dangerous work they do."[61]

Bloomberg continued by insisting that under his administration the city had banned racial profiling in 2004; he and Commissioner Ray Kelly had "zero tolerance for it" and "worked hard to strengthen police-community relations, which are better today than at any point since the 1960s." Part of the work to improve police–community relations, he wrote, was to provide the service that the black and Latino communities desired: "stronger police presence."[62]

Bloomberg promised to appeal, arguing that the ruling would lead to more gun violence in the city and make it a "more dangerous place."[63] On August 27, 2013, the Bloomberg administration moved in District Court to stay Scheindlin's decision in *Floyd et al.* Scheindlin ruled against the request. On September 23, 2013, the city filed an appeal in the U.S. Circuit Court of Appeals for the Second District requesting a stay in both *Ligon* and *Floyd*. In late October, a three-judge panel in that court ruled that Judge Scheindlin's conduct seemed improper. She may have violated the judicial code of conduct by appearing to be partial in the litigation in *Floyd et al.* Judges John M. Walker Jr., Jose J. Cabranes, and Barrington G. Parker accused her of steering the case to her courtroom when it was first filed almost six years earlier, and they criticized her for speaking publicly on the case, including granting media interviews. They stayed her decisions in *Ligon* and *Floyd* and stopped the city from implementing her remedies to reform stop, question, and frisk, including appointing a monitor. The panel then removed Scheindlin from *Floyd* and ordered that it be randomly reassigned. The new judge was ordered to postpone all proceedings and wait for further action by the three-judge panel. However, the federal court did not at this point hand down a decision on whether Scheindlin was correct that the NYPD's practice of stop, question, and frisk violated the constitutional rights of the plaintiffs. The panel set a schedule for the appeals process that extended beyond January 2014, which was the end of Bloomberg's term in office.[64]

Commissioner Kelly was elated by the panel's decision, claiming that it was "an important decision for all New Yorkers" and saying he had always been concerned about the "partiality of Judge Scheindlin." His jubilation was short-lived.[65] During his campaign to succeed Bloomberg as mayor, Bill de Blasio promised to drop the city's appeal of the *Floyd* decision. After de Blasio was elected on November 4, 2013, on November 9 Bloomberg asked the Court of Appeals to vacate Judge Scheindlin's decision. After making the request, the city's corporation counsel told the press that Judge Scheindlin's ruling created an unfair perception of the NYPD.[66] Bloomberg's purpose, however, was to avoid having the incoming mayor drop the appeal.

However, on November 21 the three-judge panel of the Court of Appeals made it clear that it did not make any "findings of misconduct, actual bias, or actual partiality on the part of Judge Scheindlin. . . . We now clarify that we did not intend to imply in our previous order that Judge Scheindlin engaged in misconduct."[67] In the interest of the "fair and impartial administration of justice," the panel denied the request by attorneys representing New York City to overturn Judge Scheindlin's sweeping ruling in the *Floyd* case.[68]

Bill de Blasio won the 2013 race for mayor largely due to his much more left-leaning position on a host of issues, including policing. On the campaign trail he promised that if elected, he would end racial profiling in stop, question, and frisk and create an inspector general position.[69] In his campaign literature he called for greater transparency and accountability for police officers, and supported greater prosecutorial authority for the civilian complaint review board.[70] In an effort to convince the mayor-elect to take a tough position on stop, question, and frisk, in December 2013 the Black, Latino/a, and Asian Caucus (BLA) sent him a letter asking that he drop the city's appeals of *Floyd* and *Ligon*. On January 21 BLA sent the now-seated mayor another letter noting that it had not received a response to the December request: "As a former member of the legislative body, you are keenly aware that the better a representative is able to engage his or her constituents, the better he or she can address the needs of the community. The longer this wedge between communities and police exists, the longer these issues of engagement persist."[71]

Speaking in Brownsville, Brooklyn, on January 30, de Blasio said, "We are here today to turn the page on one of the most divisive problems in our city." Referencing a theme of his campaign—"one city where everyone rises together"—the new mayor continued, "We believe in ending the overuse of stop and frisk, which has unfairly targeted young African American and Latino men." Declaring stop and frisk a broken policy that does not keep New Yorkers safe, de Blasio maintained that neither he nor police commissioner William Bratton, who had first served under Rudolph Giuliani, believed that a policy was acceptable when nearly 90 percent of the people stopped were innocent of any crime: "So we are taking significant corrective action to fix what is broken." He announced that the city was ending the years-long battle over stop, question, and frisk and had reached a settlement with the plaintiffs in the *Floyd* case: "We are doing it through a collective commitment to fix the fundamental problems that enabled stop and frisk to grow out of control and violate the rights of innocent New Yorkers. . . . What we are doing here today will increase the quality of policing in New York City."[72]

Mayor de Blasio insisted that he and the new police commissioner Bill Bratton were going to adopt effective policing without violating the constitutional rights of citizens: "The agreement we are announcing today accepts the facts and the roadmap laid out in last August's landmark federal court ruling." The first step of the agreement was "a joint and ongoing reform process with direct community and police dialogue ensuring the policies which are driving police and community apart are raised through a direct line of communications with the police leadership." The second step will be three years of "a court appointed monitor to assure the police department's compliance with the United States

Constitution and that limited period of oversight is contingent upon us meeting out obligations." Step three was to have a monitor, "assuring that the police department would carry out the orders of the decree." Monitoring would be done by an independent NYPD inspector general. The last point assured New Yorkers that "once the federal district court confirms the accord, the City will officially drop its appeal of the *Floyd* case."[73]

Bratton agreed with the mayor regarding his steps to reform stop, question, and frisk and was happy to help implement Judge Scheindlin's decision. He also agreed that the first obligation in a democracy was to keep people safe and that the policy had failed in that regard. Instead of creating confidence in the police, the program had even raised doubts within the NYPD. Not only were young men of color asking why they were being stopped when crimes were at historic lows, but police officers, too, were asking why, given the drop in crime, they were being encouraged to make more stops and arrests. The "public and police . . . shared a commonality of concern." Bratton characterized the resolution that the city was seeking as something essential to "assure that the fabric of society that must exist between the police and community is in fact rewoven so we come out of this process stronger than before."[74]

Bratton, however, created a false equivalency when he portrayed the police as also being victims of the city's earlier practice of stop, question, and frisk in being required to do as they did. Black people, as Judge Scheindlin rightfully noted, were humiliated and in some cases traumatized by stops made in broad daylight when simply going to school, work, the store, or other destinations.

Vincent Warren, executive director of the Center for Constitutional Rights, praised the new administration at a gathering at the Brownsville Boys' Club, saying it was a "major step that de Blasio accepted the district court's decision and was willing to adopt important steps to end racial profiling." Pointing out that the city was approaching the fifteenth anniversary of the Amadou Diallo murder, Warren noted that that incident had crystalized the relationship between the police and communities of color; now, he said, community activists would have a say in shaping the reforms with de Blasio.[75]

Donna Lieberman of the New York Civil Liberties Union characterized the Brownsville gathering as a good day and said she was happy to be in the same place with the mayor, the commissioner, the attorneys, and the advocates. It was a good day because the changes that New Yorkers fought for were actually taking place; because New York was "closing the book" on the "tale of two cities"; because the city was withdrawing its appeal of *Floyd* and *Ligon*. Lieberman was excited that the communities that experienced racial profiling were to have a hand in solving the problem.[76]

Conclusion

One important step toward advancing the police reform agenda was taken during Bloomberg's administration, and its impact is ongoing. The measure was spearheaded by a very old New York City organization, the Citizens Union (CU), which was founded in 1897 as a political party and became a watchdog group advocating good government practices. Among the issues the CU campaigns for are voting rights, "working to reduce the corrosive impact of money in politics," and pressing for "stronger ethics and oversight."[77] One area of success has been in curbing police brutality. After doing its own research and meeting with representatives of Mayor Bloomberg's administration, members of the City Council, district attorneys, and CCRB members, the Citizens Union produced a number of recommendations for overseeing the NYPD, including strengthening the CCRB. In March 2012 mayor Michael Bloomberg, City Council Speaker Christine Quinn, and police commissioner Raymond Kelly signed a memorandum of understanding accepting the CU's recommendation that the right to prosecute police officers for misconduct in cases that the CCRB has substantiated should be taken away from employees of the NYPD and put in the hands of the CCRB.[78] CCRB lawyers would prosecute cases for which the recommendation was that the most serious internal or administrative discipline should be applied.

As the CU's research noted, between 2002 and 2010 the CCRB had recommended severe punishment in 2,078 of the cases it had reviewed, but the NYPD had only followed through on 151 of them. In praising the memorandum of understanding, the CU said that "giving the CCRB prosecutorial powers is an important milestone in the ongoing march forward to bring greater accountability to the way in which the NYPD polices itself."[79] Civil rights and civil liberty organizations, activists, and City Council members have to be given credit for the relentless pressure they put on the Bloomberg administration. It was their efforts that finally got the city's administration to agree—after decades of resistance—to the terms in the memorandum of understanding.

The Bloomberg administration should also be credited for ending the Street Crimes Unit, the group regularly accused of violating the constitutional rights of black and Latino New York and for the horrendous killing of Amadou Diallo. Mayor Bloomberg also changed the tone of City Hall from the confrontational one adopted by Mayor Giuliani to a conciliatory attitude, especially in the administration's public reactions to police shootings.

However, Bloomberg's unquestioned support for stop, question, and frisk, which targeted mainly innocent blacks and Latinos, demonstrated his willingness to accept a policy that violated the constitutional rights of hundreds of thousands of New Yorkers. Thanks to the monumental efforts of grassroots, civil rights, and civil liberty organizations as well as individual New Yorkers challenging stop, question, and frisk, the most significant curtailing of police abuse and dominance of black and brown people in the long struggle against police brutality was achieved.

The *Ligon* and *Floyd* decisions handed down by the U.S. District Court for the Southern District of New York managed to end the city's sanctioned policies that were racially discriminatory. Mayor de Blasio's decision not to appeal the *Floyd* decision demonstrated that he was going forward with his police reform agenda. The January 30 event in Brownsville, Brooklyn, at which Mayor de Blasio announced his decision to drop the city appeal of judge Shira Scheindlin's rulings was a "Kumbayah" moment. For some, the hopeful sentiment expressed on that day was not going to last for long.

11

The Limits of Mayor de Blasio's Police Reform Agenda

Since 2013 the work of civil rights and civil liberties groups, grassroots organizations, elected city officials, and political leaders has led to measures to ensure greater accountability and monitoring of the NYPD. Mayor Bill de Blasio made police reform a hallmark of his election campaign, and his agenda for improving relations between the police and communities of color had some success. But after the murder of two police officers in the winter of 2014, coupled with police protests against his reforms, de Blasio proved unwilling to implement a more in-depth agenda to limit police power. The mayor's reluctance to support efforts that would help to make police officers more accountable to citizens, such as the Right to Know Act, indicated his concern about being labeled "anti-police." The mayor's reluctance to substantially curb police power also signified the NYPD's political influence.

Advances in Accountability Made by de Blasio

After the *Floyd* decision a federal monitor was assigned to ensure that the city and the NYPD took meaningful steps to end racial profiling. The City Council added additional oversight in 2014 when it passed Local Law 70, authorizing the Department of Investigation (DOI) to oversee the NYPD via an Office of the Inspector General for the NYPD (NYPD-OIG). Local Law 70 was passed in response to public outcry over the abuses of stop, question, and frisk, the revelation that the NYPD was spying on Muslim groups (including student groups at CUNY), and other police department abuses. The DOI is an independent city agency created in the 1870s to investigate corruption among city officials and those doing business with the city. As a law enforcement agency, the DOI can arrest individuals who are discovered to be violating anti-corruption laws; it issues its findings on "systematic government failure" to the mayor and City Council.[1] Local Law 70 mandates that the DOI "investigate, review, study, audit, and make recommendations relating to the operations, policies, programs and practices, including ongoing partnerships with other law enforcement agencies, of the New York City Police Department with the goal of enhancing the effectiveness of the department, increasing public safety, protecting civil liberties and civil rights and increasing the public confidence in the police force, thus building stronger police–community relations."[2]

In addition to the law imposing regulations aimed at stopping the city's use of racial profiling when it came to stop, question, and frisk, in November 2016 Mayor de Blasio and Police Commissioner Bratton took a major step toward cutting the number of arrests by announcing that people carrying twenty-five grams or less of marijuana would just receive a summons rather than be arrested. The mayor hailed the change as another example of how the city was keeping New Yorkers safe and "building a closer relationship between the police and community." Many in the black and Latino communities had been arrested for possession of small amounts of marijuana, thus hurting their chances of getting a job, completing their education, and finding housing. The following month, de Blasio took the first step toward having all police officers wear body cameras. He selected the six precincts with the highest number of stop, question, and frisk incidents and instructed a total of sixty officers from those precincts to wear the devices.[3]

Another important change happened in 2015 when an NYPD-OIG investigation noted that the Police Patrol Guide did not contain a definition of force or of "what actions constitute force," though the guide maintained that excessive force would not be tolerated. The NYPD lacked a "separate, centralized, and mandatory use of force form for documenting when physical force has been used." And while de-escalation strategies "have a proven record of not only limiting force but also ensuring officer safety," the "investigation suggests that NYPD officers rarely use de-escalation and that the Department's policy and training currently do not adequately address de-escalation as a useful tactic for officers in the field." CCRB reports also showed that "officers too often did not de-escalate encounters."[4]

To his credit, within hours of the OIG's report Commissioner Bratton announced that the NYPD acknowledged the deficiencies in police policy and said the department was overhauling its manual to create a "state of the art" approach on all "elements of use of force by officers in this department." The commissioner told the press that the department would need to overhaul its use of force policies. He maintained that many of the reforms he announced were already in progress and were intended to better track and investigate police officers' use of force. For example, officers would now be required to fill out a "Force Incident Report." The changes, Bratton said, were not just reacting to the OIG's report, in which he claimed the general inspector was "grandstanding."[5]

In 2015, NYPD chief James O'Neil proposed a neighborhood policing program.[6] O'Neil, who became police commissioner in September 2016, has implemented a program that splits precincts into four or five subdivisions or sectors that resemble the boundaries of neighborhoods. Each sector is fully staffed with two cops in a patrol car, along with officers and supervisors. Police officers assigned to the precincts are required to work the same beat, allowing them to become familiar with the neighborhood and people who live in the areas. The officers work with radio dispatchers and supervisors only in those sectors. They maintain "sector integrity," keeping the patrol cars in the sectors to which they are assigned.[7] The NYPD asserts that neighborhood policing seeks to foster a sense of ownership among sector officers for the police, the problems, and even the perpetrators in a particular sector, along with a sense of geographic responsibility and accountability. A significant amount of time is provided to the sector officer to interact with residents and learn about the crime problems of the neighborhood. The NYPD and de Blasio have asserted that neighborhood policing has closed the divide between the police and the community.[8] De Blasio and O'Neil have credited the program for the decrease in violent crime, including the drop in murders to their lowest rate since the 1950s: "We are giving our cops the opportunity to make relationships and build on those relationships."[9]

Enacting another aspect of his police reform agenda, in October 2016 Mayor de Blasio called for the New York State Assembly to amend section 50a of the New York State Civil Rights Law to make the disciplinary records of law enforcement officers and other uniformed personnel subject to public disclosure. Under the law as it stood, those personnel records could only be made public pursuant to a court order or with the written permission of the person to whom the records pertain. Mayor de Blasio released a statement maintaining that his administration "is committed to bringing greater transparency to the disciplinary records of law enforcement and other uniformed personnel." He called for the removal of "confidentiality protections currently applicable to disciplinary records, including all cases prosecuted by the New York City Civilian Complaint Review Board (CCRB) in the trial room, thereby subjecting the full public record of the disciplinary proceeding and the result of such disciplinary proceeding to public disclosure."[10]

Police reform advocates criticized de Blasio for not taking stronger action to create more transparency regarding the records of police who had been charged with misconduct. Communities United for Police Reform issued a statement declaring that de Blasio's call for the state to take action was "not substantive reform or a genuine commitment to full transparency." Christopher Dunn of the American Civil Liberties Union complained that "we'll all be dead and buried" before the state amends the law.[11]

Modifying the Reform Agenda

Despite the quite meaningful advances made toward increasing police accountability under de Blasio, they were not nearly as far-reaching as many people had surmised when listening to him make the historic announcement in Brownsville that he was dropping the city's appeal of the *Ligon* and *Floyd* decisions. Just five months after that event, the reform movement would be put to the test when another black man died at the hands of white officers.

On July 17, 2014, forty-three-year-old Eric Garner was walking on Bay Street in Staten Island when two officers, Justin Damico and Daniel Pantaleo, got out of their police car and approached him. They suspected that he was selling "loosies," single cigarettes from a pack, which was illegal and for which he had been arrested twice the previous May. As the two white officers approached Garner, who was African American, and attempted to arrest him, Garner's friend Ramsey Orta began filming the incident on his phone. Garner told Orta that he was not selling cigarettes and he was tired of the police harassing him, and then he told the cops, "I'm minding my own business, please leave me alone." When Pantaleo attempted to handcuff Garner, he raised his arms in the air to evade the cuffs. The video shows that several more officers came on the scene when Pantaleo placed Garner in a choke hold, cutting off his oxygen. At least four of them forced Garner to the ground, at which point Pantaleo released the choke hold and pushed Garner's face to ground. Other officer moved in to restrain Garner on the ground.[12]

While held there, Garner said eleven times, "I can't breathe." Eventually he lost consciousness. Although emergency medical technicians arrived on the scene, neither they nor any of the police officers attempted to perform CPR on the unconscious man or tried to assist him in any way other than when officers turned Garner on his side in an attempt to help him breathe, apparently not grasping how serious the situation was. Eventually an ambulance arrived and Garner was taken to the emergency room, where he was pronounced dead an hour later.[13] Millions of people saw the horrific event thanks to Orta's video and were outraged.[14]

New York did not explode the way Ferguson, Missouri, did just three weeks later, after police officer Darren Wilson shot and killed eighteen-year-old Michael Brown. Brown had recently stolen packets of cigarillos when Patrolman Wilson pulled up beside him and attempted to exit his police car, but when he opened the door it bumped into Brown. Wilson, along with witnesses, claimed that the teen reached into the SUV and began punching him. Wilson reached for his gun, and Brown grabbed his hand, but Wilson managed to shoot Brown in the hand. No witnesses saw Wilson shoot Brown, who then ran about 180 feet away and turned to face Wilson, who fired at least ten shots, killing Brown.[15] Ferguson erupted into days of protests and eventual rioting, which were calmed after the governor sent in the National Guard but reignited on November 25 when a grand jury decided not to indict Wilson.[16]

That New York did not experience a similarly violent reaction after Garner's death was likely one of the fruits of de Blasio's emphasis on police reform. Commissioner Bratton's immediate response was to order retraining for every police officer when it came to making arrests. On July 23, just five days after Garner's death, Bratton said he would implement the Los Angeles Police Department's modified use of force protocols, noting that they were the best in the country. The emphasis, Bratton said, had to be placed on training, and he stressed that the NYPD was learning from the "Staten Island incident and [would] move forward."[17]

Another contributing factor to New York's relatively calm reaction was that Staten Island district attorney Daniel Donovan met personally with the Garner family to assure them that he was moving forward with an investigation into Eric's death.[18] And there were additional indications that the city would, indeed, seek justice. In August the medical examiner declared that Garner died from compression of his neck, caused by the choke hold, and compression to his chest when he was being restrained. When he classified Garner's death as "homicide," Mayor de Blasio released a statement expressing his "deepest sympathies to the family of Eric Garner" and promised to work with District Attorney Donovan to "ensure a fair and justified outcome."[19]

Donovan wasted little time. Just a month after Garner's death, he made a strongly worded announcement designed to convince doubters that he was, indeed, committed to seeking justice: "Based upon the investigation that my office has conducted to date regarding the July 17, 2014, death of Eric Garner, and after a careful review of the recent findings of the Medical Examiner regarding the cause or manner of Mr. Garner's death, I have determined it is appropriate to present evidence regarding the circumstances of his death to a Richmond County Grand Jury. . . . Mindful of the solemn oath to enforce the law I took when I was first sworn into office as District Attorney in January 2004, and with a full appreciation that no person is above the law, nor beneath its protection, I assure the public that I am committed to conducting a fair, thorough and responsible investigation into Mr. Garner's death, and that I will go wherever the evidence takes me, without fear or favor."[20]

The focus of the grand jury's probe was Daniel Pantaleo, the officer who applied the choke hold. The jury met for nine weeks, hearing testimony from witnesses. Four police officers involved in the incident were given immunity from prosecution in exchange for their testimony.[21] It seemed to many that Pantaleo was going to pay for essentially strangling Garner.

That hope evaporated when the grand jury decided in early December not to bring charges against Pantaleo due to lack of sufficient evidence to indict.[22] Street demonstrations erupted immediately. In Brooklyn, protesters conducted a "die-in," lying in the street on Atlantic Avenue in the downtown hub and stopping traffic. Other protesters carried cardboard coffins symbolizing the numbers of innocent black people killed by the police; some marched to the Brooklyn Bridge and occupied the eastbound traffic lines. In Manhattan, there were demonstrations on Broadway and clashes with police near the West Side Highway on Fifty-Ninth Street. A common chant was "I can't breathe"—Eric Garner's last words.[23]

Despite the Eric Garner incident and subsequent protests, the very policing approach that led to his death—broken windows—was not in any danger of being abandoned. In an August television interview for NBC, Commissioner Bratton said, "Stop, question and frisk did not go away. It is here to stay. I'm sorry. It is part of what we do. Quality of life focus did not go away. It's what we do." On several occasions right after Garner's death, the commissioner argued that the city black and Latino communities demanded broken windows–type policing because more calls came from residents in those neighborhoods complaining about low-level criminal activity. "It is the law abiding" residents of black and Latino communities who wish "to be free of some of the disorders that are disturbing their lives." So the police, he explained, were not targeting those areas but simply responding to the demand from residents to end annoying or quality-of-life offenses. Bratton went so far as to blame Garner himself for the tragic confrontation, maintaining that such quality-of-life acts are criminal or city ordinance offenses and the job of police is to enforce the law: "If people would obey the law, they would not draw the attention of the police."[24]

Mayor de Blasio also defended broken windows. Speaking on a radio program in the fall of 2015, he said he associates the program with "successful policing." He elaborated by explaining that "Bill Bratton is the person who brought in CompStat and Broken Windows and the strategies that turned around the crime situation, and we're going to continue with those strategies because they work."[25]

The de Blasio administration's primary response to Garner's killing was not to address the negative effects of broken windows on communities of color but to offer improved training to police officers. In December 2014, after the grand jury cleared Officer Pantaleo, de Blasio again announced the retraining plans that had first been touted in July, and Bratton said that twenty-two thousand officers would be required to complete a three-day course. The course included de-escalation techniques that Bratton admitted had already been taught to the officers at the police academy, such as assuming a nonjudgmental posture.[26] First deputy commissioner Ben Tucker, in charge of the retraining, told reporters that the "Partner Officer Program" training had actually started in March, months before Garner's death, and was designed to raise "community trust and confidence and collaboration." Senior officers would serve as mentors to "new graduates" and community members would "host" officers new to their command. Those citizens would help the officers understand the "culture of the community, have an understanding of the issues of that community—in those communities—work on and attend events in those communities, get to know the business community as well as the schools and so forth."[27]

The training for patrol officers would also include instruction on how to talk suspects "into compliance, as opposed to taking people down, going to physical, hands on use of force, if there's a possibility that that can be avoided." Another element of the training would "strengthen their problem-solving skills," which would help officers "think through how to approach a particular challenge that they face while they're on patrol." Tucker declared that the department wanted patrol officers to be "positive and have positive social engagements." At the heart of "smart policing techniques," he said, was the need for police officers to "exercise discretion."[28]

According to a February 2015 article in the *New York Post*, 80 percent of the police who went through the retraining thought it was "a waste of time." The *Post* reported that a high-ranking police official, who noted that some officers fell asleep during the three-day session, called the $35 million program a failure and said that eight out of ten cops gave it a negative rating. Instead of the hands-on training the officers thought they were going to get, they had to sit through hours of lectures.[29] The Reverend Al Sharpton voiced his own criticism of the training program shortly after the mayor first announced it. In the wake of Garner's death, at a conference the mayor arranged at City Hall on July 31, Sharpton told Bratton that while training was important, "I also think, Commissioner, that the best way to make police stop using illegal chokeholds is to perp-walk one of them that did." Such a step would "send a lesson that ten trainings will not give them."[30]

Mayor de Blasio gave another indication that he was modifying his reform agenda when he reversed his position on hiring additional police officers. Initially, in April 2014, when the crime rate was at a record low, City Council Speaker Melissa Mark-Viverito announced the council's support for hiring an additional thousand police officers. Police reform advocates maintained that adding more police to the force was not needed when crime was decreasing in this period. The money to hire more police, police reform advocates argued, could be used to address the social conditions that cause crime. Siding with those who contested hiring more cops, the mayor opposed the personnel increase, and he told recruits at the police academy that the NYPD was doing a fine job with the existing force.[31] As late as June 15, 2015, speaking on WNYC, he noted that while murder rates had increased, overall crime had dropped and there were 25 percent fewer complaints to the CCRB compared to a year earlier. New York was the safest big city in the United States and getting safer, he said. Despite the dramatic curtailment of the stop, question, and frisk policy, the police force had gotten better at reducing crime, due in large part to the reduction in stops that had nothing to do with violent crime, which freed officers to concentrate on more serious offenses. Improved technology also had led to better policing, and therefore there was no need to add a thousand police officers to a force of 34,500.[32] Taking this position sent a clear message to New Yorkers that he was on the side of police reform.

By the end of June 2015, however, the mayor announced that he had "come to a plan that allows us to strengthen our police force while encouraging a deepening of reform." The plan allowed for the hiring of nearly 1,300 police officers.[33] Bratton was elated and reported at his monthly news conference that the new budget plan allowed for the hiring of "1,297 additional officers, 415 civilianized positions that we will be implementing, coupled with the funding for technology, for capital improvements. I can safely say that I think this is probably one of the best budgets that this department has ever had."[34]

Advocates for police reform were understandably upset. Monifa Bandele, head of the Committee United for Police Reform, told the press that it was "disappointing and perplexing that the city budget will increase the NYPD head count when systemic problems with police accountability and culture, that allow New Yorkers to be abused and killed, have yet to be fixed." For "this to happen in this liberal, progressive administration is the most tone deaf response they could have had," said Josmar Trujillo, an organizer for the Coalition to End Police Brutality. "This is beyond disappointment. This is a national embarrassment."[35]

Why did de Blasio reverse himself? The pressure to do so was slow to build. On July 30, 2014, Michael Goodwin wrote an opinion piece in the *New York Post* that accused de Blasio of slandering the police when he claimed that for twelve years under Bloomberg there had been a "growing tension and a growing disconnect" between the police and New Yorkers, which his administration had fixed. But according to Goodwin, de Blasio did not recognize that "thousands of black and Latino young men are alive today because they were not killed by their peers, thanks largely to aggressive policing."[36] The Patrolmen's Benevolent Association (PBA) also saw the mayor's reform measures as an attack on the police and revived the old narrative that such measures tied the hands of the police and endangered their lives and the lives of New Yorkers. Then, in December 2014, two police officers were shot and killed while sitting in a patrol car by a man the *New York Daily News* characterized as a "career criminal who was seeking revenge for the killing of Eric Garner."[37] Patrick Lynch, the head of the PBA, claimed that there was "blood on many hands," including the street demonstrators protesting the deaths of Eric Garner and other deaths caused by NYPD officers: "The blood on hands starts at the steps of City Hall in the office of the Mayor." Hundreds of police officers turned their backs on de Blasio as he eulogized the two slain officers at their funeral.[38]

A November 17, 2015, article in the *New York Times* asserted that according to a poll conducted by the paper and Sienna College, de Blasio had lost support among white New Yorkers. Only 28 percent of them approved while 59 percent disapproved of his performance. Among the white New Yorkers polled, 51 percent thought the city was less safe and 62 percent thought it was heading in the wrong direction under de Blasio's leadership.[39] The mayor's negative ratings were highest in a March 2016 survey conducted by the PBA: 87 percent of police officers polled felt that under de Blasio the city was less safe, and 96 percent felt that the police relationship with the public had gotten worse.[40]

The PBA protests in particular made the mayor move more cautiously with his reform efforts, but he also was facing a perception problem. The false narrative that crime was on the rise and the city was less safe was harming de Blasio's image; especially if he wanted a second term, he needed to be seen as a crime fighter.[41]

Encouraged by his advisers, de Blasio challenged the perception that he was anti-cop. One adviser, Phil Walzak, maintained that the mayor was "absolutely focused on strengthening the quality of life for every New Yorker."[42] Although de Blasio and Bratton claimed that broken windows was effective because there had been a dramatic decrease in the number of arrests and summonses, the Department of Investigation's Office of the Inspector General (OIG) for the NYPD released a report titled *An Analysis of Quality-of-Life Summonses, Quality-of-Life Misdemeanors, Arrests, and Felony Crime in New York City* that examined the relationship among those elements from 2010 to 2015.[43] After months of looking at the data, the OIG declared that there was "no empirical evidence demonstrating a clear and direct link between an increase in summons and misdemeanor arrest activity and a related drop in felony crimes."[44]

Confronted with the report's evidence, de Blasio responded that he "believes in Broken Windows as a strategy because it is part of what has made us so safe as a city." Along with CompStat, he insisted, Broken Windows made New York one of the safest big cities in America and "we're going to stick by them." He did state that the policy was not static and should be updated, but he insisted that "Broken Windows not only helped in terms of decreasing quality-of-life offenses, but also helped to reduce the atmosphere of disorder and violence that pervaded the City a couple of decades ago."[45]

Mayor de Blasio's adamant defense of broken windows predicted ongoing harassment of black and brown people. The Police Reform Organizing Project (PROP) and its founder, Robert Gangi, responded by turning their attention to the everyday abuse that blacks and Latinos face from broken windows–type policing. In an October 2016 report, PROP documented the number of "punitive actions" that took place between the police and New York residents in 2015. PROP defined punitive action as an interaction between a police officer and a citizen that results in a moving violation summons, criminal summons, juvenile arrest, Transit Adjudication Bureau summons, felony arrest, misdemeanor arrest, or stop, question, and frisk. The number in 2015 was 1,783,414. This was down slightly from the 1,913,015 recorded in 2014, but PROP stressed that this was not progress, as there were still far too many incidents overall. In terms of monthly averages, moving violation summonses totaled 85,587, misdemeanor arrests 18,897, and Transit Adjudication Bureau summonses 11,602.[46]

PROP noted that 94.9 percent of juvenile arrests involved blacks and Latinos. Of the 297,413 criminal summonses that police issued, 104,859 were for open alcohol container charges—and one judge noted that in his experience, the NYPD specifically singled out blacks and Latinos for such alcohol-related summonses. The city paid $202.6 million to settle claims against the NYPD in 2015, compared to $154.1 million the previous year.[47]

Right to Know

In an attempt to assure that police would not abuse their power in interactions with citizens, in March 2014 city councilmember Ritchie Torres introduced a bill that would require police officers who make a stop and wished to frisk a person to provide their rank, command, and a specific reason for conducting the search. Thirty-seven of the fifty-one council members cosponsored Torres's bill.[48]

Also in 2014, in November, city councilmember Antonio Reynoso introduced a bill that would require police officers to receive a person's consent before carrying out a search on the person if the officer or officers had no legal right to search. The searcher would be obliged to inform the person that he or she had the right to refuse to be searched and/or to withdraw consent during the search. If consent is given, the police officer would have to produce an audio or signed record of consent. Thirty-two members of the council joined Reynoso in sponsoring the bill.[49]

The main objective of the bills would curtail the ability of the police to randomly stop, question, and frisk people, and they were jointly referred to as the "Right to Know" legislation. In addition to its overwhelming support in the City Council, Right to Know received support from over two hundred racially, religiously, and politically diverse organizations, including the NAACP, the Center for Constitutional Rights, the New York City Congress of Puerto Rican Rights, the National Latino Officers Association, the Council on Islamic Relations, and Jewish Voice for Peace NYC.[50]

In response to the media coverage of and protests against police killings of unarmed black people throughout the United States, in December 2014 president Barack Obama created the Task Force on 21st Century Policing and charged it with finding solutions to end police brutality and improve relations between law enforcement agencies and communities of color. Its objective was to find ways for better collaboration between law enforcement and communities in order to reduce crime while building trust. In its final report, released in May 2015, the task force made far-reaching recommendations that could dramatically decrease police brutality. Like Right to Know supporters, the task force advocated that law enforcement throughout the country "should be required to seek consent before a search and explain that a person has the right to refuse when there is no warrant or probable cause." Furthermore, officers should ideally obtain written acknowledgment that they have sought consent to a search in these circumstances. Moreover, it recommended that "law enforcement agencies should adopt policies requiring officers to identify themselves by full name, rank, and command (as applicable) and provide the information in writing to individuals they have stopped." One way of providing those who are stopped with the identity of the officer would be for police to carry and distribute business cards.[51]

Despite the broad support for Right to Know and de Blasio's rhetoric about police reform, the mayor joined the PBA, Commissioner Bratton, and City Council Speaker Mark-Viverito in opposing the proposed legislation, which Bratton referred to as "unprecedented intrusions." In a closed-door meeting in July 2016, Mark-Viverito told City Council members that the provisions in the Right to Know legislation would be handled internally by the NYPD and therefore there was no need for legislation. The de Blasio administration, the speaker, and leaders of the NYPD struck a verbal deal and agreed to require that police officers who wish to search a car, a home, or a person request permission. They would have to confirm that the person agreed to the search and provide a business card after it was completed. The new rules would be added to the Police Patrol Guide. Though the NYPD agreed to require police officers to identify themselves before carrying out a search, this was not backed up by law and would be left solely to the NYPD to enforce. The police would monitor their own behavior. When criticizing the agreement among the mayor, police commissioner, and leaders of the City Council, Ritchie Torres observed, "Legislative reform is protected by law, whereas administrative reform can be reversed at will."[52]

The verbal deal Torres referred to did little to change the power relationship between citizens and the police. As the *New York Times* noted, the power was with the NYPD, and the commissioner gained far too much of it under the deal because he could "impose, enforce, change or reverse the rules at will—and rank-and-file officers could ignore them with impunity."[53] Communities United for Police Reform summed up its reaction to the "unwritten deal" by saying it was not "accessible to the public" and "stripped of meaningful changes," and that it "removed any reliable measures of police accountability and the most important protections of the Right to Know Act, including policies explicitly prioritized by President Obama's Task Force on 21st Century Policing."[54] These two bills were part of the police reform effort that the mayor initially supported, but he later asked the City Council not to vote on them.[55]

The call for the City Council to approve Right to Know from dozens of organizations, including Communities United for Police Reform, the New York Civil Liberties Union, and the Center of Constitutional Rights, as well as Councilman Reynoso and other members of the City Council, placed a great deal of pressure on the body to act. In December 2017 the City Council leadership, in a closed-door meeting, worked out a compromise on Right to Know. The agreement brokered between council president Mark-Viverito, Councilman Torres, the Mayor, and the NYPD, amended the Torres bill by excluding car stops and nonemergency or low-level interactions, allowing police officers to question someone without suspicion that the person committed any crime.[56]

The New York Civil Liberties Union, one of the supporters of the original bill, pointed out that there was no systematic accounting of nonemergency encounters: "We do know of countless reports of officers responding to a request for their name and badge number as an affront or challenge to their authority." According to the NYCLU, women were more likely to experience sexual harassment by police officers. The revised bill would put women who encounter such harassment at a disadvantage because police officers would not have to identify themselves.[57]

Monifa Bandele—of Communities United for Police Reform and vice president of and equity officer at MomsRising.org, a group of over one million members dedicated to ending discrimination of women and mothers and promoting economic security for families—accused Torres of allowing his bill to be gutted by the NYPD and City Council leaders. Writing in the *Huffington Post* on December 17, 2017, she asserted that the new bill "has removed the core protections of the legislation and allowed loopholes that ensure it will provide no change for New Yorkers in their abusive policing interactions." The revised bill was dangerous and "increased the likelihood of escalation and even violence in the majority of low-level encounters where New Yorkers most frequently experience abuse." Bandele declared that none of the two hundred groups that supported the original bill was in support of the compromise.[58]

On December 18, 2017, the City Council passed Intro 541-C by an overwhelming 37–13 vote. Despite widespread opposition from antipolice brutality groups, the council in a close vote, 27–20, also adopted Intro 182-D.[59] Although Mayor de Blasio withheld his support for the original version of Intro 182-D, he supported the revised one. Brooklyn council member Jumaane Williams said in his opposition to the vote on Intro 182-D, "It's a shame and sham."[60] The mayor's support of the revised Intro 182-D as well as his unwavering backing of broken windows demonstrated that he would only go so far when challenging police power. Even after he was easily elected for a second term de Blasio was unwilling to oppose the NYPD's attempt to undermine measures to curtail its power.

Conclusion

By 2017 Mayor de Blasio's police reform agenda had produced positive results. His withdrawal of the city's appeal of the *Floyd* decision, allowing the NYPD to be federally monitored to assure that it would not practice racial profiling, was a major victory. The city's decriminalizing of marijuana possession decreased the number of arrests. Moreover, the city's announcement in July 2017 that it would support the district attorneys of Brooklyn, the Bronx, Manhattan, and Queens in their decision to dismiss 750,000 outstanding warrants for minor offenses that are a decade or more old was also a major victory for those opposed to broken windows, resulting in hundreds of thousands of people, mostly black and Latino, who would no longer face arrest if stopped by a police officer who ran their name through a database. Those minor offenses included riding a bike on the sidewalk, drinking an alcoholic beverage in public, and urinating in the street.[61]

However, the mayor still embraced broken windows, the very policy that is responsible for the hundreds of thousands of warrants he supported dismissing. When Manhattan district attorney Cyrus Vance announced in late June 2017 that he would no longer prosecute people trying to beat paying the fare to ride on city trains and buses, in an effort to scale back on the number of people criminally prosecuted for what is considered a minor offense, Mayor de Blasio objected. "There is no way in hell anyone should be evading the fare," he said, because that "would create chaos."[62] De Blasio has argued that many of those apprehended for fare evasion "have a lot of money on them so the issue is not poverty.[63] Joseph Lhota, chairman of the Metropolitan Transit Authority, agreed with the mayor. In a letter to Vance, Lhota wrote, "Allowing ever more widespread fare-beating by adopting and touting a policy of non-prosecution in most cases unquestionably sends a loud a loud and clear signal to those who would flout the law."[64]

Vance objected to the claim that not prosecuting fare beaters would lead to more crime on the subways: "Police officers may continue to enforce the law exactly as they always have; when an individual is observed jumping a turnstile, that person may be stopped, questioned, and if found to possess weapons or contraband, or to haven an open bench warren, he or she will be arrested, brought to court, and prosecuted by my office."[65]

Prosecuting fare beaters was a major focus of the broken windows policy. In his announcement of the end of criminally prosecuting fare beaters, Vance argued that "the criminal prosecution of these low-level, non-violent offenses should not be part of a reformed 21st-century justice system. Absent a demonstrated public safety risk, criminally prosecuting New Yorkers accused of these offenses does not make us safer."[66] Even though tens of thousands are apprehended and many are prosecuted, de Blasio insisted on maintaining this broken windows policy.

While the NYPD has dramatically decreased the numbers of people who are stopped, questioned, and frisked, federal monitor Peter J. Zimroth reported that the department underreported the number of stops. According to Zimroth, in the second quarter of 2017 auditors were able to identify 154 arrests that seemed to have been initiated by a stop. However, only in "13 of those instances, a stop report was on file." The "commands" were ordered to investigate, and they determined that 104 cases "did not require a stop report."[67] The auditors identified in the second quarter of 2017 sixty-two arrests in NYCHA buildings that required a stop report. However, the police failed to file the required report.[68] Zimroth also reported that the team of auditors heard from some officers that they do not fill it the required stop report forms because it "is not worth the trouble."[69] The federal monitor pointed out that underreported stops is a significant problem because not having such information "will undermine the Department's and the monitor's ability to assess complaints with the court order."[70]

No mayor has done more to help eliminate police abuse of citizens than de Blasio. Neighborhood policing; banning racial profiling as a component of stop, question, and frisk; and other initiatives have made New York City one of the safest big cities in the United States. Nevertheless, De Blasio's unwavering support for broken windows and his 2015 decision to expand the police force by 1,300 officers demonstrated his reliance on policing to fight crime and helped him easily win a second term. But the question remains for many who are involved in the campaign to end all forms of police domination of citizens: Will the mayor support their efforts and end broken windows–style policing?[71] In May 2018 de Blasio acknowledged that there is racial disparity in marijuana police actions, and he ordered the NYPD to come up with a plan to end "unnecessary arrests." In addition, Manhattan district attorney Cyrus Vance said he was going to stop prosecuting those arrested for possessing and using marijuana.[72] The New York Civil Liberties Union urged de Blasio to "reduce the enforcement against low level offenses like farebeating which funnels people into the criminal justice and flags immigrants for Trump's deportation agenda. The NYCLU also asked the mayor to assure that police are held "accountable for misconduct" and to stop the "NYPD from targeting protesters or subjecting them to unequal treatment."[73] As this chapter notes, although there have been accomplishments in curbing police brutality during the de Blasio administration, not enough has been done to eliminate it and it remains a major social plague in this city.

Conclusion

Where Do We Go from Here?

New York City has been an important battleground in the campaign to end police brutality. The struggle has been a long and arduous one. Police brutality has been a pivotal issue among African Americans and other people of color because they have been its main targets. I have argued that at the very core of police brutality is the intertwining of race and the criminal justice. But this volume has addressed only the tip of the iceberg when examining the many forces in the city fighting police abuse. A major goal of this book has been to help bring attention to this long fight. The anti–police brutality campaign has been creating ways to dramatically reduce the amount of power police have over citizens. The *People's Voice*, the Communist Party, the Nation of Islam, civil rights leaders, civil liberty organizations, grassroots activists, and others examined in this book courageously fought against police dominance over individuals because a product of police dominance is abuse.

Although the campaigns against police brutality covered in this work did not meet with immediate success, it would be a mistake to see the earlier campaigns as a failure. Despite the resistance crusade by the pro-police network that included the NYPD, the PBA, and their ardent supporters in government and among the public, the anti-police brutality movement made significant gains. It gave voice to victims of unwarranted police assaults and consistently kept the issue in the public's eye despite the claim that police brutality did not exist. The movement to end police brutality publicized ways to end the horror of police attacks that would eventually be adopted. The long struggle was responsible for placing citizens on the civilian complaint review board and in 1993 for the creation of an all-civilian complaint review board. Another objective of the early movement was to get the NYPD to hire black officers. By 2013, 47.8 percent of the force identified as a racial minority; blacks made up 16.1 percent while Latinos constituted 26.1 percent and people of Asian origins 5.5 percent.[1]

As illustrated in this volume, the relentless anti–police brutality campaign led to the most important police reform measures in the city's history. Policies that would not have been imagined by many New Yorkers in the 1970s and 1980s have become reality. The federal monitoring of the NYPD, the creation of an inspector general, an end to racial profiling, the decriminalizing of certain nonviolent offenses, and the establishment of an all-civilian complaint review board with prosecutorial power have helped to change the way police operate in the city.

Yet, despite the gains made by the anti–police brutality movement, such abuse continues to plague New York City. As we have seen, it takes many forms: excessive physical force, false arrest and imprisonment, unreasonable search, harassment, sexual misconduct, intimidation, and verbal abuse are among the abuses that people not only experience, but in some cases have come to expect. Blacks and Latinos, who are subject to the greatest amount of abuse, are joined by Asians, Muslims, members of the LGBTQ communities, and others who are marginalized in some way. Despite recent moves toward transparency and accountability regarding police brutality, far stronger measures need to be enacted to empower communities to confront the problem.

In the long struggle against police brutality, the various crusading groups and individuals examined in this book have shared a core objective: to empower people who, historically, have been the victims of police abuse. This victimization has been at the heart of the struggle for institutional reform and citizen oversight in New York City and elsewhere for decades. While there have been significant accomplishments, especially in the areas of monitoring and police accountability, there is still far too much abuse. New York's CCRB reported that in the first half of 2016, 2,343 complaints were filed, a 12 percent increase over the same period in the previous year. It also noted that the "average number of complaints filed per month was 391, which is higher than the 348 average complaints per month from the first half of 2015." This was considered disturbing, since there had been a steady decline in complaints since 2010, when the CCRB received around three thousand complaints biannually. The increase was across all boroughs, with Manhattan producing the highest numbers: a 26 percent increase, up from 496 in the first half of 2015 to 593 in the first half of 2016. In the same time frame, there was a 9 percent increase in Brooklyn (708 complaints compared to 650), a 9 percent increase in the Bronx, and a 5 percent increase in both Queens and Staten Island.[2]

While allegations of excessive use of force dropped from 48 percent in the first half of 2015 to 43 percent a year later, abuse of authority allegations increased in the same time period from 60 percent to 70 percent. Black people filed 54 percent of the cases, Latinos 25 percent, whites 14 percent, and Asians 2 percent (4 percent were files by those in the "other" category). Men filed 89 percent of the cases, women 11 percent.[3]

In late June 2017, the CCRB released *Worth a Thousand Words: Examining Officer Interference with Civilian Recordings of Police*, a report that examined the 257 complaints involving officer interference with recording incidents. Among the complaints were those of officers directing people to stop recording, "knocking a recording device out of a civilian's hands, seizing a recording devise, detaining someone recording, blocking recordings by physically obstructing a civilian's camera view of a scene; and intimidation like threatening to arrest or detain a civilian for recording an interaction." The CCRB reported that 24 percent of the 257 cases involved verbal interference while 46 percent included physical interference.[4]

The decriminalizing of marijuana by Mayor de Blasio also came under attack when in July 2017 the Drug Policy Alliance and Marijuana Arrest Research Policy reported that between 2014 and 2016, 52,730 blacks and Latinos were arrested for marijuana offences, accounting for 86 percent of such actions. During the same period 8,260 whites and "all others" were arrested for marijuana offenses, accounting for just 14 percent. This racial disparity in marijuana arrests persists despite national studies showing that whites and others tend to smoke marijuana in about the same proportion as do blacks and Latinos.[5]

The reason for the racial disparity was a "'willful indifference' by top city and police officials to the unwarranted and unconstitutional racial discrimination built into these routine police enforcement patterns and policies."[6] The mayor criticized the study because the Drug Policy Alliance looked at marijuana arrests from 2014 to 2016; he noted on the television program *Road to City Hall* that his policy of not arresting people for low levels of marijuana possession started in 2015. However, the report noted that in 2016, of the 18,121 arrests for "lowest-level" marijuana possession in 2016, 46 percent were black, 39 percent were Latino, and just 10 percent were white (5 percent were Asian and a small percentage were classified as "other"). The racial disparity in the number of marijuana arrests was quite alarming in a city where blacks and Latinos make up 51 percent of the population and whites make up 49 percent.[7]

Clearly the existing officer accountability measures need to be strengthened. Civilians United against Police Brutality (CUAPB), an organization based in Minnesota, has called for police officers to carry personal liability or malpractice insurance, which would create "real consequences for officers, rather than the current practice where taxpayers foot the bill and the officers never receive any discipline." CUAPB also calls for reforming the police contract—in the context of New York City, that would include getting rid of problematic practices such as the forty-eight-hour rule, which prohibits interrogations by prosecutors of those accused of police brutality for two days after the alleged event.[8]

Involving citizens in the hiring process of police who will operate in their communities is one of the proposals put forth by the Independent Institute in Oakland, California. The institute is a nonpartisan public policy research and educational organization that mainly focuses on private security forces but examines all types of policing and believes that "citizens deserve a better system [of policing] that puts them in control."[9]

Another necessary form of community involvement would be a system by which the public could evaluate police performance in their communities on a regular basis. Calling itself "the public safety solution," the Virginia-based Commission on Accreditation of Law Enforcement Agencies (CALEA), established in 1979, has advocated for having the performance of law enforcement be evaluated by the communities served.[10] While measuring police performance is nothing new and has included the use of citizen surveys, the performance evaluations would go further in that, once measured by the public, the outcome should have an impact on future assignments, promotions, and the like. According to CALEA, "A comprehensive suite of performance measures needs to account for a broader spectrum of the work that police do, not just that part of their work related to issuing citations and arresting offenders. If police are supposed to prevent crime and motor vehicle accidents, solve community problems, reduce disorder, and build lasting community relationships, then performance measures should reflect their success in producing these and other valuable outcomes."[11] Such performance measures should not be limited to looking at entire precincts but also extend to individual officers.

The public should also play a role in the disciplinary process. In New York City, even though on August 12, 2012, thanks to the memorandum of understanding signed by the NYPD and the CCRB, the board was granted prosecutorial powers, it can still only recommend action, not enforce it.[12] To quote Udi Ofer, deputy national political director of the ACLU's Campaign for Smart Justice, "An independent investigation will be meaningful only if its findings then form the basis for deciding whether and to what extent to discipline an officer." The New York CCRB fails, he says, because the "police commissioner has full discretion to ignore the board's fact-finding or to impose no discipline, even when the board has found that wrongdoing occurred."[13] In order to make the CCRB more effective, according to Ofer, its findings would have to be binding on the NYPD once the board's professional staff completed an investigation and the board substantiated an allegation of misconduct. The commissioner would then determine the discipline from a range of options included in a "pre-negotiated disciplinary matrix."[14]

Echoing a demand of many New York City police reform groups and activists, President Obama's Task Force on 21st Century Policing recommended that "law enforcement agencies should institute residency incentive programs" requiring police officers to live in the city they serve. New Yorkers long urged residency in the very borough where the officer's precinct is located, stressing that this important reform could help to bridge the gap between the police and the communities they serve. One step toward implementing a residency requirement would be for the city to provide rent and housing subsidies to assure that officers could afford to live in certain areas.[15]

Clearly, as this book has demonstrated, the push to end police brutality cannot reliably depend on federal, state, or local officials to do the right thing. Even when a sympathetic administration is in power, as with Mayor de Blasio in New York City, there is no assurance that it will adopt effective measures to end police abuse. This book has chronicled the efforts of some of the most influential forces in that crusade. Leading black Communists, prominent black religious figures, the black press, the Congress of Racial Equality and other civil rights organizations, political leaders, members of the New York City Council, and grassroots activists and civil liberties groups have all conducted a relentless campaign over the past several decades to end one of the great civil rights abuses taking place in New York City. The groups that led the campaign against police brutality from the 1940s through the 1960s should be recognized for having been the first to articulate many of the remedies advocated by later groups which were eventually adopted, at least in part, in an effort to curb police abuse. Just as important, those early groups should be given credit for bold leadership in a period when it was much more difficult to be involved in such a battle. They were able to frame the struggle, noting that at its root was the power police and other institutions had over black and brown people. While they fell short of obtaining their goal, their determination kept the struggle alive to be taken up by activists in the late twentieth and early twenty-first century, who have achieved some measure of success in decreasing police power.

More recent actors, such as those associated with the protest organization Black Lives Matter, have demonstrated they understand that change comes about only when those in power are pressured to make change. Black Lives Matter has shown how crucial it is to put pressure even on those in powerful positions who profess to be in support of ending police brutality and other injustices. Social protest such as demonstrations, strikes, and boycotts has always been an effective way to force those with power to act for social justice.

Right-wing critics of Black Lives Matter have generally not offered any thoughtful critiques of the group. Instead, they have presented nothing more than nonsensical accusations, such as claiming the organization is anti-white and anti-police.[16] More serious critics of Black Lives Matter have considered its antiracist approach detrimental to the anti–police brutality cause. Political scientist Adolph Reed, probably the most outspoken proponent of this view, maintains that the failure of Black Lives Matter and others who argue that racism is the major cause of police brutality is that data demonstrates that nearly half of those killed annually by the police are white. Moreover, Reed insists that the group's focus on race as a cause for police killings does not lead to the building of a broad coalition of others who are victimized by police violence.[17]

One major problem with Reed's argument is its lack of information on the circumstances of police killing of civilians. He does not tell us how many of these killings were of armed or unarmed people. Reed is also silent on how many killings were done in self-defense or an attempt to protect the life of another. As my work and the work of others have noted, police killing is not the only form of police brutality and abuse. Excessive and discriminatory use of force does not always lead to death. Using a number of data sets in his July 2016 study, Harvard University economics professor Ronald G. Fryer found that there was a racial differ-ence in "lower levels" of police force.[18] One data set used in the study was from the Stop, Question, and Frisk program. A second data set used was the Police Public Survey Contact Survey (PPCS), a triennial survey of a national representative sample of civilians' interpretation of interaction with police officers collected by the Bureau of Justice Statistics. Moreover, two other data sets comprised officer-involved shootings in ten cities, including Austin, Dallas, Houston, Los Angeles, and Orlando.[19]

A team of researchers collected the data, read arrest records, and gath-ered almost three hundred variables on the incidents in the report. The study revealed that there was no racial bias when it came to lethal shoot-ings. However, the story was different when it came to nonlethal incidents.

Examining five million observations under the Stop, Question, and Frisk program from 2003 to 2013, the study showed that blacks were 50 percent more likely to be slapped, pushed into a wall, or experience some other violent encounter with police.[20] Even though there were fewer events taking place in the more severe categories, such as pointing a weapon at a suspect, the racial differences were constant. Fryer noted that "blacks are 21.3 percent more likely to be involved in an incident where a weapon is drawn.[21] He also reported that "black civilians are 21.2 percent more likely to have any force used against them in an inter-action compared to white civilians with the same reported compliance behavior."[22] The PPCS of 2011 showed that black people were more likely to experience violent encounters with the police than were whites.[23]

Contrary to Reed's claim that Black Lives Matter has made ambigu-ous and unrealistic demands, the Movement for Black Lives, a collec-tive of over fifty groups (including Black Lives Matter), issued in 2016 a number of concrete and reasonable policy demands. For example, its call for reparations and long-term investment in black communities has been made by others long before Black Lives Matter. The demand for reparations was not a wild, pie in the sky idea. The group called for support of H.R. 40, the Commission to Study and Develop Reparation Proposals for African Americans Act.[24] Leaders of the civil rights movement, including Martin Luther King's GI Bill for the poor and Whitney Young's Marshall Plan for poor urban areas, are examples of a similar call for investments fifty years earlier.

The Movement for Black Lives' solution to police domination of black people is also specific and has been advocated by others in the anti–police brutality movement—they call for an end to "zero-tolerance school policies and the arrest of students, the removal of police from school, and the reallocation of funds from police and punitive school discipline practices to restorative services."[25] Under the subheading "Community Control," the Movement for Black Lives calls for "direct democratic community control" over law enforcement agencies to ensure that the communities "most harmed by destructive policing have the power to hire and fire officers, and subpoena relevant agency information."[26] Just as important, the demands made by the Movement for Black Lives will address police brutality not only of black people but of all who are victims of police abuse.

The Movement for Black Lives is also attempting to broaden its strategies. In addition to disruptive protest, it has gotten involved in electoral activities, including endorsing candidates and members running for office. Besides demonstrations, using the courts, voting, and running for office are crucial means in the ongoing battle against police domination of citizens.

The continued criminalization of black and brown people, the huge investment in law enforcement, and the overuse of police to handle crime while at the same time not investing in neighborhoods all assures that police brutality and mass incarceration, especially of people of color, will remain a problem that plagues the United States. While blacks and Latinos continue to disproportionally experience abuse at the hands of the police, victims of police brutality cross race, ethnicity, and gender lines. Whites, Asians, women, and others have suffered police assaults and misconduct. Ending police brutality is in the interest of everyone, not just those who have historically been victims. As this book has noted, vigilance and determination on the part of the public has been one of the best ways to eradicate the scourge of police domination over the people they are sworn to protect.

ACKNOWLEDGMENTS

This writing of this book would not have been possible without the backing of my many friends and colleagues. I wish to thank Jennifer Hammer for her encouragement and support for this project. Jennifer first contacted me just as I got started writing and expressed great enthusiasm for the book. During the research and writing phase, Jennifer gave me extremely helpful advice and suggested that I submit the draft for review to New York University Press.

I am extremely grateful to Jill Hannum for her editing of the manuscript. Jill's careful reading of each chapter and numerous recommendations has made this a better book. I am indebted to Nicholas Taylor for his wonderful copyediting of the book. V. P. Franklin's careful reading and suggestions for the second chapter of the book were very helpful. I am very grateful to Fred Jerome for sharing his files on the William Epton, the Harlem Defense Council, and the Progressive Labor Movement.

I owe a great debt to Jeanne Theoharis and Komozi Woodard. In the summer of 2015, Jeanne and Komozi organized and conducted an NEH Summer Faculty Seminar and invited me to present my work to a group of leading scholars in modern African American history. The feedback, comments, and suggestions from that presentation were invaluable.

I am grateful to Jocelyn Jerome, Dave Dubnow, and Johanna Fernandez for their insight and willingness to share with me a number sources. Their analysis on policing has influenced my thinking about the subject. My discussions on policing and police brutality with Khalil Gibran Muhammad, Jerald Podair, Douglas Egerton, Leigh Fought, Carol Smith, Joe Esposito, Kristopher Burrell, Jane Latour, Tim Johnson, and Michael Koncewicz were immeasurably helpful as well.

I also benefited from discussions on policing and race with my good friend Felton O. Best and his students at Central Connecticut State University. I similarly profited from Alex Vitale's comments on chapter 3 and from his new book on policing. I wish to thank Pedro Hernandez and Juber Ayala Millas at the Centro de Estudios Puertorriqueños for help with the Richie Pérez Papers. I also wish to thank the archivists at the State University of New York in Albany for their assistance with the Papers of the New York Conservative Party. I also benefited from the work of Robert Gangi and PROP.

Last but not least, I wish to give special thanks to Marsha for her patience and understanding as I labored these last few years to complete this book.

NOTES

INTRODUCTION

1 "Shielded from Justice: Police Brutality and Accountability in the United States," Human Rights Watch, July 1, 1998, www.hrw.org.

2 "Investigation of the Ferguson Police Department," United States Department of Justice, March 4, 2015, www.justice.gov.

3 Matthew Mathias and Carly Schwartz, "The NYPD Has a Long History of Killing Unarmed Black Men," *Huffington Post* (blog), July 19, 2014, www.huffingtonpost.com; American Civil Liberties Union, "Fighting Police Abuse: A Community Action Manual," 1997, www.aclu.org.

4 Natasha Bach, "Police Violence Has Been Going On Forever: No Wonder People Are Fed Up with It," *Huffington Post* (blog), August 23, 2014, www.huffingtonpost.com.

5 Bryan Burrough, "Today, a Softer Response to Police Violence Than in the 1960s and 70s," *Los Angeles Times*, May 2, 2015.

6 Jamilah King, "Before Freddie Gray: A Timeline of American Unrest," TakePark (blog), April 29, 2015, www.takepart.com.

7 Sam Roberts, "No Longer Majority Black, Harlem Is in Transition," *New York Times*, January 5, 2010. All *New York Times* quotations are drawn from www.nytimes.com.

8 "Population of the 20 Largest U.S. Cities 1900–2012," Infoplease, n.d., www.infoplease.com.

9 Clarence Taylor, *The Black Churches of Brooklyn* (New York: Columbia University Press, 1997), 123.

10 Charles Crawford, "Law Enforcement and Popular Movies: Hollywood as a Teaching Tool in the Classroom," *Journal of Criminal Justice and Popular Culture* 6, no. 2 (1999): 46–57, available at www.albany.edu.

11 Harry S. Truman, "Address before the Attorneys General Conference on Law Enforcement Problems," February 15, 1950, www.presidency.ucsb.edu.

CHAPTER 1. THE *PEOPLE'S VOICE* AND POLICE BRUTALITY

1 Martha Biondi, *To Stand and Fight: The Struggle for Civil Rights in Postwar New York City* (Cambridge, MA: Harvard University Press, 2006), 70.

2 Warren H. Brown, "A Negro Looks at the Negro Press," *Saturday Review*, December 19, 1942, 5.

3 Maxwell R. Brooks, *The Negro Press Re-examined: Political Content of Leading Negro Newspapers* (Boston: Christopher Publishing House, 1959), 67.

4 Louis E. Lomax, *The Negro Revolt* (New York: Signet Books, 1963), 72–73.

5 Al Nall, "Reports of Police Brutality Prove Some Cops Shouldn't Be on the Force," *New York Amsterdam News*, September 7, 1957.

6 "Police Brutality," *Crisis*, March 1953, 164–65.

7 Wil Haygood, *King of the Cats: The Life and Times of Adam Clayton Powell Jr.* (New York: Amistad, 2006), 88; Kathleen Curire, Interview with Marvel Cooke for the Washington Press Club Foundation, transcript, October 6, 1989, http://beta.wpcf.org ; Brian Dolinar, *The Black Cultural Front: Black Artists and Writers of the Depression Generation* (Jackson: University Press of Mississippi, 2012), 180.

8 Bruce Lambert, "Doxey Wilkerson Is Dead; Educator and Advocate Rights," *New York Times*, June 18, 1993; Tony Pecinovsky, "Communist Party and African American Equality: A Focus Unequal in U.S. History," *People's World*, February 3, 2010; Lawrence P. Jackson, *The Indignant Generation: A Narrative History of African American Writers and Critics, 1934–1960* (Princeton, NJ: Princeton University Press, 2011), 306.

9 Barbara Harris, "Harrington, Oliver W. (14 Feb. 1912–2 Nov. 1995," in *African American Lives*, ed. Henry Louis Gates and Evelyn Brooks Higginbotham (New York: Oxford University Press, 2004), 375–76.

10 "The Editorial Policy of the *Voice*," *People's Voice*, February 14, 1942, 20.

11 James G. Thompson, letter to editor, *Pittsburgh Courier*, January 31, 1942.

12 Thompson.

13 "Editorial Policy of the *Voice*."

14 "Editorial Policy of the *Voice*."

15 Richard Robbins, "Counter-Assertion in the New York Negro Press," *Phylon* 10, no. 2 (1949).

16 Robbins; Haygood, *King of the Cats*, 90.

17 "Man Charges Cops Brutally Beat Him Up," *People's Voice*, February 28, 1942, 1.

18 James S. Ettema and Theodore L. Glasser, *Custodians of Conscience: Investigative Journalism and Public Virtue* (New York: Columbia University Press, 1998), 193.

19 Llewellyn Ransom, "Angry Mob Circled Hospital as Crazed Man Is Slain by Cop," *People's Voice*, May 16, 1942, 2.

20 Ransom.

21 For an example of a police version of a killing of a Harlem resident see, "Police Shoot into Rioters; Kill Negro in Harlem Mob," *New York Times*, May 20, 1935; "Patrolman Cleared in Harlem Shooting," *New York Times*, November 15, 1949.

22 James W. Douglas Jr., "I Saw a Harlem Cop Slay a Helpless Man," *People's Voice*, May 23, 1942, 3.

23 Douglas.

24 Thomas Kessner, *Fiorello H. La Guardia and the Making of Modern New York* (New York: McGraw Hill, 1989), 371–72; Cheryl Greenberg, *Or Does It Explode? Black Harlem in the Great Depression* (New York: Oxford University Press, 1991), 294.

25 A. G. Sulzberger, "La Guardia's Tough and Incorruptible Police Commissioner," *New York Times*, November 11, 2009.

26 "Four Lawyers Volunteer to Aid McCullom as Court Hears Case," *People's Voice*, December 12, 1942, 5.

27 Llewellyn Ransom, "Eyewitness to Shooting of Youth Swears Policeman Was Drunk," *People's Voice*, November 21, 1941, 3.

28 "Four Lawyers Volunteer to Aid McCullom as Court Hears Case," *People's Voice*, December 12, 1942, 5.

29 "McCullum Back on Job Employer Held for Him," *People's Voice*, December 12, 1942, 8.

30 Llewellyn Ransom, "4 Teen-Age Boys Beaten, Spit Upon; Detective Had Been Warned by Judge," *People's Voice*, April 10, 1943, 3.

31 "New Here?" St. Philips Church, 2017. http://stphilipsharlem.org/new-here/.

32 "Juvenile or Police Delinquency—Which?" *People's Voice*, July 22, 1944, 2.

33 Llewellyn Ransom, "Regarded as Criminals Even before They Err: Black Squad Tactic Harmful to Our Youth," *People's Voice*, August 19,1944, 7.

34 "Woman Attacked by Negro," *New York Times*, March 11, 1898.

35 "Negroes Stab a White Man," *New York Times*, August 20, 1900; "Frightened Negro Kills Girl," *New York Times*, August 20, 1900.

36 "Woman Slain in Park: Stabbed by Negro in Morningside—Her Escort Beaten," *New York Times*, July 16, 1935.

37 "One-Man Offensive Halted by Bullet," *New York Times*, April 23, 1945.

38 David V. Walcott, *Cops and Kids: Policing, Juvenile Delinquency, in Urban America, 1890–1940* (Columbus: Ohio State University Press, 2005), 193–94.

39 "Muggings Are Laid to New Arrivals," *New York Times*, March 27, 1943.

40 "Crime Smear," *Crisis*, December 1941, 375.

41 John Louis Clarke, "Daily News under Fire for Smearing," *People's Voice*, August 15, 1942, 2.

42 "Editorial Policy of the *Voice*," *People Voice*, February 14, 1942, 34.

43 Joe Bostic, "Police Commissioner Denies Press Stories," *People's Voice*, August 15, 1942, 3.

44 Bostic.

45 Clarence Taylor, *Reds at the Blackboard: Communism, Civil Rights, and the New York City Teachers Union* (New York: Columbia University Press, 2011), 80.

46 Adam Clayton Powell, "Soapbox," *People's Voice*, November 27, 1943, 5; Taylor, 80.

47 Powell.

48 Laurie Leach, "Margie Polite, the Riot Starter: Harlem, 1943," *Studies in the Literary Imagination* 40, no. 2 (Fall 2007): 25–48.

49 Adam Clayton Powell, "Soapbox," *People's Voice*, June 17, 1944, 5.

50 "No Time for Complacency," *New York Times*, August 4, 1943.

51 Adam Clayton Powell, "Soapbox," *People's Voice*, July 24, 1943.

52 "Disappearing Act: Whites Replacing Negroes on Harlem Detective Force," *People's Voice*, September 11, 1943, 3.

53 "Disappearing Act."

54 "Valentine Willing to Add More Negroes to Police Force," *People's Voice*, July 10, 1943.

55 Joe Bostic, "More Negro Detectives for Harlem, Ryan Promises: Not Sure When or How Many," *People's Voice*, September 18, 1943, 4.

56 Joe Bostic, "Ryan Fails to Name Negro Detectives," *People's Voice*, October 2, 1943, 4.

57 "Valentine Willing to Add More Negroes to Police Force," *People's Voice*, July 10, 1943, 3; Andrew Darien, *Becoming New York's Finest: Race, Gender, and the Integration of the NYPD, 1935–1980* (New York: Palgrave Macmillan, 2013), 29.

58 "Whites Replacing Negroes on Harlem Detective Force," *People's Voice*, September 1, 1943, 3.

59 Andrew Darien, "Police Fraternity and the Politics of Race and Class in New York City, 1941–1960," *Labor History Regional Labor Review* 2, no. 2 (Spring/Summer 2000): 29–37; Darien, *Becoming New York's Finest*, 30–31.

60 William M. Kephart, "Integration of Negroes into the Urban Police Force," *Journal of Criminal Law* 45, no. 3 (1954): 329–30.

61 Dominic J. Capeci Jr., "From Harlem to Montgomery: The Bus Boycotts and Leadership of Adam Clayton Powell Jr. and Martin Luther King Jr.," *Historian* 41, no. 4 (1979): 723–29.

62 Adam Clayton Powell, "Soapbox," *People's Voice*, May 30, 1942, 5.

63 Powell.

64 Powell.

65 Lewis J. Valentine to F. H. La Guardia, May 15, 1942, Harlem—Powell, Adam Clayton folder, box 3531, folder 10, La Guardia and Wagner Archives.

66 Stone Phone Call to Adam Clayton Powell, Transcript, n.d., Harlem—Powell, Adam Clayton folder, box 3531, folder 10, La Guardia and Wagner Archives.

67 Frank Shilbersky to Commanding Officer of the Criminal Alien Squad, May 17, 1942, Harlem—Powell, Adam Clayton folder, box 3531, folder 10, La Guardia and Wagner Archives.

68 Shilbersky.

CHAPTER 2. THE COMMUNIST PARTY AND POLICE BRUTALITY

1 Carl Lawrence, "Discharged GI Killed by Harlem Cops: Corpse Shipped Home," *New York Amsterdam News*, December 16, 1950, 1; "Eyewitness Tells How Cops Slew Negro Vet," *Daily Worker*, December 11, 1950.

2 For report on affidavits of witnesses, see Lawrence; and "Eyewitness Tells How Cops Slew Negro Vet." For statement by district attorney, see "Indictment Denied in Death of Ex-G.I.," *New York Times*, February 17, 1951.

3 "John Derrick's Corpse Shipped Home; "NAACP Demands Probe of Cops," *New York Amsterdam News*, December 16, 1950, 1; John Hudson Jones, "Cops Who Killed Derrick Still Kept on Duty in Harlem," *New York Amsterdam News*, December 21, 1950, 1.

4 "Mass Meeting Friday to Protest Killing, Demand Indictment," *New York Amsterdam News*, December 30, 1950.

5 Abner Berry, "Cop Killing of Negro Vet Rouses Storm of Protests," *Daily Worker*, December 17, 1950, 1.

6 Harry Haywood, *Black Bolshevik: Autobiography of an Afro-American Communist* (Chicago: Liberator Press, 1978), 436–37.

7 Carl Vedro, "The Menace of White Chauvinism," *Jewish Currents*, June 1950.

8 Mark Solomon, *The Cry Was Unity: Communists and African Americans, 1917–1936* (Jackson: University Press of Mississippi, 1998), 156–57; Marilynn Johnson, *Street Justice: A History of Police Violence in New York City* (Boston: Beacon Press, 2003), 162–63; Haywood, *Black Bolshevik*, 437.

9 "Communist Killed by Gotham Officer," *Pittsburgh Press*, July 1, 1930; "To Investigate Gonzales' Death," *Daily Star*, July 1, 1930.

10 A. B. Magil and Joseph North, "Steve Katovis: Life and Death of a Worker," *International Pamphlets*, 1930, 28.

11 American Civil Liberties Union, "The Fight for Civil Liberty, 1930–1931," June 1932, 19–20, http://babel.hathitrust.org.

12 Solomon, *Cry Was Unity*, 189.

13 Paul D'Amato, "The Communist Party and Black Liberation in the 1930s," *International Socialist Review* 1 (Summer 1997): www.isreview.org.

14 D'Amato.

15 William Z. Foster, "Problems of Solidarity," in *Strike Strategy* (Chicago: Trade Union Education League, 1926), chap. 2, www.marxists.org.

16 Clarence Taylor, *Reds at the Blackboard: Communism, Civil Rights, and the New York City Teachers Union* (New York: Columbia University Press, 2011), 37–39.

17 Dan T. Carter, *Scottsboro: A Tragedy of the American South* (Baton Rouge: Louisiana State University Press, 1979), 3–99.

18 Carter, 186–87, 225–26, 229.

19 Resolutions of the National Negro Congress, February 14–16, 1936, Woodson-Harsh Collection, Chicago Public Library; Erik Gillman, *Death Blow to Jim Crow: The National Negro Congress and the Militant Fight for Civil Rights* (Chapel Hill: University of North Carolina Press, 2012), 30–56.

20 David Garrow, "Randolph, A. Phillip (1889–1979)," in *Biographical Dictionary of the American Left*, ed. Bernard K. Johnpoll and Harvey Klehr (New York: ABC-CLIO, 1986), 329.

21 Daniel W. Aldridge III, "A Militant Liberalism: Anti-Communism and the African American Intelligential, 1939–1955" (paper presented at the American Historical Association, 2004), users.wfu.edu.

22 Eric Arnesen, "No 'Graver Danger': Black Anticommunism, the Communist Party, and the Race Question," *Labor Studies in Working Class History of the Americas* 3, no. 4 (2006): 15.

23 A. Philip Randolph, Excerpts from Keynote Address to the Policy Conference of the March on Washington Movement Meeting in Detroit, Michigan, September 26, 1942, www.bsos.umd.edu.

24 Judith Stepan-Norris and Maurice Zeitlin, *Left Out: Reds and America's Industrial Unions* (Cambridge, UK: Cambridge University Press, 2003), 254; Aldridge, "Militant Liberalism."

25 "Second Dying, 3rd Wounded, after Arrest," *Nassau Daily Review Star*, February 5, 1946.

26 "Jim Crow Pulled the Trigger," *Daily Worker*, February 10, 1946.

27 Kimberly L. Phillips, *War! What Is It Good For? Black Freedom Struggles and the U.S. Military from World War II to Iraq* (Chapel Hill: University of North Carolina Press, 2012), 91–93.

28 Phillips, 91–93; "New Unit Replaces Communist League: American Youth for Democracy Organized Here—Soviet Friendship Stressed," *New York Times*, October 18, 1943.

29 House Reports, 78th Congress, 2nd Session, January 10–December 19, 1944, Miscellaneous, vol. 2, 152.

30 John Simon, "Rebel in the House: The Life and Times of Vito Marcantonio," *Monthly Review* 57, no. 11 (2006), http://monthlyreview.org; Vito Marcantonio, "Mark My Words," *Daily Worker*, n.d.

31 Benjamin, J. Davis, *Communist Councilman from Harlem: Autobiographical Notes Written in a Federal Penitentiary* (New York: International Publishers, 1969), 101–44, 180–86.

32 Davis, 25–26.

33 Davis, 21–22.

34 Davis, 28–40.

35 Davis, 53–62.

36 Davis, 53–100; Benjamin J. Davis, "Why I Am a Communist," *Phylon* 8, no. 2 (1947): 108–9.

37 Davis, "Why I Am a Communist," 110.

38 Davis, 107–8.

39 Davis, 110.

40 Ben Davis, "Willie McGee Lynching," *Daily Worker*, May 16, 1951; Benjamin J. Davis, *The Negro People in the Struggle for Peace and Freedom: Report to the 15th Convention, Communist Party* (New York: New Century, 1951), 8.

41 Horace Marshall, *Police Brutality, Lynching in the Northern Style* (New York: Office of Councilman Benjamin J. Davis, 1947).

42 Davis press release, April 2, 1948, Communist Party of the United States of America, box 139, folder 16, Tamiment Institute Library and Robert F. Wagner Labor Archives (hereafter cited as Tamiment Library).

43 Ben Davis, "An Answer to Wallander, End Police Brutality" *Daily Worker*, August 18, 1946.

44 Davis to "Dear Friend," n.d., Communist Party of the United States of America, box 139, folder 16, Tamiment Library; Marshall, "Police Brutality: Lynching Northern Style."

45 "'Muss Up" Hoodlums, Wallander Tells Cops," *Brooklyn Daily Eagle*, September 9, 1947.

46 "Ben Davis Will Continue to Serve the People," *New York Age*, October 29, 1949.

47 Penny M. Von Eschen, *Race against Empire: Black Americans and Anticolonialism, 1937–1957* (Ithaca, NY: Cornell University Press, 1997), 109–10.

48 Manning Marable, *Race, Reform, and Rebellion: The Second Reconstruction in Black America, 1945–1990* (Jackson: University Press of Mississippi, 1991), 22.

49 Walter Francis White, "The Negro and the Communists," *Harper's Magazine*, December 1931.

50 Hugh T. Murray Jr., "The NAACP vs. the Communist Party: The Scottsboro Rape Cases, 1931–1932," *Phylon* 28, no. 3 (1967): 276; Manfred Berg, "Black Civil Rights and Liberal Anticommunism: The NAACP in the Early Cold War," *Journal of American History* 94, no. 1 (June 1967): 75–96.

51 Ben Davis, "Truman's Betrayal Hasn't Ended Civil Rights Fight," *Daily Worker*, June 27, 1950.

52 Eric Arnesen, "Civil Rights and the Cold War at Home: Post-War Activism, Anti-communism, and the Decline of the Left," *American Communist History* 11, no. 1 (April 2012), www.tandfonline.com.

53 Patricia Sullivan, *Lift Every Voice: The NAACP and the Making of the Civil Rights Movement* (New York: New Press, 2009), 248–49.

54 Clarence Taylor, *Knocking at Our Own Door: Milton A. Galamison and the Struggle to Integrate New York City Schools* (Lanham, MD: Lexington Books, 2001), 55–65.

55 Manfred Berg, *"The Ticket to Freedom": The NAACP and the Struggle for Black Political Integration* (Gainesville: University Press of Florida, 2005), 134–36.

56 "Our New Councilman," *New York Age*, November 20, 1943.

57 Rev. Ben Richardson to Ben Davis, September 17, 1945, Communist Party of the United States of America, box 139, folder 16, Tamiment Library.

58 Dorothy M. Hayes to Ben Davis, January 10, 1947, Communist Party of the United States of America, box 139, folder 16, Tamiment Library.

59 Walter White to Ben Davis, Western Union telegram, August 5, 1946, Communist Party of the United States of America, box 139, folder 16, Tamiment Library.

60 James Powers to Ben Davis, February 9, 1949, Communist Party of the United States of America, box 139, folder 16, Tamiment Library.

61 Walter White, press release, n.d., Communist Party of the United States of America, box 139, folder 16, Tamiment Library.

62 William L. Patterson, *The Man Who Cried Genocide* (New York: International Publishers, 1991), 19–59.

63 Patterson, 77–79.

64 Patterson, 79–87.

65 Patterson, 87–93.

66 Eugene Debs, "The Negro in the Class Struggle," *International Socialist Review* 4, no. 5 (November 1903): www.marxists.org.

67 "Toward an Anti-Racist Practice," SocialistWorker.org, September 9, 2014, www.
    socialistworker.org.

68 Patterson, *Man Who Cried Genocide*, 94–103.

69 Patterson, 126–38, 161.

70 Walter T. Howard, ed., *Black Communists Speak on Scottsboro: A Documentary
    History* (Philadelphia: Temple University Press, 2007), 103–17.

71 Patterson, *Man Who Cried Genocide*, 156–66.

72 William Patterson, "William Patterson Speaks," in Black Communists Speak
    on Scottsboro: A Documentary History, ed. William T. Howard (Philadelphia:
    Temple University Press, 2008), 118.

73 Patterson, *Man Who Cried Genocide*, 91–95; Gerald Horne, *Communist Front? The
    Civil Rights Congress, 1946–1956* (Rutherford, NJ: Fairleigh Dickinson University
    Press, 1988), 29.

74 Patterson, 170.

75 Manfred Berg, "Black Civil Rights and Liberal Anticommunism: The NAACP in
    the Early Cold War," *Journal of American History* 94, no. 1 (June 2007): 75–96.

76 Civil Rights Congress, *We Charge Genocide* (New York: International Publishers,
    1970); Daniel Levitas, "Remembering Stetson Kennedy," Institute for Research and
    Education on Human Rights, October 25, 2011, www.irehr.org.

77 Civil Rights Congress, *We Charge Genocide*, xiv.

78 Taylor, *Reds at the Blackboard*, 14; Tony Pencinovsky, "Remembering James W.
    Ford," *People's World*, February 16, 2010; James H. Meriwether, *Proudly We Can Be
    Africans: Black Americans and Africa, 1935–1961* (Chapel Hill: University of North
    Carolina Press, 2002), 61; "Claudia Jones, Communist," The Marxist-Leninist: A
    Revolutionary Communist Website, March 1, 2010, www.marxistleninist.word-
    press.com; Carole Boyce Davies, *Left of Karl Marx: The Political Life of Black Com-
    munist Claudia Jones* (Durham, NC: Duke University Press, 2008); Gerald Horne,
    Ferdinand Smith and Radical Black Sailors in the United States and Jamaica (New
    York: NYU Pres, 2005); Eric Homberger, "Obituary: Howard Fast," *The Guardian*,
    March 13, 2003.

79 Civil Rights Congress, *We Charge Genocide*, xvii.

80 Civil Rights Congress, 4.

81 Civil Rights Congress, 10.

82 Civil Rights Congress, 8–9.

83 Civil Rights Congress, 12–76.

84 Patterson, *Man Who Cried Genocide*, 180; Ronald Brown and Carolyn Hartfield,
    "The Black Church Culture and Politics in the City of Detroit," Center of Urban
    Studies, October 2011, 1–5.

85 Berg, "Black Civil Rights and Liberal Anticommunism"; Aldridge, "Militant Lib-
    eralism."

86 For example, see Gerald Horne, *Black and Red: W. E. B. Du Bois and the Afro-
    American Response to the Cold War* (Albany: State University of New York Press,
    1985); Marable, *Race, Reform and Rebellion*; and Robbie Lieberman and Clar-

ence Lang, eds., *Anticommunism and the African American Freedom Movement: Another Side of the Story* (New York: Palgrave Macmillan, 2009).

87 Yama Kunichoff, "From Chicago to Geneva, a Call for Police Accountability for Violence and Torture," *Truthout*, October 15, 2014, www.truth-out.org.

88 "We Charge Genocide: The Cry Rings True 52 Years Later," *People's World*, February 3, 2003, www.peoplesworld.org.

89 "Statement to the Media by the United Nations Working Group of Experts on People of African Descent, on the Conclusion of its Official Visit to the USA, 19–29 January 2016," United Nations Human Rights Office of the High Commissioner, January 29, 2016, www.ohchr.org.

90 Christopher Magan, "Speaking in St. Paul, NAACP Leader Compares Recent Police Killings to Lynching," Twin Cities Pioneer Press, July 10, 2016, www.twincities.com.

CHAPTER 3. THE NATION OF ISLAM AND POLICE BRUTALITY

1 All Nation of Islam sites were initially called "temples"; however, in an effort increase the organization's legitimacy by adding elements from mainstream Islam, the NOI later switched to the word "mosque."

2 "April 14, 1972: The Harlem Muslim Mosque Incident: Justice for Ptl. Cardillo Pending to This Day!" *The History of Policing in the City of New York* (blog), March 22, 2017, www.nypdhistory.com.

3 Rasul Miller, "Where Did All That Power Go? Muslims in the Movement for Community Control and Police Accountability," *Sapelo Square* (blog), September 1, 2015, www.sapelosquare.com.

4 Gilbert Osofsky, *Harlem: The Making of a Ghetto* (New York: Harper Torchbooks, 1966), 128–29.

5 Andy A. Beveridge, "Harlem's Shifting Population," *Gotham Gazette* (blog), September 2, 2008, www.gothamgazette.com.

6 Gilbert Osofsky, *Harlem: The Making of a Ghetto, Negro New York, 1890–1930* (Chicago: Ivan R. Dee, 1996), 135; "Answers about Depression-Era Harlem," *New York Times*, February 19, 2009; Richard L. Hughes, "Harlem's Schools in the Great Depression: The Promise of the Agenda for Education in a Democracy in an Educational Dystopia," Miami University, n.d., www.units.miamioh.edu.

7 Jamie J. Wilson, *Building a Healthy Black Harlem: Health Politics in Harlem, New York, from the Jazz Age to the Great Depression* (Amherst, NY: Cambria Press, 2009), 24.

8 Hughes, "Harlem's Schools in the Great Depression."

9 Arthur Huff Fauset, *Black Gods of the Metropolis: Negro Religious Cults of the Urban North* (Philadelphia: University of Pennsylvania Press, 1944), 76–78.

10 Erdmann Doane Beynon, "The Voodoo Cult among Negro Migrants in Detroit," *American Journal of Sociology* 43, no. 6 (1938): 894.

11 Beynon, 895–902.

12 Fauset, *Black Gods of the Metropolis*, 41–51; Howard M. Brotz, "Negro 'Jews' in the United States," in *The Black Church in America*, ed. Hart M. Nelsen, Raytha L.

Yokley, and Anne K. Nelsen (New York: Basic Books, 1971), 195–209; Ernest Allen Jr., "When Japan Was 'Champion of the Darker Races': Satokata Takahashi and Flowering of Black Messianic Nationalism," *The Black Scholar* 24, no. 1 (Winter 1994): 26–28.

13 "Nation of Islam: Cult of the Black Muslims/Chapter 5," Wikisource, last modified August 5, 2011, http://en.wikisource.org.

14 Southern Poverty Law Center, "The Nation of Islam," n.d., www.spicenter.org; Khuram Hussain, "The Radical Black Press: Forgotten Legacy of Malcolm X," *Black Press Collective*, June 2014.

15 Wayne Taylor "Premillennium Tension: Malcolm X and the Eschatology of the Nation of Islam," *Souls* 7, no. 1 (2005): 53.

16 Manning Marable, *Malcolm X: A Life of Reinvention* (New York: Viking, 2011), 207.

17 "Nation of Islam," part 2, 52, FBI Records: The Vault, n.d., http://vault.fbi.gov.

18 "Nation of Islam," part 1, 37.

19 "Nation of Islam," part 1, 38.

20 "Nation of Islam," part 2, 52–54.

21 "The Hate That Hate Produced (1959): Malcom X First TV Appearance," YouTube, June 28, 2017, http://www.youtube.com/watch?v=BsYWD2EqavQ.

22 "Races: The Black Supremacists," *Time*, August 10, 1959, 4–5.

23 "Recruits behind Bars" *Time*, March 31, 1961, http://www.time.com.

24 C. Eric Lincoln, *The Black Muslims in America* (Boston: Beacon Press, 1961), 156; see also E. U. Essien-Udom, *Black Nationalism: A Search for an Identity in America* (Chicago: University of Chicago Press, 1962), 293.

25 Lee P. Brown, "Black Muslims and the Police," *Journal of Criminal Law and Criminology* 56, no. 1 (Spring 1965): 119–22.

26 Lincoln, *Black Muslims in America*, 3.

27 Elijah Muhammad, *Message to the Blackman in America* (Chicago: Muhammad's Temple No. 2, 1965), 211–15.

28 Muhammad, 216.

29 Elijah Muhammad, "The Black Policeman and What He Polices," *Muhammad Speaks*, December 13, 1968, www.elijahmuhammadspeaks.com.

30 Muhammad.

31 Muhammad.

32 File 100-6989, part 8, 42, "FBI File on Elijah Muhammad," Internet Archive, www.archive.org (hereafter cited as "FBI File on Elijah Muhammad").

33 File 100-6989, "FBI File on Elijah Muhammad."

34 Section 8, 10, "FBI File on Elijah Muhammad."

35 Muhammad, *Message to the Blackman in America*, 315.

36 "MGT Laws," *Muhammad Speaks*, n.d., www.elijahmuhammadspeaks.com.

37 Muhammad, *Message to the Blackman*, 315.

38 Part 8, 52, "FBI File on Elijah Muhammad."

39 Muhammad, *Message to the Blackman*, 319.

40 Muhammad, 316.

41 Muhammad, 211.

42 Elijah Muhammad, *Police Brutality* (1964; repr., Glendale, AZ: Scretarius Memps, 1997), Kindle ed., 8.

43 "Elijah Muhammad: Messenger Meets the Press," *Muhammad Speaks*, January 28, 1972, www.elijahmuhammadspeaks.com. (The last line was a reference to NOI founder Wallace Fard's mysterious disappearance in 1934.)

44 "Elijah Muhammad."

45 Martin Luther King Jr., "The Social Organization of Nonviolence," in *Civil Rights since 1787: A Reader on the Black Struggle*, ed. Jonathan Birnbaum and Clarence Taylor (New York: NYU Press, 2000), 459; "SCLC and 'The Beloved Community,'" in Birnbaum and Taylor, 461.

46 "Malcolm X: Make It Plain," YouTube, March 7, 2013, www.youtube.com/watch?v=zGCygxs5ZqI.

47 Malcolm X to Dear Brother, n.d., file 100-399321, section 1, serials 1–17, 8, "Malcolm X FBI Files," Internet Archive, www.archive.org (hereafter cited as "Malcolm X FBI Files").

48 Memorandum, SLC, Philadelphia, to Director, FBI, April 4, 1954, file 100-399321, section 1, 33–34, "Malcolm X FBI Files."

49 New York City Meeting in June 1959, file 105-8999, "Malcolm X FBI Files."

50 Marable, *Malcolm X*, 207–11.

51 "Malcolm X: Harlem Unity Rally Excerpt 1963," YouTube, September 15, 2016, http://www.youtube.com/watch?v=xMHzLFmMfRw

52 "Malcolm X."

53 "Bayard Rustin Debate (November, 1960)," Malcolm X Files, www.malcolmxfiles.blogspot.com; Robert Penn Warren Interviews, Roy Wilkins, April 1, 1964, Who Speaks for the Negro? An Archival Collection, whospeaks.library.vanderbilt.edu; Michael G. Long, ed., *First Class Citizenship: The Civil Rights Letters of Jackie Robinson* (New York: Time Books, 2007), 148–49.

54 Martin Luther King Jr., "Address at the Thirty-Fourth Annual Convention of the National Bar Association," August 20, 1959, Martin Luther King Jr. Research and Education Institute, http://kinginstitute.stanford.edu.

55 Some of those writing on the Hinton case claim that Hinton said to Dolan, "This is not Alabama, this is New York." For example, see Marable, *Malcolm X*, 127. However, in an affidavit, Hinton testified that he only asked Dolan "Why don't you carry the man to jail?" "Moslem Victim's Own Story of Cop's Brutality," *New York Amsterdam News*, May 18, 1957, 1.

56 "Moslem Victim's Own Story," 1.

57 "Moslem Victim's Own Story."

58 James L. Hicks, "Riot Threat as Cops Beat Moslem," *New York Amsterdam News*, May 4, 1957; Mariame Kaba, *An Abridged History of Resisting Police Violence in Harlem* (Chicago: Project NIA, 2012), www.policeviolence.files.wordpress.com.

59 *Hinton v. City of New York*, March 21, 1961, Leagle, www.leagle.com.

60 Malcom X and Alex Haley, *The Autobiography of Malcolm X* (New York: Ballantine Books, 1965), 233–34.

61 Peter Goldman, *The Death and Life of Malcolm X* (Urbana: University of Illinois Press, 1979), 55–56.

62 Goldman, 56–59.

63 Hicks, "Riot Threat as Cops Beat Moslem"; "Moslem Victim's Own Story," 1, 32.

64 Hicks, 1, 32.

65 See Spike Lee's film *Malcolm X*; and Hicks, "Riot Threat as Cops Beat Moslem."

66 Fredrick Knight, "Justifiable Homicide, Police Brutality, or Governmental Repression? The 1962 Los Angeles Police Shooting of Seven Members of the Nation of Islam," *Journal of Negro History* 79, no. 2 (Spring 1994): 184.

67 "The Day That Malcolm Won Harlem Over," *Prison Culture*, August 12, 2012, www.usprisonculture.com.

68 Justin Charity, "In 1957, Malcolm X Stared Down the NYPD—and Won," *Complex*, May 19, 2015, www.complex.com.

69 Hicks, "Riot Threat as Cops Beat Moslem."

70 File 100-399321, section 3, 10, "Malcolm X FBI Files."

71 File 105-6999, section 3, 80, "Malcolm X FBI Files."

72 File 105-6999.

73 File 105-6999, 21–22.

74 "Cops Quiz Moslems: New Hearing Slated," *New York Amsterdam News*, May 2, 1959.

75 "Moslems Confer with Top Cop," *New York Amsterdam News*, April 11, 1959.

76 Section 3, 94, "Malcolm X FBI Files.".

77 "Moslems Confer with Top Cop."

78 "Cops Quiz Moslems."

79 "Moslems Didn't Get to See Commissioner," *New York Amsterdam News*, June 27, 1959, 20.

80 "Moslems Didn't Get to See Commissioner," 20.

81 "Muslim Charges Police Brutality," *New York Amsterdam News*, August 19, 1961, 18.

82 "Muslim Charges Police Brutality."

83 Report of (Name Redacted) to (Name Blanked), November 17, 1959, 38, FBI Records: The Vault, http://vault.fbi.gov.

84 "Say NY Cops KKK Members: Top Cop Denies Charge," *New York Amsterdam News*, September 12, 1959, 1. The letter can also be found in Rodnell P. Collins, *Seventh Child: A Family Memoir of Malcolm X* (New York: Citadel, 2000), 213–18.

85 Subject file Malcolm Little, 5 of 27, 77–78, FBI Records: The Vault, http://vault.fbi.gov.

86 "Say NY Cops KKK Members."

87 Marable, *Malcolm X*, 191–93.

88 Malachi D. Crawford, "Neo-Houstonian Studies: The Nation of Islam, Edward W. Jacko Jr., and the Struggle for Afro-Muslim Civil Liberties," in *Charles H. Houston:*

An Interdisciplinary Study of Civil Rights Leadership, ed. James L. Conyors (Lanham, MD: Lexington Books, 2012), 238–41; Malachi D. Crawford, *Black Muslims and the Law: Civil Liberties from Elijah Muhammad to Muhammad Ali* (Lanham, MD: Lexington Books, 2015), 50–51.

89 Crawford, 59.
90 "Muslim Wins $75,000 in Damages from City," *New York Amsterdam News*, May 7, 1960; *Hinton v. City of New York* .

CHAPTER 4. CIVIL RIGHTS, COMMUNITY ACTIVISTS, AND POLICE BRUTALITY

 1 Clarence Taylor, *Knocking at Our Own Door: Milton A. Galamison and the Struggle to Integrate New York City Schools* (Lanham, MD: Lexington Books, 2001), 48–49.
 2 Themis Chronopoulos, "Police Misconduct, Community Opposition, and Urban Governance in New York City, 1945–1965," *Journal of Urban History* (2015): 5, http://journals.sagepub.com.
 3 Martha Biondi, "How New York Changes the Story of the Civil Rights Movement," *Afro-Americans in New York Life and History* 31, no. 2 (2007): 15–31.
 4 *The Complete Report of Mayor La Guardia's Commission on the Harlem Riot of March 19, 1935* (New York: Arno Press, 1969), 122, 133–34.
 5 *Complete Report of Mayor La Guardia's Commission*, 134–35.
 6 On June 22, 1943, Detroit erupted in "race riots." Over six thousand federal troops were sent to restore order.
 7 "No Detroit in New York," *People's Voice*, August 7, 1943, 1; Llewelyn Ransom, "Racial Element Not Present in Harlem, Leaders Act Quickly to Restore," *People's Voice*, August 7, 1943, 3; Marvel Cooke, "Riots Express Resentment against Existing Social Ills," *People's Voice*, August 7, 1943, 4.
 8 Cooke, 4.
 9 "Police Commissioner Kills Cop Brutality Committee, *People's Voice*, March 20, 1948.
10 "NAACP Organizes Police Committee," *People's Voice*, March 27, 1948.
11 John J. Cassese to the Mayor and Council of the City of New York, May 21, 1964, Legislative Materials, Police Civilian Complaint Review Board, 1964–1965, box 14, folder 278, LaGuardia and Wagner Archives; Andrew T. Darien, *Becoming New York's Finest: Race, Gender, and the Integration of the NYPD, 1935–1980* (New York: Palgrave, 2013), 35.
12 Cedric Larson, "New York City Launches New Public Relations Policy," *Journal of Criminal Law and Criminality* 41, no. 3 (1950): 375.
13 Larson, 369–70.
14 Larson, 372–73.
15 From the Desk of the P.C. [Police Commissioner], "The Police and the Public," January 1950, www.archive.org.

16 "New York NAACP Opens Drive against Cop Brutality," *People's Voice*, March 6, 1948, 9; "Police Commissioner Kills Cop Brutality Committee".

17 Malachi D. Crawford, "Neo-Houstonian Studies: The Nation of Islam, Edward W. Jacko Jr., and the Struggle for Afro-Muslim Civil Liberties," in *Charles H. Houston: An Interdisciplinary Study of Civil Rights Leadership*, ed. James L. Conyors (Lanham, MD: Lexington Books, 2012), 238–41; Malachi D. Crawford, *Black Muslims and the Law: Civil Liberties from Elijah Muhammad to Muhammad Ali* (Lanham, MD: Lexington Books, 2015), 50–51.

18 "Win $130Gs Damages," *New York Amsterdam News*, February 9, 1957, 1, 31; "Convict Former Cop for Shooting Fields," *New York Amsterdam News*, July 6, 1957.

19 "Cop Victim Wins $50,000 in Court," *New York Amsterdam News*, September 28, 1957, 2.

20 "Police Brutality," *Crisis*, March 1953, 164–65.

21 "Brutality Charges against City Police under U.S. Inquiry," *New York Times*, February 17, 1953; "Cop Victim Wins $50,000 in Court"; Marilynn Johnson, *Street Justice: A History of Police Violence in New York City* (Boston: Beacon Press, 2003), 222–26.

22 "Brutality Charges against City Police under U.S. Inquiry."

23 "Brutality Charges against City Police under U.S. Inquiry."

24 "Police Brutality," 165.

25 Charles Grutzner, "Halley Urges City Sift 'Deal' on FBI; Mayor Disagrees," *New York Times*, February 19, 1953.

26 Grutzner.

27 Grutzner.

28 Grutzner.

29 Majority Report of a Special Subcommittee to Study the Feasibility of Creating an Independent Civilian Complaint Review Board to Investigate, Hear, and Make Recommendations Concerning Allegations of Police Brutality, Bill No. 498, City Counsel Special Committee, May 18, 1965, box 14, folder 278, La Guardia and Wagner Archives. .

30 Majority Report.

31 "Boy, 9, Says Cops Brutally Beat Him," *New York Amsterdam News*, May 21, 1955, 1; "Grand Jury Fails to Indict Cop," *New York Amsterdam News*, June 11, 1955, 1.

32 Michael Nash, "Pregnant, Says Cop Beat Her," *New York Amsterdam News*, April 27, 1957, 1.

33 Les Matthews, "It Was Police Brutality," *New York Amsterdam News*, August 29, 1959, 1, 9.

34 "Miles Davis Seized," *New York Times*, August 26, 1959.

35 Matthews, "It Was Police Brutality," 1, 9.

36 Fred Powledge, "Brutality Cases Urged for Study," *New York Times*, April 7, 1964.

37 Richard J. H. Johnston, "Murphy Charges Attack on Police," *New York Times*, April 29, 1964.

CHAPTER 5. POLICE BRUTALITY, THE HARLEM AND BEDFORD-STUYVESANT RIOTS, AND THE NATIONAL CIVIL RIGHTS MOVEMENT

1 Al Nall, "Reports of Police Brutality Prove Some Cops Shouldn't Be on Force," *New York Amsterdam News*, September 7, 1957, 2; "Police Brutality Called Old Issue," *New York Times*, March 22, 1953.

2 Milton Nallory, "Sidewalk Interview," *New York Amsterdam News*, May 18, 1957, 11.

3 Michael Flamm, *In the Heat of the Summer: The New York Riots of 1964 and the War on Crime* (Philadelphia: University of Pennsylvania Press, 2017), 12–13.

4 Gilligan Report, September 1, 1964–September 3, 1964, box 60228, folder 16, La Guardia and Wagner Archives.

5 Carol J. Pelleck and Ted Poston, "City Probes Slaying of Boy, 15," *New York Post*, July 17, 1964. All *New York Post* quotations are drawn from http://nypost.com. See also Gilligan Report.

6 Gilligan Report; Flamm, *In the Heat of the Summer*, 28.

7 Paul L. Montgomery and Frances X. Clines, "Thousands Riot in Harlem Area: Scores Are Hurt," *New York Times*, July 19, 1964; Paul Montgomery, "Night of Riots Began with Calm Rally, *New York Times*, July 20, 1964.

8 "Negroes, Police Turn Harlem into Battlefield," *Asahi Evening News*, July 20, 1964, 1.

9 Robert L. Muller, "Virtual Guerrilla Warfare Rocks Harlem," *Windsor-Star*, July 20, 1964, 28.

10 Peter Kihss, "Screvane Links Reds to Rioting," *New York Times*, July 22, 1964.

11 "The Campaign," *Time*, July 31, 1964, 10.

12 R. W. Apple Jr., "Violence Flares Again in Harlem; Restraint Urged," *New York Times*, July 20, 1964; Robert Wagner, "Statement on the Harlem Riot, July 22, 1964," New York City Municipal Archives WNYC Collection.

13 Wagner.

14 Paul Screvane, "Statement on the Harlem Riots, July 19, 1964," New York City Municipal Archives WNYC Collection.

15 Kihss, "Screvane Links Reds to Rioting," 1.

16 Author interview with Fred Jerome, June 5, 2017.

17 Peter Kihss, "Wagner Asserts Disorders Harm Negroes' Cause," *New York Times*, July 23, 1964.

18 William Borders, "More Than 100 Injured Get Aid at 2 City Hospitals in Harlem," *New York Times*, July 20, 1964.

19 Francis X. Clines, "Policemen Exhaust Their Ammunition in All-Night Battle," *New York Times*, July 20, 1964.

20 Simone Montgomery to Mayor Wagner and Commissioner Murphy, July 22, 1964, CORE Papers, reel 3, Schomburg Center for Research in Black Culture (hereafter cited as Schomburg).

21 "Freedom Funders: Philanthropy and the Civil Rights Movement, 1955–1965," *National Committee for Responsive Philanthropy*, June 2014.

22 Ray Arsenault, *Freedom Riders: 1961 and the Struggle for Racial Justice* (New York: Oxford University Press, 2006), 11–22, 33–93, 207.

23 "Farmer and Murphy Discuss Complaints Board," *New York Times*, April 28, 1964.

24 "Farmer and Murphy Discuss Complaints Board."

25 Pelleck and Poston, "City Probes Slaying of Boy."

26 Apple, "Violence Flares Again in Harlem," 1.

27 Fred Powledge, "Screvane to Meet Rights Leaders," *New York Times*, July 20, 1964.

28 List of July 20 Meeting, President of the City Council (Paul Screvane, 1962–1965), Series: Press Releases, box 52517, folder 32, Harlem Riots, July 25, 1964, La Guardia and Wagner Archives; Powledge, 1.

29 Meeting July 20, 1964, Hildebrand's Group, President of the City Council (Paul Screvane, 1962–1965), Series: Press Releases, box 52517, folder 32, Harlem Riots, July 25, 1964, La Guardia and Wagner Archives; Peter Kihss, "City to Increase Negro Policemen on Harlem Duty," *New York Times*, July 21, 1964.

30 Kihss.

31 Kihss.

32 Warren Weaver Jr., "Powell Says Riots Can End If Mayor Meets 5 Demands," *New York Times*, July 23, 1964.

33 Arthur C. Logan, "Statement from Board of Directors, HARYOU-ACT, Inc., of Conflict in Harlem," press release, n.d., Robert F. Wagner Documents Collection, box 60228, folder 18, Harlem Riots, La Guardia and Wagner Archives.

34 Christopher Hayes, "The Heart of the City: Civil Rights, Resistance, and Police Reform in New York City, 1945–1966" (PhD diss., Rutgers University, 2012), 194–95.

35 *Police Power and Citizens' Rights: The Case for an Independent Police Review Board* (New York: American Civil Liberties Union, 1966), 3.

36 "Riots in Harlem and Other Sections of New York," Robert F. Wagner Documents Collection, box 60228, folder 19, Harlem Riots—Statements, July 21, 1964, La Guardia and Wagner Archives.

37 "Riots in Harlem and Other Sections of New York."

38 "Riots in Harlem and Other Sections of New York."

39 "Riots in Harlem and Other Sections of New York."

40 "Riots in Harlem and Other Sections of New York."

41 "WSB-TV Newsfilm Clip of Dr. Martin Luther King Jr. Speaking about Race Riots in Rochester and New York City, New York, 1964 July 27," Civil Rights Digital Library, n.d., http://crdl.usg.edu.

42 "WSB-TV Newsfilm Clip of Dr. Martin Luther King."

43 Peter Kihss "Harlem Killings Reported Urged," *New York Times*, July 28, 1964.

44 Paul L. Montgomery, "CORE to Continue Its Direct Action," *New York Times*, August 10, 1964.

45 Philip Benjamin, "Dr. King Confers with Mayor on City and U.S. Rights Issues," *New York Times*, July 28, 1964; Philip Benjamin, "Harlem Leaders Charge Dr. King Is Ignoring Them," *New York Times*, July 29, 1964.

46 Benjamin.

47 "Key Negro Groups Call on Members to Curb Protests," *New York Times*, July 30, 1964.

48 To JCCE, Telephone Conversation Message from Mrs. Roy Wilkins, n.d., box 60224, folder 5, Robert F. Wagner Documents Collection, 37–44, La Guardia and Wagner Archives.

49 To JCCE, Telephone Conversation Message from Mrs. Roy Wilkins.

50 Author interview with Fred Jerome, June 5, 2017; R. W. Apple Jr., "Police Ban March in Harlem Today; Sponsors Defiant," *New York Times*, July 25, 1964; "Jesse Gray, 64, Leader of Harlem Rent Strike," *New York Times*, August 5, 1988.

51 Apple.

52 R. W. Apple Jr., "Protest Leaders Seized in Harlem: Two Leftist Arrested after Defying Police and Ignoring Pleas for Negro Unity," *New York Times*, July 26, 1964.

53 M. S. Handler, "Negro Factions Are Considering a United Front," *New York Times*, July 29, 1964.

54 President Lyndon Baines Johnson, State of the Union Address, January 8, 1964, MP503, Lyndon Baines Johnson Library and Museum.

55 "MLK on the Republican Nomination of Barry Goldwater," July 16, 1964, King Library and Archives, www.thekingcenter.org.

56 Roy Wilkins to Senator Barry Goldwater, May 13, 1964, Telegram, NAACP Collection, Manuscript Division, Library of Congress, www.loc.gov.

57 Apple, "Police Ban March in Harlem Today."

58 Apple.

59 "Key Negro Groups Call on Members to Curb Protests," *New York Times*, July 30, 1964.

60 "Key Negro Groups Call on Members to Curb Protests"; R. W Apple Jr., "Negro Leaders Split over Call to Curtail Drive," *New York Times*, July 31, 1964.

61 Andrew Young, "Whitney Young: Working from the Middle," *Life* 70/11 (March 26, 1971), 4; Whitney Young Interview with Robert Penn Warren, April 13, 1964, Who Speaks for the Negro? An Archival Collection, whospeaks.library.vanderbilt.edu.

62 Lyndon Johnson Conversation with A. Philip Randolph, November 29, 1963, tape K6311.05, Miller Center, University of Virginia.

63 Apple, "Negro Leaders Split over the Call to Curtail Drive," 1.

64 Bayard Rustin, "From Protest to Politics: The Future of the Civil Rights Movement," *Commentary* 39, no. 2 (February 1965), www.crmvet.org.

65 Martin Luther King Jr., "Letter from a Birmingham Jail," in *Civil Rights since 1787: A Reader in the Black Struggle*, ed. Jonathan Birnbaum and Clarence Taylor (New York: NYU Press, 2000), 478–80.

66 Statement from Dr. Martin Luther King Jr. on Republican Nomination of Senator Barry Goldwater.

67 Clarence Taylor, "'Whatever the Cost We Will Set the Nation Straight': The Ministers Committee for Job Opportunities and the Downstate Medical Center Jobs Campaign," *Long Historical Journal* 1, no. 2 (Spring 1989): 136–46.

68 Roy Wilkins, "What Now! One Negro Leader's Answer," *New York Times Magazine*, August 1, 1964.

69 Brian Purnell, *Fighting Jim Crow in the County of Kings: The Congress of Racial Equality in Brooklyn* (Lexington: University Press of Kentucky, 2013).

70 Purnell.

71 Purnell.

72 Paul L. Montgomery, "CORE to Continue Its Direct Action," *New York Times*, August 10, 1964.

73 James Farmer, *Freedom When?* (New York: Random House, 1966), 26–28.

74 Farmer, 28–31.

75 James Farmer, *Lay Bare the Heart: An Autobiography of the Civil Rights Movement* (Fort Worth: Texas Christian University Press, 1985), 279–80.

76 Woody Klein, "James Farmer: Non-violent Pied Piper," *New York World and Sun*, July 25, 1964.

77 Fred Howard to James Farmer, July 23, 1964, CORE Papers, reel 3, Schomburg.

78 Ronald S. Freund to James Farmer, July 21, 1964, CORE Papers, reel 3, Schomburg.

79 Blaine Lotz to James Farmer, n.d., CORE Papers, reel 3, Schomburg.

80 Milton Ellenbogen to James Farmer, July 19, 1964, CORE Papers reel 3, Schomburg.

81 Perry S. Samuels to James Farmer, July 21, 1964, CORE Papers, reel 3, Schomburg.

82 James Marshall to Farmer, July 21, 1964, CORE Papers, reel 3, Schomburg.

83 Justin G. Ferguson to James Farmer, n.d., CORE Papers, reel 3, Schomburg.

84 Herbert B. Geist to James Farmer, July 23, 1964, CORE Papers, reel 3, Schomburg.

85 G. Louis Schata to James Farmer, July 24, 1964; G. Blaine Lotz to James Farmer, n.d., CORE Papers, reel 3, Schomburg.

86 Joanne Ferrera to James Farmer, July 27, 1964, CORE Papers, reel 3, Schomburg.

87 Anne C. Jordan to James Farmer, July 27, 1964, CORE Papers, reel 3, Schomburg.

88 Pat Matteo to James Farmer, July 29, 1964, CORE Papers, reel 4, Schomburg.

89 Fred Powledge, "Poll Shows Whites in City Resent Civil Rights Drive," *New York Times*, September 21, 1964.

90 Thomas Hudson McKee to James Farmer, July 23, 1964, CORE Papers, reel 3, Schomburg.

CHAPTER 6. JOHN LINDSAY, RACIAL POLITICS, AND THE CIVILIAN COMPLAINT REVIEW BOARD

1 Lynda Richardson, "Michael J. Murphy, 83, Dies, Led New York Police in 1960s," *New York Times*, May 18, 1997.

2 John Lindsay, "Address to New York Lawyers," *New York Times*, May 21, 1965.

3 Geoffrey Kabaservice, "On Principle: A Progressive Republican," in *Summer in the City: John Lindsay, New York, and the American Dream*, ed. Joseph P. Viteritti (Baltimore: Johns Hopkins University Press, 2014), 27–28.

4 Eric Pace, "Herbert Brownell, 92, Eisenhower Attorney General, Dies," *New York Times*, May 2, 1992.

5 "Civil Rights Act of 1957," Dwight D. Eisenhower Presidential Library, www.eisen-hower.archives.gov.

6 "John Lindsay (R-NY) and Emmanuel Celler (D-NY) on the Compromise Bill," Civil Rights Act of 1964: A Long Struggle for Freedom, January 15, 1964, Library of Congress. www.loc.gov.

7 Interviews of John Lindsay by Seymour Siegel, "Close Up," WNYC, May 3, 1964, New York City Municipal Archives WNYC Collection.

8 Ronald Sullivan, "Lindsay Rejects National Ticket," New York Times, August 4, 1964.

9 Lindsay, "Address to New York Lawyers."

10 Lindsay.

11 "Lindsay Proposes Adding Civilians to Police Board," New York Times, May 21, 1965.

12 Clayton Knowles, "City Bar Urges Civilian Control of Police Review," New York Times, August 6, 1965; "The Democrats on Public Safety," New York Times, September 10, 1965.

13 Charles G. Bennett, "Police Reform on Board Hailed," New York Times, July 23, 1965.

14 "Lindsay Proposes Adding Civilians to Police Board," 1.

15 Thomas Buckley, "Joint Drive Is On for Review Board," New York Times, May 27, 1965; Edward J. Blum and Paul Harvey, "How (George) Romney Championed Civil Rights and Challenged His Church," The Atlantic, August 13, 2012, www.theatlantic.com.

16 Buckley, "Joint Drive Is on for Review Board"; "Lindsay Is Assailed for Stand on Police," New York Times, May 24, 1965.

17 Homer Bigart, "5,000 Policemen Picket City Hall," New York Times, June 30, 1965.

18 "Off Duty Police Officers against Civilian Review Board City Hall—June 29, 1965," serial file Jul 21965 FOIA: JBS-NYC, Internet Archive, www.archive.org.

19 "Off Duty Police Officers against Civilian Review Board City Hall."

20 Homer Bigart "Inquiry Is Sought on Police Racism," New York Times, July 1, 1965.

21 Peter Kihss, "Negro Policemen Here Ask for a Civilian Review Board," New York Times, June 15, 1965; Bigart, "5,000 Policemen Picket City Hall."

22 William F. Buckley Jr., God and Man at Yale (Washington, DC: Regnery Publishing, 1986).

23 Russell Kirk, The Conservative Mind: From Burke to Elliot, 7th ed. (Washington, DC: Regnery Publishing, 2001); Whittaker Chambers, Witness: (Washington, DC: Regnery Publishing, 1987); Carl T. Bogus, Buckley: William F. Buckley Jr. and the Rise of American Conservatism (New York: Bloomsbury Press, 2011), 14–17, 107–11.

24 William. F. Buckley Jr. Speech to National Press Club, Washington, DC, August 4, 1965, M. E. Grenander Department of Special Collections and Archives (hereafter cited as Grenander Department). Milton Galamison was the leader of the public school integration campaign in New York City. See Clarence Taylor, Knocking at Our Own Door: Milton Galamison and the Struggle to Integrate New York City Schools (New York: Columbia University Press, 1997).

25 Buckley.

26 Statement Scheduled for Delivery by William F. Buckley Jr., Conservative Party Candidate for Mayor of New York City, to the New York City Council on Tuesday Afternoon, July 13, 1965, on the Proposal to Establish a Civilian Review Board for the New York City Police Department, Buckley Files—William F. Buckley Jr., box 18, Grenander Department.

27 Statement Scheduled for Delivery by William F. Buckley Jr.

28 Statement Scheduled for Delivery by William F. Buckley Jr.

29 William F. Buckley Jr., "Crime: In New York, It Pays," box 18, Position Papers for Mayoral Race, 1965, Grenander Department.

30 Buckley.

31 Sam Tanenhaus, "The Buckley Effect," *New York Times*, October 5, 2005.

32 Richard Wilkin, "Seesaw Contest: Vote Is Tightest Here in a Quarter Century," *New York Times*, November 2, 1965.

33 Paul Hofmann, "Sweeping Change in Police Powers Urged on Lindsay," *New York Times*, February 7, 1966.

34 Eric Pace, "Broderick Defies Lindsay on Issue of Police Review Board," *New York Times*, February 9, 1966.

35 Pace.

36 Terrence Smith, "Lindsay Declares His Record Good," *New York Times*, April 6, 1966.

37 Murray Schumach, "Choice Is Praised by Rights Groups," *New York Times*, February 16, 1966.

38 Thomas R. Farrell letter to the editor, *New York Times*, February 18, 1966.

39 "Statements and Preamble of Order on Police Review Board," *New York Times*, May 3, 1966; Paul Hofmann, "Civilian Control of Police Review Is Set Up by City," *New York Times*, May 3, 1966.

40 General Order No. 14, Amendments to the Rules and Procedures, Civilian Complaints—Revised Procedures, May 17, 1966. Mayor Lindsay subject files, box 21, folder 364, Civilian Complaint Review Board, New York City Municipal Archives.

41 In addition to Brownell, the other members were Morris B. Abram, U.S. representative to the United Nations Commission on Human Rights; William H. Booth, chair of the City Commission on Human Rights; Vincent J. Cuttis, member of the Catholic Lawyers Guild; John Patrick Hogan, assistant principal of P.S. 65 in the Bronx; Donald S. Harrington, minister of the Community Churches of New York; Orin Lehman, a Democrat who ran and lost the race to fill Lindsay's congressional seat; William Hughes Mulligan, a law professor at Fordham University; Raymond Fernandez Narrel, vice president of the Puerto Rican Bar Association; C. B. Powell, editor of the *Amsterdam News*; and Sandy F. Ray, pastor of Cornerstone Baptist Church. See General Order No. 14.

42 "A Modern Review Board," *New York Times*, May 3, 1966.

CHAPTER 7. THE TRIUMPH OF A FALSE NARRATIVE

1 Peter Kihss, "NAACP Attacks New Police Plan," *New York Times*, May 4, 1966.

2 "Cassese Balks at a TV Debate with Mayor on Review Board," *New York Times*, October 30, 1966.

3 Kihss, "NAACP Attacks New Police Plan," 1.

4 Peter Kihss, "CORE Assails Lack of Voice for Ghettos on Police Panel," *New York Times*, May 5, 1966.

5 Eric Pace, "Suit Threatened on Police Board," *New York Times*, February 15, 1966.

6 Paul Hofmann, "Civilian Control of Police Review Is Set Up by City," *New York Times*, May 3, 1966.

7 Eric Pace, "Suit Threatened on Police Board."

8 Will Lissner, "Policemen to Sue for Writ Barring Civilian Review Board," *New York Times*, May 9, 1966.

9 Lissner.

10 Eric Pace, "PBA Gets Writ Ordering City to Court Today on Its Review Board Plan," *New York Times*, May 10, 1966.

11 *John J. Cassese et al., on Behalf of Themselves and All Members of the Police Department of the City of New York Similarly Situated, Plaintiffs v. John V. Lindsay as Mayor of the City of New York, et al. Defendants*, Supreme Court Special Term, New York County, June 23, 1966; Robert E. Tomasson, "Court Hears Police Board Plan; Ruling Is Expected Next Month," *New York Times*, May 21, 1966.

12 *John J. Cassese et al. v. John V. Lindsay as Mayor of the City of New York, et al.*; Tomasson.

13 "Battler for Police Rights: John Joseph Cassese," *New York Times*, May 9, 1966.

14 Lissner, "Policemen to Sue for Writ Barring Civilian Review," 1.

15 Lissner.

16 Eric Pace, "PBA Asks Public to Oppose Board," *New York Times*, June 3, 1966.

17 Pace.

18 *John J. Cassese et al. v. John V. Lindsay as Mayor of the City of New York, et al.*

19 Eric Pace, "PBA Asks Public to Oppose Board."

20 Sidney E. Zion, "Civilian Review Board: Now a Nasty Campaign," *New York Times*, July 3, 1966.

21 Bernard Weinraub, "Lindsay to Fight Police Issue," *New York Times*, July 9, 1966.

22 Author interview with Jay Kriegel, February 12, 2012.

23 Herbert Brownell to John V. Lindsay, May 27, 1966; and Biographical Data on Algernon Black, Kenneth Clark, Manuel Diaz, Thomas R. Farrell, Helen Hall, Theodore W. Kheel, both in Mayor Lindsay subject files, box 21, folder 364, Civilian Complaint Review Board, New York City Municipal Archives (hereafter cited as Civilian Complaint Review Board); Emanuel Perlmutter, "Lindsay to Name 4 Civilians Today for Police Board," *New York Times*, July 11, 1966; Bernard Weinraub, "New Police Board Has Two Negroes and Puerto Rican," *New York Times*, July 12, 1966.

24 Weinraub, "New Police Board Has Two Negroes and Puerto Rican."

25 Weinraub.

26 Bernard Weinraub, "Racism Laid to PBA Head in Review Board Stand," *New York Times*, July 13, 1966.

27 Petition for the Submission to the Electors of the City of New York, Mayor Lindsay subject files, box 21, folder 364, Civilian Complaint Review Board.

28 Conservative Party Petition for the Submission to the Electors of the City of New York at the General Election to Be Held November 8, 1966, Concerning Control of Disciplinary Proceedings within the Police Department of the City of New York, Mayor Lindsay subject files, box 21, folder 364, Civilian Complaint Review Board .

29 Bernard Weinraub, "Leary Assails PBA Accusations," *New York Times*, September 28, 1966.

30 Weinraub.

31 Sidney E. Zion, "Civilian Review Board: FAIR Fights for It," *New York Times*, September 11, 1966.

32 American Jewish Committee, "Review of the Year: United States Other Countries," *American Jewish Year Book* 68 (1967): 90–91, www.ajcarchives.org.

33 Jonathan Randal, "Mayor Sees Chances of Civilian Review Board Improving 'Every Minute,'" *New York Times*, September 11, 1966.

34 "Myths about the Review Board," Mayor Lindsay subject files, box 21, folder 364.

35 "City Loses Again on Police Board," *New York Times*, October 1, 1966.

36 Robert Alden, "Lindsay Seeks Aid on Review Board," *New York Times*, October 3, 1966.

37 Bernard Weinraub, "Poll Favors Foes of Review Board," *New York Times*, October 14, 1966.

38 Thomas R. Brooks, "25,000 Police against the Review Board: No! Says the PBA, *New York Times*, October 16, 1966.

39 Eric Pace, "PBA Asks Public to Oppose Board," *New York Times*, June 3, 1966.

40 Herman Katz, Letter, August 4, 1964, Legislative Materials: Parents and Taxpayers, box 14, folder 274, La Guardia and Wagner Archives.

41 "PAT Denounces City Clerk's Decision on Neighborhood School Referendum: Attacks Mayor and 'Political Cronies' for Defying Will of the Majority," August 4, 1964, Legislative Materials: Parents and Taxpayers, box 14, folder 274, La Guardia and Wagner Archives.

42 Clarence Taylor, "Conservative and Liberal Opposition to the New York City School Integration Campaign," in *Civil Rights in New York City: From World War II to the Giuliani Era*, ed. Clarence Taylor (New York: Fordham University Press, 2011), 106–9.

43 Will Bunch, "Gathering Storm: The Philly Riots of 1964," *Inquirer Daily News*, August 29, 1964; "Rochester Police Battle Race Riot," *New York Times*, July 25, 1964; "300 Negroes Riot in Philadelphia," *New York Times*, August 29, 1964; "2 New Jersey Cities Racked by Race Riots," *Chicago Tribune*, August 3, 1964, 7.

44 "2,000 Troops Enter Los Angeles on Third Day of Negro Rioting; 4 Die as Fires and Looting Grow," *New York Times*, August 14, 1965; Gene Roberts, "Negroes Still Angry and Jobless Three Months after Watts Riot, *New York Times*, November 7, 1965.

45 Linda Lyons, "Gallup Brain: The Darkest Hours of Racial Unrest," Gallup, June 3, 2003, http://news.gallup.com.

46 Lyons.

47 Bernard Weinraub, "Police Review Panel Killed by Large Majority in City," *New York Times*, November 9, 1966.

48 Weinraub.

49 Brooks, "25,000 Police against the Review Board."

CHAPTER 8. MAYOR RUDOLPH GIULIANI AND POLICE BRUTALITY

1 Statement of Honorable Edward I. Koch, Mayor of the City of New York, before the City Council Committee on Public Safety, October 21, 1986, Series: Local Laws, box 50016, folder 14, Civilian Review Police Actions, 1986, La Guardia and Wagner Archives.

2 Statement of Honorable Edward I. Koch.

3 Joyce Purnick, "Koch, in Shift, Wants Private Citizens on Police Review Board," *New York Times*, June 7, 1985.

4 "Cops Plead Innocent in Torture Case," *Chicago Tribune*, May 3, 1985, www.chicagotribune.com.

5 Joyce Purnick, "Koch, in Shift, Wants Private Citizens on Police Review Board," *New York Times*, June 7, 1985.

6 The Council of the City of New York Intl. No. 583, A Local Law, December 20, 1990, Series: Local Laws, box 50045, folder 11, Accounting for Revenues and Expenditures Associated with the Safe Streets / Safe City Omnibus Criminal Justice Program, 1991, La Guardia and Wagner Archives; Ralph Blumenthal, "Dinkins on Crime: Dinkins Proposes Record Expansion of Police Forces," *New York Times*, October 3, 1990.

7 William Bratton, *Broken Windows and Quality-of-Life Policing in New York City* (New York: NYPD, 2015), 1, www.nyc.gov.

8 "Lee Brown's Legacy," *New York Times*, August 4, 1992.

9 James G. McKinley, "Dinkins Denounces Police Protest as Furthering Images of Racism," *New York Times*, September 16, 1992; Catherine Manegold, "Rally Puts Police under New Scrutiny," *New York Times*, September 27, 1992.

10 James C. McKinley Jr., "Officers Rally and Dinkins Is Their Target," *New York Times*, September 17, 1992; Manegold, "Rally Puts Police under New Scrutiny."

11 Local Laws of the City of New York for the Year 1993, Chapter 18—Civilian Complaint Review Board, Office of the Vice-Chair / Maj. Leaders—Cuite / Vallone (1969–89), Office of the Speaker—Vallone (1990–2001), box 52456. La Guardia and Wagner Archives.

12 James C. McKinley Jr., "Giuliani Imposes Curbs on Hiring by Agencies, *New York Times*, January 5, 1994.

13 Norman Siegel to Peter Vallone, March 9, 1994, Series: Committee Files, box 50215, folder 24, Civilian Complaint Review Board (CCRB), 1994, La Guardia and Wagner Archives.

14 Norman Siegel to Edward Silver and Hector Soto, January 7, 1994, Committee Files, box 50218, folder 44, Miscellaneous—Civilian Complaint Review Board (CCRB); Abortion Clinic Access; Gun Control, 1994, La Guardia and Wagner Archives.

15 Norman Siegel to Edward Silver and Hector Soto, January 7, 1994.

16 Testimony of David M. Zornow before the Public Safety Committee of the New York City Council, March 15, 1995, Committee Files, box 50212, folder 2, Oversight Preliminary Budget for Fiscal Year 1995, La Guardia and Wagner Archives.

17 Jonathan P. Hicks, "Mayor Accused of Sabotaging Civilian Board," *New York Times*, March 10, 1994.

18 Alison Mitchell, "Giuliani Urges Street Policing Refocused on Crime," *New York Times*, January 25, 1994.

19 William Bratton, *Turnaround: How America's Top Cop Reversed the Crime Epidemic* (New York: Random House, 1998), 198–99; Judith Greene, "Zero Tolerance: A Case Study of Police Policies and Practices in New York City," *Crime and Delinquency* 45, no. 2 (April 1999): http://crab.rutgers.edu/~goertzel/ZeroNYC.htm.

20 William Bratton, Testimony before the Committee on Public Safety of the New York City Council on Police Productivity, Monday May 9, 1994, Series: Committee Files, box 50152, folder 27, Oversight: Citizens Budget Commission Report on New York Police Department, May 9, 1994, La Guardia and Wagner Archives.

21 Gary Pierre-Pierre, "They're Tried, They're True, but How Long Do They Last?" *New York Times*, October 8, 1995; *Congressional Record*, March 28, 2000, H3794.

22 George L. Kelling and James Q. Wilson, "Broken Windows: The Police and Neighborhood Safety," *The Atlantic*, March 1982, www.theatlantic.com.

23 Bratton, *Broken Windows and Quality-of-Life Policing in New York City*.

24 *CompStat: Its Origins, Evolution, and Future in Law Enforcement Agencies* (Washington, DC: Bureau of Justice Assistance, 2013), vii.

25 *CompStat*, 4.

26 Greene, "Zero Tolerance."

27 George L. Kelling and William J. Bratton, "Why We Need Broken Windows Policing," *City Journal*, Winter 2015, www.city-journal.org.

28 Freda F. Solomon, "The Impact of Quality-of-Life Policing," CJA Research Brief, August 2003, 1–2; K. Babe Howell, "Broken Lives from Broken Windows: The Hidden Cost of Aggressive Order-Maintenance Policing," *New York University Review of Law and Social Change* 33 (2009): 271, 281.

29 New York State Law: Penal Law, Consolidated Laws of New York Penal Code, n.d., www.ypdcrime.com; "Marijuana Possession Arrests in New York City in Three Decades," Brown University, May 31, 2007, www.brown.edu.

30 Howell, "Broken Lives from Broken Windows," 81–82.

31 Kelling and Bratton, "Why We Need Broken Windows Policing."

32 Greene, "Zero Tolerance."

33 Commission to Investigate Allegations of Corruption and the Anti-corruption Procedures of the Police Department Commission Report (Mollen Commission Report), July 7, 1994, 2–8, www.scribd.com (hereafter cited as Mollen Commission Report).

34 Mollen Commission Report, 1–2.

35 Mollen Commission Report, 2–3.

36 Mollen Commission Report, 43–44.

37 Mollen Commission Report, 44–45.

38 Mollen Commission Report, 47.

39 Mollen Commission Report, 47–48.

40 Mollen Commission Report, 50.

41 Mollen Commission Report, 142.

42 Mollen Commission Report, 122–28.

43 Mollen Commission Report, 143.

44 Mollen Commission Report.

45 Mollen Commission Report, 152.

46 George James, "Investigating by a Monitor Is Opposed by Bratton," *New York Times*, April 25, 1994; Alison Mitchell, "Corruption in Uniform: The Mayor; Giuliani Promises to Fight to Root Out Police Corruption," *New York Times*, July 8, 1994.

47 Int. No. 961, A Local Law to Amend the New York City Charter, in Relation to the Establishment of an Independent Police Investigation and Audit Board, May 14, 1997, Series: Local Laws, box 51913, Local Laws 91, Independent Police Investigation and Audit Board, 1997, La Guardia and Wagner Archives.

48 Int. No. 961.

49 *Supreme Court, New York County, New York, Mayor of the City of New York, et al., Plaintiffs, v. Council of the City of New York, Defendant*, Decided August 21, 1999.

50 *Supreme Court, New York County, et al. v. Council of the City of New York.*

51 Int. No. 961.

52 Int. No. 961.

53 *Mayor of the City of New York et al., Plaintiff, v. Council of the City of New York, Defendant*, Decided August 31, 1999.

54 *Mayor of the City of New York et al. v. Council of the City of New York.*

55 *Congressional Record*, March 28, 2000, H3794.

CHAPTER 9. ABNER LOUIMA, AMADOU DIALLO, AND THE RESISTANCE TO GIULIANI

1 Wayne Barrett, "Rudy's Milky Way," *Village Voice*, January 19, 1999; Perry Bacon, "Giuliani's Ties to Black New York Troubled," *Washington Post*, June 10, 2007. All *Washington Post* quotations are drawn from www.washingtonpost.com.

2 Mark Green, Public Advocate for the City of New York, Trend Analysis of Complaints Received by the New York Civilian Complaint Review Board, 1992–1996,

September 11, 1997, Series: Committee Files, box 50215, folder 2, La Guardia and Wagner Archives.

3 Michael Fletcher, "Changes in Police Tactics Trigger Charges of Brutality," *Washington Post*, April 27, 1997.

4 "Mayor Defends Cops After Boy Shot," United Press International, April 8, 1997.

5 Barbara Ross, Stephen McFarland, James Ruttenberg, and Alice McQuillan, "Cop Who Shot Teen Cleared," *New York Daily News*, July 2, 1997. All *New York Daily News* quotations are drawn from www.nydailynews.com.

6 United States Court of Appeals, Second Circuit, *United States of America, Appellee v. Francis X. Livoti, Defendant-Appellant*, Docket No. 981608, Decided November 8, 1999.

7 *Police Brutality and Excessive Force in the New York City Police Department* (London: Amnesty International, 1996), 29–30.

8 Cathy Lisa Schneider, *Police Power and Race Riots: Urban Unrest in Paris and New York* (Philadelphia: University of Pennsylvania Press, 2014), 170.

9 *Police Brutality and Excessive Force in the New York City Police Department*, 1–6.

10 *Police Brutality and Excessive Force in the New York City Police Department*.

11 *Police Brutality and Excessive Force in the New York City Police Department*.

12 *Police Brutality and Excessive Force in the New York City Police Department*, 11.

13 *Police Brutality and Excessive Force in the New York City Police Department*, 12–13.

14 *Police Brutality and Excessive Force in the New York City Police Department*, 13–14.

15 *Police Brutality and Excessive Force in the New York City Police Department*, 55.

16 "Amadou Diallo Was Not the First: Selected Police Brutality Cases—NYC (1994–1998)," National Congress for Puerto Rican Rights, Justice Committee—New York City Chapter, n.d., Richie Pérez Papers, box 6, folder 7, Archives of the Puerto Rican Diaspora.

17 *Police Brutality and Excessive Force in the New York City Police Department*, 56–57.

18 *Police Brutality and Excessive Force in the New York City Police Department*, 56–58.

19 *Police Brutality and Excessive Force in the New York City Police Department*, 58–59.

20 *Police Brutality and Excessive Force in the New York City Police Department*, 59–60.

21 *Police Brutality and Excessive Force in the New York City Police Department*, 60–61.

22 *Police Brutality and Excessive Force in the New York City Police Department*, 65.

23 *Police Brutality and Excessive Force in the New York City Police Department*, 66.

24 Clifford Krauss, "Rights Group Finds Abuse of Suspects by City Police," *New York Times*, June 26, 1996; David Firestone, "Poll of Voters Gives Giuliani an Early Lead," *New York Times*, November 20, 1996.

25 Gary Pierre-Pierre, "Settling Suits for Brutality Rises in Cost," *New York Times*, August 2, 1995; "Shielded from Justice: Police Brutality and Accountability in the United States," Human Rights Watch, July 1, 1998, www.hrw.org.

26 Marie Brenner, "Incident in the 70th Precinct," *Vanity Fair*, December 1997, www.vanityfair.com.

27 United States District Court Eastern District of New York, Abner Louima and Micheline Louima, Plaintiffs, against the City of New York, the Patrolmen's Benevolent Association, Individually and in Their Official Capacity as New York City Police Officers, Justin Volpe, Charles Schwarz, Thomas Bruder, et al., Third Supplemental Summons and Third Complaint, Testimony of the Center for Law and Social Justice before the City Council Hearings on Police Brutality, August 28, 1997, at Brooklyn College, Series: Committee Files, box 50215, folder 2, Oversight: Police Abuse And Brutality—Searching for Solutions, September 11, 1997, La Guardia and Wagner Archives (hereafter cited as Abner Louima and Micheline Louima, Plaintiffs, against the City of New York).

28 Abner Louima and Micheline Louima, Plaintiffs, against the City of New York.

29 Abner Louima and Micheline Louima, Plaintiffs, against the City of New York.

30 Abner Louima and Micheline Louima, Plaintiffs, against the City of New York; Brenner, "Incident in the 70th Precinct."

31 Abner Louima and Micheline Louima, Plaintiffs, against the City of New York.

32 Michael Meyers, Margaret Fung, and Norman Siegel, *Deflecting Blame: The Dissenting Report of the Mayor's Task Force on Police/Community Relations* (New York: New York Civil Liberties Union, 1998), 13, www.nycivilrights.org.

33 Dan Barry, "Leaders in Precinct Are Swept Out in Torture Inquiry," *New York Times*, August 15, 1997.

34 Meyers, Fung, and Siegel, *Deflecting Blame*; 15 Dan Barry, "Giuliani Dismisses Police Proposals by His Task Force, *New York Times*, March 27, 1998.

35 David Firestone, "Skepticism and Fiery Debate Mark First Session of Panel," *New York Times*, August 22, 1997.

36 Meyers, Fung, and Siegel, *Deflecting Blame*, 15; Firestone.

37 Meyers, Fung, and Siegel, 15–17.

38 Meyers, Fung, and Siegel, 17–24.

39 Meyers, Fung, and Siegel, 3–5.

40 Barry, "Giuliani Dismisses Police Proposals."

41 Committee on Public Safety, Oversight: Police Abuse and Brutality—Searching for Solutions, September 11, 1997, box 050215, folder 2, La Guardia and Wagner Archives.

42 "The Role of the Public Advocate," NYC Public Advocate, n.d., http://archive.advocate.nyc.gov.

43 Testimony of Mark Green, Public Advocate for the City of New York, before the City Council Committee on Public Safety, Series: Committee Files, box 50215, folder 2, September 11, 1997, La Guardia and Wagner Archives.

44 Testimony of Mark Green.

45 Testimony of the Center for Law and Social Justice before the City Council Hearings on Police Brutality, August 28, 1997, at Brooklyn College Prepared by Esmeralda Simmons, Esq., Executive Director, Joan P. Gibbs, Esq., General Counsel, Ruth Lateefah Carter, Project Associate, 4, 5, Series: Committee Files, box 50215,

folder 2, Oversight: Police Abuse and Brutality—Searching for Solutions, September 11, 1997.

46 Testimony of the Center for Law and Social Justice, box 50215, folder 2, September 11, 1997, La Guardia and Wagner Archives, 5

47 Testimony of the Center for Law and Social Justice, 7–8.

48 100 Blacks in Law Enforcement Who Care, "Mutual Respect through Proper Monitoring," Series: Committee Files, box 50215, folder 2, September 11, 1997, La Guardia and Wagner Archives.

49 Latino Officers Association, City of New York, Inc., "Police Abuse and Brutality: Searching for Solutions," August 28, 1997, Series: Committee Files, box 50215, folder 2, La Guardia and Wagner Archives.

50 Latino Officers Association.

51 Testimony of Ray LaForest before the New York City Council Committee on Public Safety, September 11, 1997, Series Committee Files, box 50215, folder 2, La Guardia and Wagner Archives.

52 John Kifner, "Thousands March to Protest Police," *New York Times*, August 17, 1997; Chrisena Coleman et al., "City Grids for Protest Tide," *New York Daily News*, August 29, 1997.

53 Kifner.

54 Meyers, Fung, and Siegel, *Deflecting Blame*, 10–11.

55 Randy Kennedy, "Haitians Press Mayor on Issue of Brutality by Police," *New York Times*, September 1, 1997.

56 Kennedy; Gary Pierre-Pierre, "For Haitians, Leadership Split Is a Generation Gap," *New York Times*, September 24, 1997.

57 Pierre-Pierre.

58 John Kifner, "Thousands Call on City Hall to Confront Police Brutality," *New York Times*, August 30, 1997.

59 Kifner; Kennedy, "Haitians Press Mayor on Issue of Brutality by Police."

60 Kifner.

61 "NY Officer to Plead Guilty in Brutality Case," *Baltimore Sun*, May 25, 1999.

62 Devlin Barrett, "Tearful Volpe Confesses: Apologizes to Own Family, Not Louima," *New York Post*, May 26, 1999; Joseph P. Fried, "Volpe Sentenced to a 30-Year Term in the Louima Torture," *New York Times*, December 14, 1998.

63 *United States v. Volpe*, 62 F. Supp. 2d 887 (E.D.N.Y. 1999).

64 "Court Overturns 3 Convictions in NY Police Torture Case," CNN, February 26, 2002, www.cnn.com.

65 Joseph P. Fried and Blaine Harden, "The Louima Case: The Overview; Officer Is Guilty in Torture of Louima," *New York Times*, June 9, 1999.

66 Timothy Lynch, "We Own the Night: Amadou Diallo's Deadly Encounter with New York City Special Crime Unit," Cato Institute Briefing Paper, March 31, 2000.

67 Tara George, "Cops Tell Their Story Officer's Frantic Plea: 'Please Don't Die,'" *New York Daily News*, February 15, 2000; "Opening Statements: The Amadou Diallo Killing," Diallo, 2012, www.criminaldefense.com.

68 Jane Fritsch, "Diallo Witness: Man Cried 'Gun!' but Police Shot without Warning," *New York Times*, February 10, 2000; Michael Cooper, "Officers in Bronx Fire
41 Shots, and an Unarmed Man Is Killed," *New York Times*, February 5, 1999.

69 Rafael A. Olmeda and John Marzulli, "Unarmed Man Amadou Diallo Is Killed by
Four Officers Who Shot at Him 41 Times in 1999," *New York Daily News*, February
3, 2015.

70 Marilyn Vogt-Downey, "New Yorkers Protest Cop Killing of Ahmed Diallo,"
Socialist Action, March 3, 1999.

71 Ginger Thompson, "1,000 Rally to Condemn Shooting of Unarmed Man by
Police," *New York Times*, February 8, 1999; Michael Cooper, "12 Arrested during
Sit-In to Protest Diallo Killing," *New York Times*, March 10, 1999.

72 Michael Copper, "12 Arrested during Sit-In to Protest Diallo Killing," *New York
Times*, March 10, 1999.

73 Dave Saltonstall, "Inside Al's Protest Machine Rev. Al's Line Getting Long," *New
York Daily News*, March 21, 1999.

74 "History," National Action Network History, n.d., www.nationalactionnetwork.
net; Clarence Taylor, *Black Religious Intellectuals* (New York: Routledge, 2002),
138–39.

75 Taylor, 138.

76 Michael Litwin, "Labor Joins Protest over New York Police Killing," May 1999,
http://michaelletwin.wordpress.com.

77 Shan-san Wu, "'Books, Not Bullets' Demand CUNY Students and Faculty," *The
Ticker*, April 14, 1999, 1, 5.

78 "U.S. Commission on Civil Rights to Investigate Diallo Shooting," 15.

79 Scott Sherman, "He Has a Dream: The Grand Ambition of the Rev. Al Sharpton,"
The Nation, March 30, 2001, www.thenation.com.

80 "Life after Diallo: Officials Ponder Why NYPD Arrest Numbers Are Down," *Law
Enforcement News* 25, nos. 511–12 (May 1999): 1.

81 Katherine Finkelstein, "Rookies Told to Serve, Protect and Respect," *New York
Times*, May 7, 1999.

82 "NYPD's 'Streetwise' Cultural Sensitivity Training Gets Renewed Impetus," *Law
Enforcement News* 25, nos. 511–12 (May 1999): 1.

83 "Trials Put Giuliani, NYPD on Defensive," *Washington Post*, March 30, 1999.

84 Tom Topousis, "Rudy Job Rating Hits a New Low; Bad News in Post Diallo Poll,"
New York Post, April 9, 1999; "Despite Crime Approval, Mayor's Job Rating Is
Negative, Quinnipiac College Poll Finds; New Yorkers Concerned With Race
Relations, Police," Quinnipiac University Poll, April 8, 1999, http://poll.qu.edu.

85 Eric Lipton, "Giuliani Cites Criminal Past of Slain Man," *New York Times*, March
20, 2000; Bill Vann, "The Killing of Patrick Dorismond: New York Police Violence
Escalates in Wake of Diallo Verdict," World Socialist Web Site, March 22, 2000,
www.wsws.org.

86 Transcript, "New York Police Arrest Protestors at Funeral of Patrick Dorismond,"
Democracy Now! March 27, 2000. www.democracynow.org.

87 Lipton, "Giuliani Cites Criminal Past of Slain Man."

88 *In the Matter of Mark Green, as Public Advocate of the City of New York, Petitioner, v. Rudolph Giuliani, as Mayor of the City of New York, Respondent,* Supreme Court, New York County, November 21, 2000, Leagle, www.leagle.com.

89 *Mark Green v. Rudolph Giuliani.*

90 *Mark Green v. Rudolph Giuliani.*

91 C. J. Chivers, "Grand Jury Clears Detective in Killing of Unarmed Guard," *New York Times,* July 28, 2000.

92 William Clarkson, "City Settles Suit in Guard's Death by Police Bullet," *New York Times,* March 13, 2003.

93 Rudolph Giuliani, "The City of New York Mayor's Management Report Fiscal 2001," City of New York, September 12, 2001, 1–16, www1.nyc.gov.

94 *New York City Civilian Complaint Review Board Status Report, January–December 2002* (New York: City of New York, 2003), xvii, www1.nyc.gov.

95 Giuliani, "City of New York Mayor's Management Report," 17.

96 Giuliani.

97 Giuliani.

CHAPTER 10. THE CAMPAIGN TO END STOP, QUESTION, AND FRISK

1 Testimony of Mark Green, Public Advocate for the City of New York, before the City Council Committee on Public Safety, Series: Committee Files, box 50215, folder 2, September 11, 1997, La Guardia and Wagner Archives.

2 Testimony of Mark Green.

3 Testimony of Mark Green.

4 Alice McQuillan, "Street Crime Unit Dumped: Kelly Sending Cops to Detective, Plainclothes Squad," *New York Daily News,* April 10, 2002.

5 *Daniels et al. v. City of New York,* Center of Constitutional Rights, 1999, http://ccrjustice.org; *Winston Daniels Jr., Appellant v. City of New York, Defendant, New York City Transit Authority,* Leagle, February 14, 2002, www.leagle.com.

6 *Daniels et al. v. City of New York.*

7 Michael Myers, *Special Report: Mayor Bloomberg and Civil Rights—an Assessment of the First Year* (New York: New York Civil Rights Coalition, 2003); Diane Cardwell, "Mayor to Mark King's Birthday with Sharpton," *New York Times,* January 19, 2002.

8 Diane Cardwell and Sewell Chan, "Mayor Calls 50 Shots by the Police Unacceptable," *New York Times,* November 28, 2006.

9 "Bloomberg and NY Police Shooting," *American Spectator,* November 27, 2006.

10 *New York City Civilian Complaint Review Board Status Report, January–December 2002* (New York: City of New York, 2003), www1.nyc.gov.

11 *New York City Civilian Complaint Review Board Status Report, January–December 2003* (New York: City of New York, 2004), xvii–xviii, www1.nyc.gov.

12 Ernie Naspretto, "The Real History of Stop and Frisk," *New York Daily News,* June 3, 2002.

13 *New York City Civilian Complaint Review Board Status Report, January–December 2005* (New York: City of New York, 2006), 1, www1.nyc.gov.

14 *Terry v. Ohio*, 392 U.S. 1 (1968), Argued December 12, 1967, Decided June 10, 1968, www.law.cornell.edu.

15 Interview with Bill Bratton, *Here and Now*, February 25, 2014, www.wbur.org.

16 "Stop-and-Frisk Data," New York Civil Liberties Union, n.d., www.nyclu.org.

17 "Stop-and-Frisk Data."

18 Al Baker and Emily Vasquez, "Police Report Far More Stops and Searches," *New York Times*, February 3, 2007; Michael D. White and Henry F. Fradella, *Stop and Frisk: The Use and Abuse of a Controversial Policing Tactic* (New York: NYU Press, 2016).

19 Eliot Spitzer, *The New York City Police Department's Stop and Frisk Practices: A Report to the People of the State of New York from the Office of the Attorney General* (New York: Civil Rights Bureau, 1999), v–vii, 5, http://ag.ny.gov.

20 Spitzer, ix.

21 "Richie Pérez (1944–2004)," Virtual Boricua, March 30, 2004, www.virtual.boricua.org.

22 Richie Pérez, "Police Brutality and the Black and Latino Coalition," January 11, 1980, Richie Pérez Papers, box 6, folder 2, Archives of the Puerto Rican Diaspora; Richie Pérez Interview, Tape 2, Voces Digital Audio Archive, 1988, Richie Pérez Interviews, VOCES Digital Audio Archive, www.voces.prattsi.org; Joseph P. Field, "Police Ruled Not Liable in Killing," *New York Times*, November 21, 1979.

23 "Interview with Richie Pérez, Founder, National Congress for Puerto Rican Rights, and the Justice Committee," ed. Blanca Vazquez, 2004, Anderson Gold Films, www.andersongoldfilms.com.

24 National Congress for Puerto Rican Rights, Justice Committee, NYC Chapter, August 2, 1988, Richie Pérez Papers, box 10, folder 1, Archives of the Puerto Rican Diaspora.

25 "Interview with Richie Pérez."

26 Richie Pérez to Malcolm X Grassroots Movement, August 27, 1996; and Adele Mora di Puma, "Adopt a Day in Court," September 5, 1996, both in Richie Pérez Papers, box 14, folder 2, Archives of the Puerto Rican Diaspora.

27 Matthew Purdy, "Judges Rule Clerical Error Voids Officer's Homicide Charges," *New York Times*, September 6, 1996.

28 Press Release, Committee to Remember Anthony Baez, September 16, 1996, Richie Pérez Papers, box 4, folder 1, Archives of the Puerto Rican Diaspora.

29 Richie Pérez Interview.

30 Copies of *Justicia* can be found in the Richie Pérez Papers, box 14, folder 2, Archives of the Puerto Rican Diaspora.

31 David M. Herszenhorn, "Judge Assails but Acquits Officer in Man's Choking Death in Bronx," *New York Times*, October 8, 1996.

32 David Gonzalez, "Not Innocent, Not Guilty: No Comfort," *New York Times*, October 9, 1996.

33 *United States of America v. Francis X. Livoti*, 25 F. Supp. 2d 390 (S.D.N.Y. 1998), Court Listener, www.courtlistener.com.

34 Benjamin Weiser, "Former Officer Gets 7 ½ Years In Man's Death," *New York Times*, October 9, 1998.

35 Richie Pérez Interview.

36 Richie Pérez Interview.

37 "Mission and History," Center for Constitutional Rights, May 27, 2015, www.ccrjustice.org.

38 "Daniels, et al. v. the City of New York," Center for Constitutional Rights, 1999, www.ccrjustice.org.

39 "Daniels, et al. v. the City of New York."

40 "Daniels, et al. v. the City of New York."

41 "Floyd, et al., v. City of New York, et at.," Center for Constitutional Rights, 2008, www.ccrjustice.org.

42 *Davis v. City of New York*, 10 Civ. 0699 (SAS). (S.D.N.Y. May. 5, 2011), Casetext, 1–4, http://casetext.com.

43 *Davis v. City of New York*, 4–13.

44 *Davis v. City of New York*, 15–16.

45 *Jaenean Ligon, Individually, et al. v. the City of New York et al.*, New York Civil Liberties Union, March 28, 2012, 1–2, www.nyclu.org.

46 *Jaenean Ligon* (March 28, 2012), 3.

47 *Jaenean Ligon* (March 28, 2012), 4.

48 *Jaenean Ligon* (March 28, 2012), 10.

49 *Jaenean Ligon et al. v. the City of New York et al.*, New York Civil Liberties Union, January 8, 2013, 1–10, www.nyclu.org.

50 *Jaenean Ligon* (January 8, 2013), 134–47.

51 *Jaenean Ligon* (January 8, 2013).

52 *Jaenean Ligon* (January 8, 2013), 1–3.

53 *Jaenean Ligon* (January 8, 2013), 6–7.

54 *Jaenean Ligon* (January 8, 2013), 7–8.

55 *Jaenean Ligon* (January 8, 2013), 13–14.

56 *Jaenean Ligon* (January 8, 2013), 22–23.

57 *Jaenean Ligon* (January 8, 2013), 178.

58 *Jaenean Ligon* (January 8, 2013), 178–87.

59 *Opinion and Order, David Floyd, et al., Plaintiffs, against City of New York, Defendant*, New York Civil Liberties Union, August 12, 2013, www.nyclu.org.

60 *Davis v. City of New York*—Joint Letter to the Court re: Settlement, NAACP LDF, January 7, 2015, www.naacpldf.org.

61 Michael R. Bloomberg, "Michael Bloomberg: 'Stop and Frisk' Keeps New York Safe," *Washington Post*, August 18, 2013.

62 Bloomberg.

63 Christopher Mathlas, "Bloomberg Decries 'Dangerous' Stop-and-Frisk Ruling, Promises Appeal," *Huffington Post* (blog), August 12, 2013, www.huffingtonpost.com.

64 *In re: Reassignment in Cases: Ligon; Floyd et al. v. City of New York et al.*, United
States Court of Appeals for the Second Circuit, Filed November 13, 2013, docket
13-3123-3088, FindLaw, http://caselaw.findlaw.com; Joseph Goldstein, "Court
Blocks Stop and Frisk Changes of New York Police," *New York Times*, October 31,
2013.

65 Goldstein.

66 Benjamin Weisner and Joseph Goldstein, "New York City Asks Court to Vacate
Rulings on Stop-and-Frisk Tactics," *New York Times*, November 9, 2013.

67 *In re: Reassignment in Cases: Ligon; Floyd et al. v. City of New York et al.*

68 Benjamin Weiser, "Judges Decline to Reverse Stop-and-Frisk Ruling, All but Ending Mayor's Fight," *New York Times*, November 22, 2013.

69 Michael Barbaro, "The Ad Campaign: De Blasio Speaks against Stop and Frisk
Tactics," *New York Times*, August 18, 2013.

70 *One New York Rising Together* (New York: Bill de Blasio for Mayor, 2013), 20–21,
www.marijuana-arrests.com.

71 Black, Latino/a, and Asian Caucus to Mayor Bill de Blasio, January 21, 2014,
Scribd, www.scribd.com.

72 "Transcript: Mayor Bill de Blasio Announces Agreement in Landmark Stop-
And-Frisk Case," City of New York, January 30, 2014, www.1.nyc.gov; Benjamin
Weiser, "Mayor Says New York Will Settle Suits on Stop and Frisk Tactics," *New
York Times*, January 30, 2014; Black, Latino/a, and Asian Caucus to Mayor Bill de
Blasio.

73 "Transcript: Mayor Bill de Blasio."

74 "Transcript: Mayor Bill de Blasio."

75 "Transcript: Mayor Bill de Blasio."

76 "Transcript: Mayor Bill de Blasio."

77 "What We Want," Citizens Union, n.d., www.citizensunion.org.

78 "Citizens Union Commends City Agreement Allowing Civilian Police Complaints
to Be Prosecuted Independently," Citizens Union, March 28, 2012, www.citizen-
sunion.org; Al Basker, "Independent Agency Gets New Powers to Prosecute New
York City Officers," *New York Times*, March 27, 2012.

79 Basker.

CHAPTER 11. THE LIMITS OF MAYOR DE BLASIO'S POLICE REFORM AGENDA

1 "DOI's Mission and History," NYC Department of Investigation, n.d., www1.nyc.
gov.

2 "Local Laws of the City of New York for the Year 2013: No. 70," City of New York,
2013, www1.nyc.gov.

3 "Transcript: Mayor de Blasio, Police Commissioner Bratton Announce Change
in Marijuana Policy," City of New York, November 10, 2014, www1.nyc.gov; "Transcript: Mayor de Blasio and Police Commissioner Bratton Host Press Conference
on Police Body Cameras," City of New York, December 3, 2014, www1.nyc.gov;

Margaret Hartman, "43 Ways New York Has Changed under Mayor de Blasio," *New York*, December 31, 2014.

4 *Police Use of Force in New York City: Findings and Recommendations on NYPD's Policies and Practices* (New York: New York City Department of Investigation Office of the Inspector General for the NYPD, 2015), 21–29, www.nyc.gov.

5 J. David Goodman and Al Baker, "Bratton, Tracking Police Use of Force, Aims to Stay Step Ahead of Watchdogs," *New York Times*, October 1, 2015; Alison Fox, "NYPD Reveals New Use of Force Guidelines, Admitting Deficiencies," *New York Times*, October 1, 2015.

6 William J. Bratton, "The NYPD Plan of Action and the Neighborhood Policing Plan: A Realistic Framework for Connecting Police and Communities," n.d., http://home.nyc.gov.

7 Bratton.

8 New York City Police Department, "Neighborhood Policing," n.d., www1.nyc.gov.

9 Ellie Kaufman, "New York City on Pace to Record Lowest Murder Tally in Decades," CNN, December 28, 2017, www.cnn.com.

10 "Mayor de Blasio Outlines Core Principles of Legislation to Make the Disciplinary Records of Law Enforcement and Other Uniformed Public Personnel Subject to Disclosure," City of New York, October 14, 2016, www1.nyc.gov.

11 "NYC Police Reform Campaign Responds to Mayor de Blasio's 'Core Principles' of State Legislation on Police Transparency, Communities United for Police Reform," Communities United for Police Reform, October 14, 2016, http://changethenypd.org; Rick Rojas and David Goodman, "De Blasio Calls for Change in Law That Blocks Release of Police Disciplinary Action," *New York Times*, October 14, 2016.

12 Al Baker, David Goodman, and Benjamin Mueller, "Beyond the Chokehold: The Path to Eric Garner's Death," *New York Times*, June 13, 2015.

13 Baker, Goodman, and Mueller.

14 In October 2016, two years after Eric Garner's death, Ramsey was convicted and sentenced to four years in prison for gun and drug possession. "Ramsey Orta, Who Filmed Death of Eric Garner, Sentenced to Four Years in Prison for Drug and Weapons Charges," *New York Daily News*, October 2, 2016.

15 *Department of Justice Report Regarding the Criminal Investigation into the Shooting Death of Michael Brown by Ferguson, Missouri Police Officer Darren Wilson* (Washington, DC: U.S. Department of Justice, 2015), 1–7, www.justice.gov.

16 Raf Sanchez and David Lawler, "Ferguson: Timeline of Events since Michael Brown's Death," *Telegraph*, August 10, 2015.

17 "NYPD Commissioner Talks about Death of Eric Garner," *News 4 New York*, August 20, 2014, www.nbcnewyork.com.

18 Erin Durkin, "Mayor de Blasio Defends 'Broken Windows' Policing Strategy after Eric Garner Death," *New York Daily News*, July 25, 2014.

19 "Statement of Mayor Bill de Blasio on the Medical Examiner's Report on the Death of Eric Garner," City of New York, August 1, 2014, www1.nyc.gov.

20 Ian Blair, "Finally,. Staten Island DA Will Convene Grand Jury in Eric Garner Chokehold Case," *Salon* (blog), August 19, 2014, www.salon.com.

21 Jeffrey Fagan and Bernard E. Harcourt, "Fact Sheet in Richmond County (Staten Island) Grand Jury in Eric Garner Homicide," Social Justice Initiatives, Columbia University Law School, n.d., www.law.columbia.edu.

22 David Goodman and Al Baker, "Waves of Protest after Grand Jury Doesn't Indict Officer in Eric Garner Chokehold Case," *New York Times*, December 3, 2014.

23 Goodman and Baker.

24 "NYPD Commissioner Talks about Death of Eric Garner"; "NYPD Commissioner Bratton on Broken Windows, Community Policing, and More," *Brian Lehrer Show*, WNYC, August 12, 2014, www.wnyc.org; Aaron Feis, "Bratton: Criminal Suspects Should Not Resist Arrest," *New York Post*, August 12, 2014.

25 "Transcript: Mayor de Blasio Appears on the Brian Lehrer Show on WNYC," City of New York, November 13, 2015, www1.nyc.gov.

26 Marc Santora, "Mayor de Blasio Announces Retraining of New York Police," *New York Times*, December 4, 2014.

27 "Transcript: Mayor de Blasio and Commissioner Bratton Host Press Conference to Discuss Police Retraining," City of New York, December 4, 2014, www1.nyc. gov; Kate Briquelet, "Cops Say Training after Eric Garner's Death Is a Waste of Time," *New York Post*, February 22, 2015; "NYPD Cops Say Training Inspired by Eric Garner's Death Is a 'Waste of Time,'" *Vice News* (blog), February 23, 2015, http://news.vice.com.

28 Briquelet.

29 Briquelet.

30 Corinne Lestch, "Rev. Sharpton Takes de Blasio, NYPD Commissioner Bratton to Task over Eric Garner's Death as Mayor Calls for Change," *New York Daily News*, August 1, 2014.

31 Yoav Gonen and Beth DeFalco, "City Council Wants to Add 1,000 Cops to NYPD," *New York Post*, April 22, 2014.

32 "A Second Summer Sit-down with the Mayor," *Brian Lehrer Show*, WNYC, June 5, 2015, www.wnyc.org.

33 Michael M. Grynbaum and Matt Flegenheimer, "Mayor de Blasio Poised to Hire Nearly 1,300 Police Officers," *New York Times*, June 22, 2015.

34 "Transcript: NYPD Commissioner William Bratton and Executive Staff Hold Briefing at 1 Police Plaza," City of New York, July 1, 2015, www1.nyc.gov.

35 Grynbaum and Flegenheimer, "Mayor de Blasio Poised to Hire"; Murray Weiss, Jeff Mays, and Trevor Kapp, "De Blasio Hired More Police to Head Off Political Fallout Sources Say," *DNAinfo* (blog), June 24, 2015, www.dnainfo.com.

36 Michael Goodwin, "Why de Blasio Smears the NYPD," *New York Post*, July 30, 2014.

37 Tina More, Dale Esinger, and Rocco Parascandola, "Two NYPD Officers 'Assassinated' while Sitting in Patrol Car in Brooklyn by Gunman Who Boasted on Instagram about 'Revenge Killing' Cops," *New York Daily News*, December 21,

2014; Benjamin Mueller and Al Baker, "2 NYPD Officers Killed in Brooklyn Ambush; Suspect Commits Suicide," *New York Times*, December 20, 2014; "NY Police Union Head Blames Mayor, Protesters for Officers' Death," YouTube, December 21, 2014, http://www.youtube.com/watch?v=bmPPUXgMNM.

38 "Hundreds of Police Turn Backs on NYC Mayor at Slain Officer's Funeral," Reuters, January 4, 2015; "Why the NYPD Turned It Back on the City," *The Atlantic*, January 5, 2015.

39 Michael Grynbaum, Alexander Burns, and Dalia Sussman, "Mayor de Blasio Has Lost Support of White New Yorkers, Poll Finds," *New York Times*, November 17, 2015.

40 Rocco Parascandola, Erin Dunkin, and Revuen Blau, "First Time PBA Union Survey Says NYPD Morale at Rock Bottom under Mayor de Blasio, *New York Daily News*, March 14, 2016.

41 Weiss, Mays, and Kapp, "De Blasio Hired More Police."

42 Grynbaum, Burns, and Sussman, "Mayor de Blasio Has Lost Support of White New Yorkers."

43 *An Analysis of Quality-of-Life Summonses, Quality-of-Life Misdemeanors, Arrests, and Felony Crime in New York City, 2010–2015* (New York: New York City Department of Investigation Office of the Inspector General for the NYPD, 2016), 1–3, www1.nyc.gov.

44 *An Analysis of Quality-of-Life Summonses*, 3.

45 "Transcript: Mayor de Blasio Appears Live on WNYC's Brian Lehrer Show," City of New York, June 23, 2016. www1.nyc.gov.

46 *Nearly 1,800,000 per Year Punitive Interactions between NYPD and New Yorkers* (New York: Police Reform Organizing Project, 2016), 1–4, www.policereformorganizingproject.org.

47 *Nearly 1,800,000 per Year Punitive Interactions*, 5.

48 File Int. 0182-2014, A Local Law to Amend the Administrative Code of the City of New York in Relation to Requiring Law Enforcement Officers to Identify Themselves to the Public, New York City Council, March 12, 2014, legistar.council.nyc.gov; J. David Goodman, "De Blasio's Police Reforms Pledges May Burden His Re-election Bid," *New York Times*, October 14, 2016.

49 File Int. 0541-2014, A Local Bill to Amend the Administrative Code of the City of New York, in Relation to Requiring Law Enforcement Officers to Provide Notice and Obtain Proof of Consent to Search Individuals, New York City Council, November 14, 2014, http://legistar.council.nyc.gov.

50 File Int. 0541-2014.

51 *Final Report of the President's Task Force on 21st Century Policing* (Washington, DC: Office of Community Oriented Policing Services, 2015, 25, http://cops.usdoj.gov.

52 J. David Goodman "New York Council Won't Vote on Police Reform Bills, but Agency Agrees to Changes," *New York Times*, July 12, 2016.

53 "New York City Policing Reform, Derailed," *New York Times*, July 26, 2016.

54 "Communities Need Legislation," Communities United for Police Reform, n.d., www.changethenypd.org.

55 Michael Garland and Yoav Gonen, "De Blasio Asking City Councilors to Delay Police Reform Bill," *New York Post*, March 7, 2017.

56 Michael Sisitzky, "A Backroom Deal Threatens to Weaken Real Police Reform in New York," New York City Liberties Union, December 15, 2017, www.nyclu.org.

57 Sisitzky.

58 Monifa Bandele, "NYC Council Shouldn't Take City backwards by Undermining Police Reform," *Huffington Post* (blog), December 17, 2017, www.huffingtonpost.com.

59 J. David Goodman, "City Council Passes Billson Police Behavior amid Outcry on Both Sides," *New York Times*, December 19, 2017.

60 Goodman.

61 Dean Meminger, "First on 1: More Than 750,000'Broken Windows' Era Warrants Tossed," NY1, www.ny1.com Access July 27, 2017.

62 James C. McKinley Jr., "For Manhattan Fare Beaters, One-Way Ticket to Court May Be Over," *New York Times*, June 30, 2017.

63 J. David Goodman, "Turnstile Jumping Pits de Blasio against Police Reformers," *New York Times*, February 7, 2017.

64 Joseph J. Lhota to Cyrus R. Vance Jr., February 5, 2017, www.politico.com.

65 Cyrus R. Vance Jr. to Joseph J. Lhota, February 5, 2017 www.politico.com/.

66 "District Attorney Vance to End Criminal Prosecution of Approximately 20,000 Low-Level, Non-Violent Misdemeanors per Year," Manhattan District Attorney's Office, June 30, 2017, www.manhattanda.org.

67 Peter L. Zimroth, "Seventh Report of the Independent Monitor," December 13, 2017, 41, http://nypdmonitor.org.

68 Zimroth, 41; Al Baker, "City Police Officers Are Not Reporting All Street Stops, Monitor Says," *New York Times*, December 13, 2017.

69 Zimroth, "Seventh Report of the Independent Monitor," 4.

70 Zimroth, 38.

71 Ginia Bellafante, "What Happened to Police Accountability? The Mayor Is Not Saying," *New York Times*, September 29, 2017.

72 Benjamin Mueller, "Mayor de Blasio and Some Prosecutors Move to Curb Marijuana Arrests," *New York Times*, May 15, 2018; "District Attorney Vance to End Prosecution of Marijuana Possession and Smoking Cases," Manhattan District Attorney's Office, May 15, 2018, www.manhattanda.org.

73 "NYCLU Issues Seven Steps Mayor Can Take for a Fairer New York City," February 13, 2018, www.nyclu.org.

CONCLUSION

1 "Police Department Race and Ethnicity Demographic Data," Governing: The States and Localities, n.d., www.governing.com.

2 *Semi-Annual Report, January–June 2016* (New York: NYC Civilian Complaint Review Board, 2016), ix, www1.nyc.gov.

3 *Semi-Annual Report*, ix–x.

4 *Worth a Thousand Words: Examining Officer Interference with Civilian Recordings of Police* (New York: NYC Civilian Complaint Review Board, 2017), 1–15, www1.nyc.gov.

5 *Unjust and Unconstitutional: 60,000 Jim Crow Marijuana Arrests in Mayor de Blasio's New York* (New York: Drug Policy Alliance and Marijuana Arrest Research Project, 2017), 1–5, www.drugpolicy.org.

6 *Unjust and Unconstitutional*, 7.

7 *Unjust and Unconstitutional*, 8.

8 *Solutions to Police Brutality, Racism and Misconduct That Could Be Implemented by the City Council and Mayor of Minneapolis* (Minneapolis: Communities United against Police Brutality, 2014), http://d3n8a8pro7vhmx.cloudfront.net.

9 Lawrence J. McQuillan and Kelly R. Lester, "Bureaucrats or Citizens: Who Should Control the Police?" Independent Institute, July 14, 2016, www.independent.org.

10 "The Commission," CALEA, n.d., www.calea.org.

11 "Measuring the Performance of Law Enforcement Agencies," CALEA, n.d., www.calea.org.

12 "Memorandum of Understanding between the Civilian Complaint Review Board (CCRB) and the Police Department (NYPD) of the City of New York concerning the Processing of Substantiated Complaints," City of New York, August 12, 2012, www1.nyc.gov.

13 Odi Ofer, "Getting It Right: Building Effective Civilian Review Boards to Oversee Police," *Seton Hall Law Review* 46, no. 1033 (May 2016): 1046–47.

14 Ofer, 1047–48.

15 M. G. Duke, "Residency Rules for Police," *New York Times*, January 21, 2015.

16 Melissa Chan, "Rudy Giuliani Says 'Black Lives Mater' Is Inherently Racist," *Time*, July 10, 2016, time.com.

17 Adolph Reed Jr., "How Racial Disparity Does Not Help Make Sense of Patterns of Police Violence," *Nonsite* (blog), September 16, 2016, www.nonsite.org.

18 Ronald G. Fryer, "An Empirical Analysis of Racial Difference in Police Use of Force," Harvard University Department of Economics, July 2016, 1–2, http://scholar.harvard.edu.

19 Fryer, 2–3, 8.

20 Fryer, 2–4.

21 Fryer, 4.

22 Fryer, 35.

23 Fryer, 3–8.

24 *A Vision for Black Lives: Policy Demands for Black Power, Freedom, and Justice* (n.p.: Movement for Black Lives, 2016), 9, http://policy.m4bl.org.

25 *A Vision for Black Lives*, 4–7.

26 *A Vision for Black Lives*, 14.

INDEX

Abyssinian Baptist Church, 11, 87, 113

ACLU. *See* American Civil Liberties Union

activism, against police brutality: acknowledgment issue, 2–3; civil rights and, 6; in North, 9, 121–22; religious, 3, 5–6; resistance to, 6–7; spectrum of people and groups in, 5; start of, 4–5. *See also* civil rights activism, police brutality and

African Affairs Council, 53

AFSCME. *See* American Federation of State, County, and Municipal Employees

AI. *See* Amnesty International

alcohol container charges, 167, 238

American Civil Liberties Union (ACLU), 2, 37, 110, 217, 230; on police commissioner power, 249

American Communist Party (Workers Party), 11–12, 85; appeal to blacks, 50; black weekly news and, 39; daily newspaper of, 35, 36; Davis, B., and, 41–49; Nazi Germany pact with, 39–40, 54; NNC affiliation with, 39; Patterson leadership in, 48–49; riots blamed on communism and, 104–5

American Federation of State, County, and Municipal Employees (AFSCME), 189

American Labor Party, 32

American Spectator, 207

Amnesty International (AI), 178–83

Amsterdam News. See *New York Amsterdam News*

Anderson, Palmer, 15

Antoine, Patrick, 192–93

Arm, Walter, 75–76, 77, 104

Armstrong, Wallace, 16–18, 31, 32

arrests, 238; B-misdemeanor, 167; decline in number of SCU, 198–99; marijuana, 228, 241, 247–48; 1990s percentage of black, 167–68; retraining on, 231; vertical patrols causing more, 215

Asahi Evening News, 102

Asian American Legal Defense and Education Fund, 186

Asians, 246

asphyxia, deaths by, 178, 179

attorney generals, 41, 130, 142, 198, 210; district, 232

The Autobiography of Malcolm X (Malcolm X), 72

Bach, Natasha, 2

Baez, Anthony, 178, 206, 212–13

Baez, Iris, 212–13

Baez, Luis, 211

Baker, Ella, 92, 98

Bandele, Monifa, 235–36, 240–41

Bandy, Robert, 87

Bates, Ruby, 38

Beame, Abraham, 133

Bedford-Stuyvesant, Pérez demonstrations in, 211

ABOUT THE AUTHOR

Clarence Taylor is an American historian and author and editor of several books, including *Civil Rights since 1787: A Reader in the Black Struggle* and *Reds at the Blackboard: Communism, Civil Rights, and the New York City Teachers Union.*